Dreamweaver 2 | H·O·T

lynda.com/books

By Lynda Weinman

Design: Ali Karp

Dreamweaver 2 | H·O·T Hands-On Training

Lynda Weinman

lynda.com/books | Peachpit Press

1249 Eighth Street • Berkeley, CA • 94710

510.524.2178 • 510.524.2221(fax)

http://www.lynda.com/books

http://www.peachpit.com

lynda.com/books are published by Peachpit Press

Peachpit Press is a division of Addison Wesley Longman

Copyright ©1999 by Lynda Weinman

ISBN 0-201-35452-7

0 9 8 7 6 5 4 3 2
Printed and bound in the
United States of America

Dreamweaver 2 | H•O•T_____

Credits

Book Design: Ali Karp (alink@earthlink.net)

Peachpit Editor: Cary Norsworthy

Peachpit Production Coordinator: Cary Norsworthy

lynda.com Editor: Kathryn Van Sant

Tech Editor: Chris Deutsch

Production Artist: Heidi Goodspeed

Cover Illustration: Bruce Heavin (bruce@stink.com)

Indexer: Steve Rath

CD-ROM **Coordinator:** Victor Gavenda

 Dreamweaver 2 | H•O•T_____

Colophon

The preliminary art direction for *Dreamweaver 2 H•O•T* was sketched on paper. The layout was heavily influenced by online communication—merging a traditional book format with a modern Web aesthetic.

The text in *Dreamweaver 2 H•O•T* was set in Akzidenz Grotesk from Adobe and Triplex from Emigre. The cover illustration was painted in Adobe Photoshop 5.5 and Adobe Illustrator 8.0.

This book was created using QuarkXPress 3.32, Adobe Photoshop 5.0, Microsoft Office 98, and Dreamweaver 2 on a MacOS G3. It was printed on 50lb. Arbor Smooth (Weyerhauser), at Edwards Brothers, Ann Arbor, Michigan.

Dreamweaver 2 H•O•T_____Table of Contents

.Introduction

• A Note From Lynda •

Dreamweaver 2

In my opinion, most people buy computer books in order to learn, yet it is amazing how few of these books are actually written by teachers. In this book, you will find carefully developed lessons and exercises that have been tested in our training center to help you learn Dreamweaver 2—one of the most well-respected HTML editors on the planet. This is the first of several H•O•T titles designed specifically for learning digital art tools and principles related to Web Design, Animation, and Digital Imaging.

This book is targeted toward beginning to intermediate-level Web developers who are looking for a great tool to speed up production, offer workflow flexibility, and create great code and results. The premise of the hands-on exercise approach is to get you up to speed quickly in Dreamweaver 2, while actively working through the book's lessons. It's one thing to read about a product, and an entirely different experience to try the product and get measurable results.

Many exercise-based books take a paint-by-numbers approach to teaching, which offer instructions that tell you what to do, but not why to do it or when to do it. While this approach sometimes works, it's often difficult to figure out how to apply those lessons to a real-world situation, or understand why or when you would use the technique again. What sets this book apart is that the lessons contain lots of background information for each given subject, which are designed to help you understand the process as well as the particular exercise.

At times, pictures are worth a lot more than words. When necessary, I have also included short QuickTime movies to show any process that's difficult to explain with words. These files are located on the *H•O•T CD-ROM* inside a folder called **movies**. It's my style to approach teaching from many different angles because I know that some people are visual learners, while others like to read, and still others like to get out there and try things. This book combines a lot of teaching approaches so you can learn Dreamweaver 2 as thoroughly as you want to.

In this book, I didn't set out to cover every single aspect of Dreamweaver. The manual and many other reference books are great for that! What I saw missing from the bookshelves was a process-oriented book that taught readers core principles, techniques, and tips in a hands-on training format.

It's my hope that this book will raise your skills in Web design, HTML, JavaScript, and publishing. If it does, then I have accomplished the job I set out to do!

I welcome your comments
lynda@lynda.com

Please visit my Web Site as well
http://www.lynda.com.

The URL for support for this book
http://www.lynda.com/books/dw2hot

—*Lynda Weinman*

How This Book Works

This book has several components, including step-by-step exercises, commentary, notes, tips, warnings, and movies. Step-by-step exercises are numbered, and file names and command keys are bolded so they pop out more easily. You might notice that certain words are capitalized, such as Tables, Frames, Layers, etc. I chose to capitalize these terms to call more attention to them, and to mimic how they appear in Dreamweaver. When you see italicized text, it either signifies a picture caption or commentary.

Whenever you're being instructed to go to a *menu* or to *multiple menu items*, it's stated like this: **File > Open…**. *Menu commands* are also bolded to make them stand out more, as are file names.

Code is in a monospace font: `<HTML></HTML>`

URLs are in a contrasting font: http://www.lynda.com

Macintosh and Windows Interface Screen Captures: Most of the screen captures in the book were taken on a Macintosh. The only time Windows shots were taken was when the interface differed from the Macintosh. I made this decision because I do most of my design work and writing on my Mac. I also own and use a Windows system, so I noted important differences when they occurred, and took screen captures accordingly.

Exercise Files and the H•O•T CD-ROM: All of your course files are located inside a folder called **exercise_files** on the *H•O•T CD-ROM*. These files are divided into chapter folders. During many of the exercises, you will be instructed to copy the chapter folders to your hard drive. **Warning:** Unfortunately, when files originate from a CD-ROM, the Windows operating system defaults to making them write-protected, meaning that you cannot alter them. If you use Windows, you will need to remove this setting, so please read the following note for instructions.

Note_____

Windows Write-Protect Solution

By default, when you copy files from a CD-ROM to your Windows 95/98 hard drive, they are set to read-only (write protected). This will cause a problem with the exercise files, because you will need to write over some of them. When you define a site (which you will learn how to do in Chapter 3, *"Site Control"*) you will notice that the files have a small lock next to them which means they have been set to read-only. To remove this setting and make them editable, follow the short procedure below.

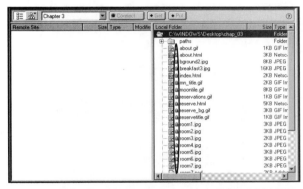

1. Define your site using the folder you copied from the *H•O•T CD-ROM*. When the Site window opens, you will see little locks next to all of the files.

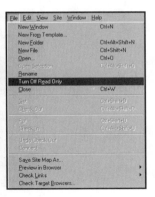

2. Ctrl+Click on each of the files that have a lock next to them.

3. Once you have all of the files selected, select **File > Turn Off Read-Only**.

Warning_____

Missing Windows File Extensions

By default, Windows 95/98 users will not be able to see file extension names, such as **.gif**, **.jpg**, or **.html**. Don't worry, you can change this setting!

Windows 95 Users:

1. Double-click on the **My Computer** icon on your desktop. (**Note:** If you or someone else has changed the name, it will not say My Computer.)

2. Select **View > Options**. This will open the **Options** dialog box.

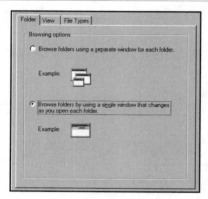

3. In the Options window, click on the **View** tab at the top. This will open the **View** options screen so you can change the view settings of Windows 95.

4. Make sure there is no checkmark in the **Hide MS-DOS file extensions for file types that are registered** option. This will ensure that the file extensions are visible, which will help you better understand the exercises in the book!

Windows 98 Users:

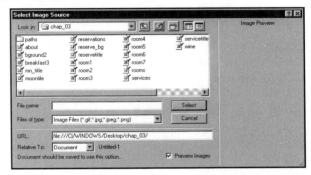

1. Double-click on the **My Computer** icon on your desktop. (**Note:** If you or someone else has changed the name, it will not say My Computer.)

2. Select **View > Folder** Options to open the **Folder Options** dialog box.

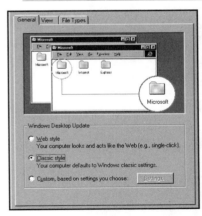 

3. Click on the **View** tab at the top. This will allow you to access the different **View** settings for your computer.

4. Uncheck the checkbox inside the **Hide File** extensions for known file types option. This will make all of the file extensions visible.

Demo Files on the CD-ROM

In addition to the exercise files, the *H•O•T CD-ROM* also contains a free 30-day trial version of Dreamweaver 2 for Mac or Windows. A Mac and Windows version of Netscape 4.6 is also on the CD. All **software** is located inside the software folder (imagine that!) on the *H•O•T CD-ROM*.

HTML Versus HTM

All of the HTML exercise files on the CD-ROM end with an .html extension. Windows users might be more used to naming files with an .htm extension. You can name your files either way, and a Web browser will be able to read them. The choice to name them with the four-letter extension represents a personal bias. The shorter .htm suffix is a throwback to the old days of DOS when file names were limited to the eight-dot-three convention. That meant that file names could be no longer than eight characters, and had to end with a dot and a three-letter extension. Those days are history since the advent of Windows 95 and Windows 98, so in this book I named all the files with the more accurate four-letter extension. It does, after all, stand for **H**yper**T**ext **M**arkup **L**anguage, not **H**yper**T**ext **M**arkup! Now you know why I chose to name the files this way, but the bottom line of this explanation is that you can use either naming method and your HTML files will still work. I simply made a choice to use the four-letter extension because that's what I prefer to use.

Troubleshooting FAQ

If you find yourself getting stuck in an exercise, be sure to read the *"Trouble-shooting FAQ,"* located in the back of the book. If you don't find your answer there, send an email to dw2faq@lynda.com, and I'll post an update on the companion Web site for the book, http://www.lynda.com/books/dw2hot as quickly as I can. Obviously, I can't offer personal technical support for everyone who reads the book, so be sure to refer to this FAQ before you request extra help.

Note: This FAQ is intended to support the exercises in this book. If you have other questions about Dreamweaver, as a registered owner of the program you can call Macromedia's technical support (415) 252-9080, or visit their excellent Web site at http://www.macromedia.com/support/dreamweaver/

System Requirements

This book requires that you use either the MacOS operating system (on a Macintosh running System 7.5.5 or later) or Windows 95, Windows 98, or Windows NT. I suggest that you have at least 64 MB of RAM in your system, because it's optimal if you can open Dreamweaver and a Web browser at the same time. More RAM is better, especially on Macintosh computers, which do not offer dynamic RAM allocation like Windows. Here is a little chart that cites Macromedia's and Netscape's system requirements, along with my recommendations.

RAM		
	Dreamweaver Requires	**Lynda Recommends**
Mac	24 MB	30 - 50 MB
Windows 95/98/NT	16 MB	24 MB
	Netscape Requires	**Lynda Recommends**
Mac	16 MB	24 MB
Windows 95/98/NT	16MB	16 MB

About lynda.com/books

lynda.com/books is dedicated to helping Web designers and developers understand tools and design principles. lynda.com also offers hands-on workshops, training seminars, on-site training, training videos, training CDs, web tips, and training products, so be sure to visit our site at http://www.lynda.com to learn more!

*A few of **Lynda Weinman's Books** include:* Designing Web Graphics—*Web graphics and design priniciples.* Coloring Web Graphics—*Information on Web color and helpful color schemes.* Creative HTML Design—*The principles of HTML and Web publishing.*

Lynda Weinman's Video Training Series, *with titles on Dreamweaver 2, Flash 4, Fireworks 2, Photoshop 5.5 / ImageReady 2.0, GoLive 4.0, and more.*

Ojai Digital Arts Center, *co-founded by Lynda Weinman and Bruce Heavin, offers classes in Web application and design.*

About Me

I've been practicing computer design and animation since 1984, when I bought one of the first Macintosh computers. I worked as an animator and motion graphics director in the special effects industry for 7 years before having a daughter in 1989. At that time, I was asked to teach my first workshop in multimedia animation, and eventually became a full-time faculty member at Art Center College of Design in Pasadena, California. I've worked as a beta tester for imaging and animation software packages since 1984, and have worked as a consultant for Adobe, Macromedia, and Microsoft. I've conducted workshops at Disney, Microsoft, Adobe, and Macromedia, and have been a keynote speaker, moderator, and/or speaker at numerous design, broadcast-design, animation, Web-design, and computer-graphics conferences. I co-founded lynda.com, LLC with my husband Bruce Heavin (who is responsible for the beautiful covers of all my books!), which specializes in Web-design training via hands-on classes, seminars, training videos, books, Web tips, and CD-ROMs. The list could go on and on, but I basically love teaching and sharing knowledge, and that's what I spend most of my waking hours doing. I hope you'll visit http://www.lynda.com, to learn more…

 Note_____

lynda.com

For more information on Lynda, her books, training videos, and classes, check out her home page **http://www.lynda.com** or go directly to the online store, **http://www.lynda.com/products**.

Lynda's daughter Jamie in a serious mood (as usual).

Lynda with book designer, Ali Karp at their combo booksigning/photo exhibit.

The Ojai Dital Arts Center offers classes in Dreamweaver, Flash, Fireworks, Photoshop, ImageReady, GoLive and Web design principles. For more information please visit: http://www.lynda.com/classes.

A blurry Bruce and Lynda at their training center via digital camera.

Acknowledgements

I could not have written this book without the help of many key people.

Special Thanks to..._____

My **writing partner** on this project, *Garo Green*, who helped develop many of the exercises, conducted research, beta tested, and was there (even at 2 a.m. when we finished our final final check of the CD-ROM files!) through both the fun and hard parts of creating this book.

My **book designer**, the always incredible *Ali Karp*, who not only laid out pages, but also beta tested, took a Dreamweaver workshop from me, and gave her usual 200% to this project. This is the 10th book that Ali and I have collaborated on in four years. Wow!

My **husband**, *Bruce Heavin*, who made the cover art, put up with the countless hours it took to complete this project, and was always there for moral support (and of couse, the ever-important foot massages!).

My **daughter**, *Jamie*, who provided much-needed cuddle time with her mom, after a hard day's work on the book. Thanks for being so understanding and always lending your wry sense of humor to carry me through my intense work load.

My **agent**, *David Rogelberg*, who helped make my dream of a **lynda.com/book** imprint come true.

My **Peachpit Press editor**, *Cary Norsworthy*, who contributed numerous great ideas, and whose opinion I always valued and appreciated. Not to mention that she's a very neat person, and someone I hope to know for a long time to come as a friend and co-worker.

My **editor**, the amazing *Kathryn Van Sant*, whose belief in this project was unending. I thank you for your enthusiasm and good humor, not to mention that you're a damn great editor, hunny!

My **technical editor**, the extraordinarily young and talented *Chris Deutsch*, who was always there to nit-pick and find the mistakes, regardless of how minor. Hey, that was your job, and we both know it, but you did it ohs o well ;-).

My **production artist**, *Heidi Goodspeed*, who Quarked until the cows came home, and beta tested, and tested, and tested again. Thanks for your great attitude and devotion to this project.

The **Macromedia folks** who made this amazing HTML editor—especially the honorable *Kevin Lynch*, whose brilliance is undisputed by all.

My fantastic **lynda.com staff**—*Tony Winecoff*, *Phillip Lantham*, *KC O'Connell*, *Shane Rebenschied*, and *Abie Arcillia*. You all make having a business much more fun than working out of my garage ;-).

I. Background

- **Roundtrip HTML • HTML**
- **File Naming • Extending Dreamweaver**
- **DHTML • XML • JavaScript**

chap_01 folder

Dreamweaver 2
H•O•T CD-ROM

I could start this book with lots of exercises, throwing you right into working with Dreamweaver 2 without any preparation. But then you would be flying blind, without understanding basic Web-design fundamentals like HTML, DHTML, XML, and JavaScript. Instead, I'm starting you off with some definitions, concepts, and guidelines to help with your hands-on Dreamweaver training. Feel free to scan this chapter for information, in the event you already know some of what's here or want the instant gratification of getting started.

What Is Dreamweaver?

Dreamweaver is a WYSIWYG (**W**hat **Y**ou **S**ee **I**s **W**hat **Y**ou **G**et) HTML generator. This means if you change something on the screen inside Dreamweaver, it will show you the results instantly. In contrast, if you were to code the HTML by hand, you would have to look at the code inside a Web browser to see the results. The instant feedback of a live design environment like Dreamweaver speeds up your workflow tremendously, because you can see whether you like the results while you are working.

RoundTrip HTML

Dreamweaver has gained a lot of great reviews and customer loyalty because of its invention of roundtrip HTML. Roundtrip HTML means you can alter the code that Dreamweaver automatically writes. Virtually all other WYSIWYG HTML editors today do not let you alter the code they produce. That's because they need to work with code that's written in a specific way, so they can offer all the WYSIWYG features. In other words, the code is self-serving to help the program, not to create the HTML.

Why is roundtrip HTML important? Because you can alter the code that Dreamweaver writes, and it will leave your changes alone, even if it doesn't understand them. This respect for your changes is key, since the program doesn't assume it knows what you want better than you do. Don't you wish all programs were so respectful?

Roundtrip HTML is especially important because HTML isn't yet a stable standard. If you've been watching the development of HTML, you might have noticed that it's changed a lot since it was first introduced in 1993. The inventors of the markup language didn't really expect that the Web would catch on as it has, or that people would want to do full-scale multimedia with HTML.

To put it politely, HTML was extremely limited when it was first released. Browsers such as Mosaic, Netscape Navigator, and Microsoft Internet Explorer pushed the early boundaries of developing HTML without the consent of the Web's formal standards committee (the **W**orld **W**ide **W**eb **C**onsortium, or W3C). So if you were using a WYSIWYG editor that didn't allow you to write your own code, you were prevented from trying some of the new markup that wasn't officially part of HTML. That meant many people who started with visual HTML editors, such as Adobe PageMill, Claris HomePage, NetObjects Fusion, and Microsoft FrontPage, couldn't always take advantage of the latest features that were supported by browsers. It was like having a tool that handcuffed you in time to whatever was possible at the moment it was released. Roundtrip HTML, on the other hand, allows you to try things that aren't even invented yet. That's pretty cool.

Programmers have looked at HTML editors with dubious eyes, because of the inflexibility of these tools and their inclusion of nonstandard HTML code. Dreamweaver is the first HTML editor to win the approval of programmers and designers alike. Programmers like the product because they are not tied to writing code in a rigid manner. Designers like Dreamweaver because it writes clean code without a lot of proprietary and self-serving tags, and because it allows them to do lots of great visual layout without understanding even a line of code. Hard to believe there could be a tool to please both these divergent groups, but there is, and Dreamweaver is it.

Do You Need to Learn HTML to Use Dreamweaver?

For most people, HTML at first glance is quite intimidating—your first reaction may be to avoid it at all costs. In order to do design work in Photoshop, QuarkXPress, or PageMaker, it isn't necessary to look at raw PostScript code anymore. However, the early pioneers of desktop publishing had to know how to program in PostScript just to create a page layout! Because we are actually still in the infancy of the Web and HTML development, most early Web developers have been programmers, not artists, because it was necessary to write the raw code to create a Web page.

HTML has come a long way since its inception, and many of its features have become standardized while others have not. In the past, if you didn't know some HTML, you were at the mercy of a programmer who might have more control over your design than you liked. Today, with Dreamweaver, you actually can get by without understanding or writing a single line of code. Attractive though it might be, I actually recommend that you do understand HTML at its simplest, so that you aren't afraid of it. No one likes to work in fear, and I find that most people who don't take the time to learn a little HTML are at a disadvantage in the workplace. When you don't understand HMTL, it's sort of like having a secret that you hope no one will discover, or feeling like a fake and worrying that you will be found out. No one likes that feeling!

How do you learn HTML? The best way is to view the source code of pages that you like. Virtually all the HTML jocks I've met have taught themselves in this way. One of the best things about HTML is that "learning by doing" is possible. If you were to try to learn other computer languages this way, you most likely could not, because the code would be compiled and hidden from your view. In HTML, the code is visible to everyone and is parsed on-the-fly by the Web browser itself. To view their source code, look under your browser's Edit menu and choose **View Page Source** (Netscape) or **View > View Source** (Internet Explorer). This will show you the raw HTML, and once you get comfortable with some of the tags you will likely be able to deconstruct how these pages were made.

HTML Resources

There are many great resources, online and off, for learning HTML. Here is a short list:

NCSA: A Beginner's Guide to HTML Home Page
http://www.ncsa.uiuc.edu/General/Internet/WWW/
HTMLPrimer.html

HTML: An Interactive Tutorial for Beginners
http://www.davesite.com/webstation/html/

The WDVL: HTML—The Hypertext Markup Language
http://www.stars.com/Tutorial/HTML/

Webmonkey: HTML Tutorial
http://www.hotwired.com/webmonkey/teachingtool/
index.html

NCDesign HTML Design Guide v4.0
http://www.ncdesign.org/html/

Index DOT HTML: The Advanced HTML Reference
http://home.webmonster.net/mirrors/bloo-html/

Resource list from, The HTML Writers Guild
http://www.hwg.org/resources/html/intros.html

What Does HTML Do?

HTML stands for **H**yper**T**ext **M**arkup **L**anguage. It is a derivative of SGML (**S**tandardized **G**eneral **M**arkup Language), an international standard for representing text in an electronic form that can be used for exchaging documents in an indepedent manner.

When I first touched computers, (way) back in 1980, we had to use a form of markup in word processor documents. If you wanted something to be bold, for example, you had to tag it with the symbol **<B>** in order to create that formatting. You would never see the actual boldfaced text until the file was printed; back then, bold type could not even be displayed on the computer screen!

We've come a long way since then, and so has HTML. That's why programs like Dreamweaver are starting to become viable alternatives to writing all the tags by hand. With maturity and established standards, HTML in its raw form will likely become as hidden away as the markup behind word processors is today.

At its heart, HTML allows for the markup of text and the inclusion of images, as well as the ability to link documents together. Hyperlinks, which are at the core of HTML's success, are what allow us to flip between pages in a site, or to view pages in outside sites. These hyperlinks are references that are contained within the markup. If the source of the link moves or the reference to the link is misspelled, it won't work. One of the great attributes of Dreamweaver is its site-management capabilities, which will help you manage your internal links so they are automatically updated if they change or are moved.

What Does HTML Look Like?

HTML uses a combination of tags, attributes, and values to generate its results. Here is a sample line of code that uses a tag, an attribute, and a value.

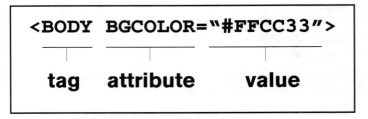

In this line of code, the *tag* is **<BODY>**, the *attribute* is **BGCOLOR**, and the *value* is **FFCC33**. When put together, this collection of items within the brackets **< >** is called an *element*.

Many tags require opening and closing *containers*, as marked here for the **<BODY>** elements:

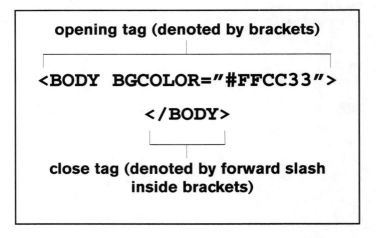

HTML Deconstructed

All HTML pages follow a basic structure. It contains the **HTML**, **HEAD**, **TITLE**, and **BODY** tags. Whenever you open a new Untitled Document in Dreamweaver, this framework is already written. It looks like this:

```
1   <HTML>
2   <HEAD>
3   <TITLE>Untitled Document</TITLE>
4   <META HTTP-EQUIV="Content-Type" CONTENT="text/html; charset=iso-8859-1">
5   </HEAD>
6   <BODY BGCOLOR="#FFFFFF">
7   </BODY>
8   </HTML>
```

1 Notice how the **<HTML>** tag is at the beginning of the Document? It signifies that this is an HTML page. Without this tag, the page could not be read by a browser. See line 8, the close **</HTML>** tag? This particular tag requires an *open* and a *close tag*. Open and close tags are required for most HTML tags, but not all.

2 The **<HEAD>** element of the Document contains the **HEAD** information. In this case the **TITLE** tag and the **META** tag are contained within the **HEAD**.

3 The **<TITLE>** is what appears at the top of the page inside a browser. If you leave the title "Untitled Document," as in the example above, that is exactly what will appear! Dreamweaver has a setting for easily changing this title. We will get to this setting in Chapter 4, "*Basics.*"

4 **META** tags are **HEAD** elements that record information about the current page, such as the character encoding, author, copyright, and Keywords. Many properties can be set here, which you will learn about in Chapter 4, "*Basics.*"

5 Here's the close tag for the **HEAD** element. Note that the **TITLE** and **META** tags were nested within the **HEAD** tag.

6 The **BODY** tag is specifying that this page will be white, instead of the default gray. If you don't enter a **BGCOLOR** value here, the page will defer to browser defaults.

7 This is the close tag for **BODY**.

8 This is the close tag for **HTML**.

Fortunately, you don't have to worry about getting this structure right. It is automatically built in to any page you create in Dreamweaver.

File-Naming Conventions

Working with HTML is much more restrictive than with other types of computer media. The strictest part about HTML is its file-naming conventions.

Don't use spaces: It's best if you save your files using no spaces in between the file-name elements. For example, the file name (**about lynda.html**) would be considered illegal because of the space between the word about and lynda. Instead, you would write this file name as **about_lynda.html** or **aboutlynda.html**.

Avoid capital letters: It is best to avoid capitalization in your file names. Although **AboutLynda.html** would work as a file name, anytime you linked to the file you would have to remember the correct capitalization, since many UNIX servers are case sensitive. It is far easier to simply use all lowercase letters.

Avoid illegal characters: Below is a chart of characters to avoid using in file names.

Character	Usage
File-Naming Conventions	
Character	**Usage**
. (dot)	Periods are reserved for filename extensions or suffixes, for example .gif and .jpg.
"	Quotes are reserved for HTML, to indicate the value of tags and attributes.
/ or \	Forward slashes (/) indicate that files are nested in folders. If you include a forward slash in your filename, HTML may lose your references, thinking you are specifying a folder. A backslash (\) won't be allowed on MS-Windows servers.
:	Colons are used to separate certain script commands on Macs and Windows. Avoid them in your filenames so as not to confuse a filename with a script command.
!	Exclamation marks are used in comment tags.

Note _____

Filename Extensions

You may be curious about the many extensions used after the dot at the end of file names. Below is a chart which lists the meaning of some extensions you'll commonly run across.

Filename Extensions	
Extension	**Usage**
.html, .htm	These two extensions are commonly used to denote an HTML file. The three-letter extension works just as well as the four-letter version. Older DOS systems didn't allow for four-letter extensions, which is why you sometimes see .html abbreviated as .htm. Dreamweaver defaults to using .htm.
.gif	GIF images
.jpg	JPEG images
.swf	Flash files
.mov	QuickTime movie files
.avi	AVI movie files
.aif	AIFF sound files

Extending Dreamweaver

One of the neatest things about the Dreamweaver community is the way people share objects, commands, and behaviors. These prebuilt elements can be shared and distributed, much the way Photoshop Plug-Ins work. If you visit the Dreamweaver section of the Macromedia site, you will find numerous listings for shared resources. Here are just a few of my favorites:

Dreamweaver Depot
http://people.netscape.com/andreww/dreamweaver/
This is one of the largest repositories of Dreamweaver actions, objects, and commands on the Internet. Many of them were developed by the site's owner, Andrew Woodbridge.

Dreamweaver Extensions Database
http://www.idest.com/cgi-bin/database.cgi
At this site you are able to search an extensive database which includes all of the Dreamweaver extensions.

Yaromat
http://www.yaromat.com/dw/index.htm
A personal home page that contains several very useful Dreamweaver extensions, including a great one for importing Fireworks-created Rollovers.

Dreamweaver's Fan Page
http://www.cybernet.ch/users/massimo/index4.htm
A great resource for Dreamweaver extensions, behaviors, commands, and objects. It has an interesting DHTML interface, too!

What Is DHTML?

Dynamic **HTML** (DHTML) is actually a collection of different technologies put together. This can include any combination of HTML, JavaScript, **C**ascading **S**tyle **S**heets (CSS), and **D**ocument **O**bject **M**odel (DOM). The purpose of combining these technologies is to allow the authoring of more dynamic content than what basic HTML affords.

Some of the things possible with DHMTL include animation, drag-and-drop, and complicated Rollovers (buttons that change when your mouse moves over them). When you want to create pages with buttons that change in more than one place on the screen at the same time, Dreamweaver uses DHTML to achieve it.

Just like HTML, if you program DHTML effects in Dreamweaver, most of the coding occurs behind the scenes. You don't have to see it unless you choose to.

There are, however, some serious cross-platform issues with DHTML, because it is supported quite differently by Navigator and Explorer (makers of the two leading browsers). Fortunately, Dreamweaver lets you target specific browsers, as well as test the cross-browser compatibility of your choices.

 Note_____

DHTML Combinations

DHTML uses a combination of HTML, JavaScript, DOM, and CSS. Below is a chart with a short definition of each.

DHTML Terms	
Technology	**Explanation**
HTML	HyperText Markup Language. The default markup for basic Web pages and the root of DHTML.
JavaScript	A scripting language that extends the capabilities of HTML.
CSS	Cascading Style Sheets. A page layout system understood by newer web browsers, which allows for better control over the appearance and positioning of elements on a web page.
DOM	Document Object Model. A hook to outside scripting protocols such as ActiveX, or external Plug-Ins such as Shockwave or Flash. It allows scripts and programs to address and update documents.

What Is XML?

XML stands for **Ex**tensible **M**arkup **L**anguage. The specifications for XML are still in development, but many people are looking to XML as a solution to improve interactivity between Web sites and databases. XML would make it possible, for example, to sort a list of names alphabetically online. It would also enable much more sophisticated searching of data, making it a boon to many Web-based forms and databases.

Dreamweaver supports templates, covered in Chapter 9, *"Templates/Libraries."* One of the advanced features of Dreamweaver 2 is the ability to import XML databases through a template. Because XML is so new, and the use of databases is outside the scope of this book, I don't include any XML exercises in any of the chapters. But you can investigate XML extensibility at the developer's area of the Dreamweaver site.

Macromedia Developer's Site
http://www.macromedia.com/support/dreamweaver/

World Wide Web Consortium
http://www.w3.org/xml/

What is JavaScript?

JavaScript was developed by Netscape in 1996, and has become almost as popular as HTML. It actually has nothing to do with the Java programming language, but Netscape licensed the name from Sun Microsystems in hopes of increasing acceptance of the new scripting protocol. I'm not sure if it was the name that did the trick, but JavaScript has almost become as widely adopted as HTML itself! The most common uses of JavaScript allow for Rollovers, resizing of browser windows, and checking for browser compatibility.

Most of the JavaScript routines are accessed by Dreamweaver's behaviors interface, which you will learn about in Chapter 11, *"Rollovers"* and Chapter 13, *"DHTML."* This is one area of Dreamweaver's product that must be previewed in a browser to be visible. This book covers many JavaScript techniques, including Rollovers (Chapter 11, *"Rollovers"*), browser-sniffing (Chapter 8, *"Style Sheets"*), and launching external browser windows (Chapter 12, *"Forms"*).

You will not have to learn to write JavaScript by hand in order to use it within Dreamweaver. This is very fortunate for those of us who are not programmers, since JavaScript programming is more complicated than HTML.

2.Interface

• Interface Tour • Objects Palette
• Launcher and Mini-Launcher • Properties Inspector
• Document Window • Preferences

chap_02 folder

Dreamweaver 2
H•O•T CD-ROM

I am a big fan of the Dreamweaver 2 interface. Other HTML editors that I've used require that you open a lot of windows and palettes in order to reach all of the features. Instead, Dreamweaver uses a few primary windows and palettes that change depending on the context of what you are doing. This saves screen real estate and makes learning the interface a lot easier than with other comparable programs. Although you might believe at this point that learning Dreamweaver represents a big learning curve, understanding the interface is probably one of the easier challenges ahead of you.

This chapter will take you through the basic concepts of the program's interface. In addition to a tour through the interface features, I've also shared how to set up my favorite Dreamweaver preference settings and configurations.

You might be antsy to start in on some of the step-by-step exercises contained in later chapters, but this chapter is needed first to establish how to use the interface.

Warning_____

Macintosh RAM Suggestion

If you are using Dreamweaver on a Macintosh, it is recommended that you assign more RAM than what Dreamweaver leads you to believe you'll need. We run a Mac and Microsoft Windows lab at our training center and have noticed many problems with Dreamweaver on our Macs when the minimum RAM is allocated. This is not an issue for PCs, since that operating system has dynamic RAM allocation; Macs do not.

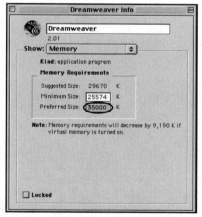

*To change the memory allocation on a Macintosh (rec-ommended!), make sure that Dreamweaver 2 is not open. Locate the program on your hard drive, and choose **File > Get Info**. Select **Show: Memory** in the pop-up menu. Change the **Preferred Size** allocation to **35,000K** or more. (I use 50,000K on my machine.)*

A Tour of the Interface

The features that Dreamweaver 2 offers are very sophisticated, but the interface to the program is actually quite simple. There are five main parts to this program, as illustrated here.

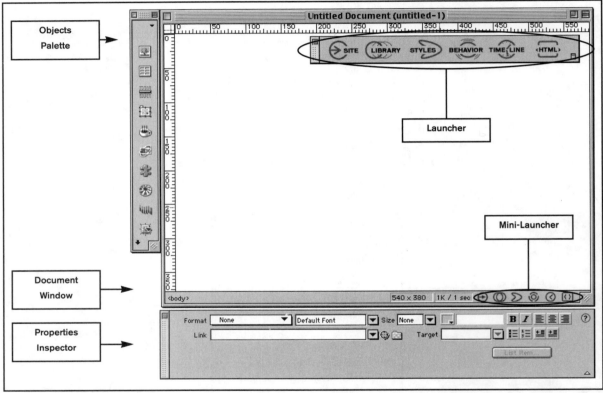

*The **Objects Palette**, **Properties Inspector**, **Launcher**, **Mini-Launcher**, and **Document Window** on a Mac. Whenever you open Dreamweaver, it defaults to opening a new Untitled Document, as shown here.*

The Objects Palette

The Objects Palette is used as a one-click stop for many operations. If you move your mouse over the Objects Palette and pause for a moment, you'll see what each one of the icons stands for.

*The **Objects Palette** in its default mode.*

You can alter the appearance of this palette in your Dreamweaver Preferences, if you'd like. To change the appearance of the Objects Palette, select **Edit > Preferences > General > Object Palette**. The Objects Palette's setting can be changed to **Icons with Text, Icons Only,** or **Text Only**.

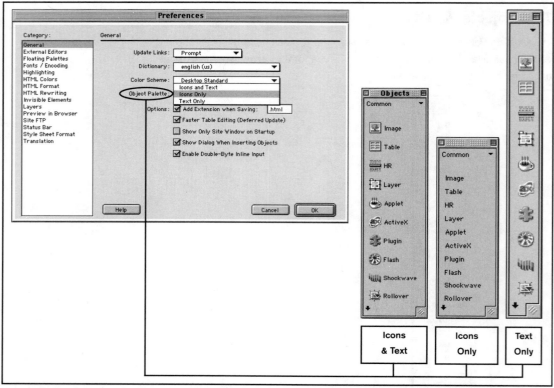

*The Objects Palette's appearance can be modified inside Dreamweaver's Preferences dialog box. The three versions of the Objects Palette shown to the right are the choices available in the Preferences. As you examine the Objects Palette, you'll see that it allows you to access essential functions, such as inserting an image, a Table, a horizontal rule, a Layer, and so on. These functions are called **objects** in the Dreamweaver 2 Objects Palette.*

Many items that exist as objects are also found under the **Insert** menu in the top menu bar. The Objects Palette exists as a one-click alternative to using the top menu bar. Some people are more comfortable clicking on the icons, and others prefer the menu access. There is no right or wrong way to do this; it is just a matter of your personal preference.

Tip_____

PC Shortcuts

PC Users: The underlined letters in the menu names and command names represent the **Alt+key** shortcuts you can use. For example, to insert an image, you can first hit **Alt+I** (for the Insert menu) and then press **I** again for the Image command. The **I** is underlined for both the menu and command. Sadly, the Mac menus cannot be accessed using this method.

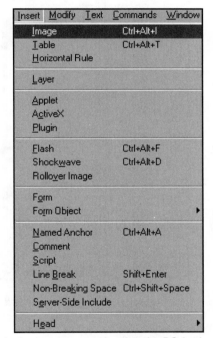

*Here's the Insert menu, showing the PC keyboard short-cuts for its commands. **Note:** The **I** is underlined in Image. Whatever letter you see underlined in a command is the **Alt+key** shortcut for that operation.*

Types of Objects

Like many of the toolbars in Dreamweaver, the Objects Palette is context sensitive. It defaults to showing what Dreamweaver calls the **Common** elements. You can change the Objects Palette to show other categories of objects when you need them.

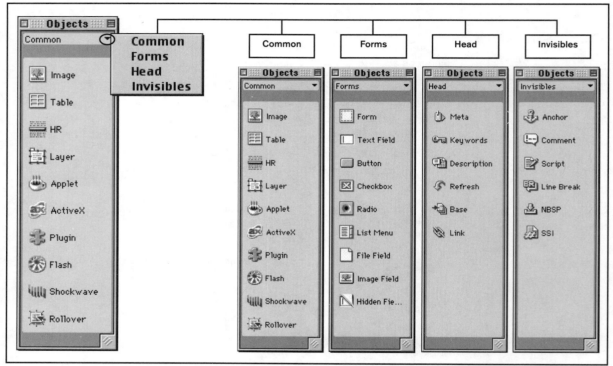

*If you hold your mouse down on the arrow at the top of the Objects Palette, notice that it says "Common"? That tells you you're looking at the **Common** tags on this toolbar. To show the other types of objects, click and hold the mouse on the pop-up menu arrow. You'll see a list of the other palettes, called **Common**, **Forms**, **Head**, and **Invisibles**.*

Object Palette Types

Palette	Description
Common	The Common Palette contains the most frequently used objects in Dreamweaver, including Images, Tables, Layers, simple Rollovers, etc. You will use this palette a lot.
Forms	The Forms Palette contains all of the objects essential for creating Forms for your Web page. These objects include text boxes, buttons, menus, etc. You'll learn about these items in Chapter 12, *"Forms."*
Head	The Head Palette contains objects that are inserted in the **HEAD** tag of your Web page. These elements, even though not visible on the page, can be an important part of your pages. These objects include **META** tags, such as Keywords, and Descriptions, etc. Many of these tags are used for search operations.
Invisibles	The Invisibles Palette is probably used the least, but it's still important. Invisible objects include Named Anchors, Server-Side Includes, Non-Breaking Spaces, etc. You will get a chance to work with some of the invisible elements in exercises later in the book.

Movie_____

properties_inspector.mov

To see how to change the context of the Properties Inspector, watch the movie **properties_inspector.mov** located in the **movies** folder of the *Dreamweaver 2 H•O•T CD-ROM*.

(Note: this movie intentionally has no sound.)

The Properties Inspector

Like the Objects Palette, the Properties Inspector is context sensitive, meaning it constantly changes depending on what type of element is selected. The Properties Inspector controls many settings, including those for Text, Tables, Alignment, and Images. Since Dreamweaver defaults to opening a blank page with the text insertion-symbol blinking, the Properties Inspector defaults to displaying text properties, as shown below.

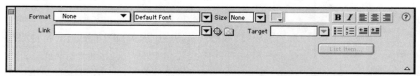

The Properties Inspector changes depending on what is being edited on screen. Since these elements change depending on context, future chapters will cover the various properties on this bar in depth.

The Launcher and Mini-Launcher

The **Launcher** allows you to access several aspects of Dreamweaver with a single click. It basically "launches" the Site, Library, Styles, Behavior, Timeline and HTML areas of the Dreamweaver 2 interface. Go ahead and try clicking on each of the buttons to see what it does. You can't hurt anything, I promise! Click on the button again, and the feature will go away.

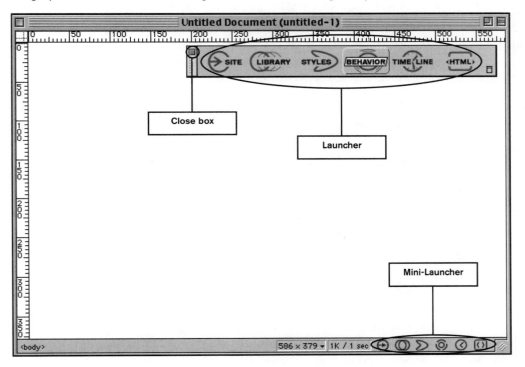

The **Mini-Launcher** at the bottom of the screen works identically to its larger counterpart. Try clicking on each of its buttons to see what I mean. If you can train yourself to understand what the icons on the Mini-Launcher represent, then you can close the larger Launcher by clicking on its close box to make more room on your screen. You can open the larger Launcher at any time by selecting **Window > Launcher**.

Launcher and Mini-Launcher Features

Site	The Site button opens the Site window, where you will control Dreamweaver's powerful site-management features. This window is covered in detail in Chapter 3, *"Site Control."*
Library	The Library button opens the Library window. You can create Library items that are shared across your site, and update them with ease. You would use Library items when you have elements of your site that are used on many pages, such as copyright notices or navigation bars. By converting these sorts of elements into Dreamweaver Library items, they can be changed once and the change will ripple through every page in which the element is present. You will learn about this in Chapter 9, *"Templates/Libraries."*
Styles	The Styles button opens the Styles window. Styles are part of **C**ascading **S**tyles **S**heets (CSS) and are an advanced feature of Dreamweaver. This feature will be covered in Chapter 8, *"Style Sheets."*
Behavior	The Behavior button opens the Behaviors window. This feature allows you to add JavaScript to your pages, even if you are not a programmer. Some of the Behaviors features will be covered in Chapter 11, *"Rollovers."*
Timeline	The Timeline button opens the Timeline window, and is used to orchestrate animation using Dynamic HTML. You will learn about this feature in Chapter 13, *"DHTML."*
HTML	The HTML button opens the HTML window, where you can view the actual code generated by Dreamweaver 2. You can even watch the HTML code be generated as you create objects on your page! You will learn about this feature in Chapter 4, *"Basics."*

Tip_____

Launcher Shortcuts

All of the Launcher features are available as items under the **Window** menu. In addition, the following function-key shortcuts are available for both Mac and PC users to access these features.

If you memorize the F-keys for the Launcher items, you'll probably never need the larger Launcher Palette again. For example, I use the Site and HTML windows more often than the others, so I have memorized **F5** and **F10** as keyboard shortcuts. Below is a handy chart of the Launcher shortcuts.

Shortcuts	
Key	**Function**
F5	Site
F6	Library
F7	Styles
F8	Behaviors
F9	Timelines
F10	HTML

 Warning_____

Redundancy in the Interface

Truth be told, there is some redundancy in the Dreamweaver 2 interface. For example, you can insert an image by clicking on the Objects Palette, or by choosing the Insert Image command from the Insert menu. You can often align objects using the Properties Inspector, or using a command on a menu. Though it's convenient at times to have different options, it can be confusing to learn a program that has two or three ways to accomplish the same task. Throughout the book I'll be citing my favorite ways to access features, but if you prefer an alternate method, don't let me stop you!

The Document Window

The Document window is where all the action happens. This is where you assemble your page elements and design your pages. The Document window is similar in appearance to the browser window when viewed from Netscape Navigator or Microsoft Internet Explorer. On both the Mac and Windows, Dreamweaver 2 will create a blank and Untitled Document each time you open the application.

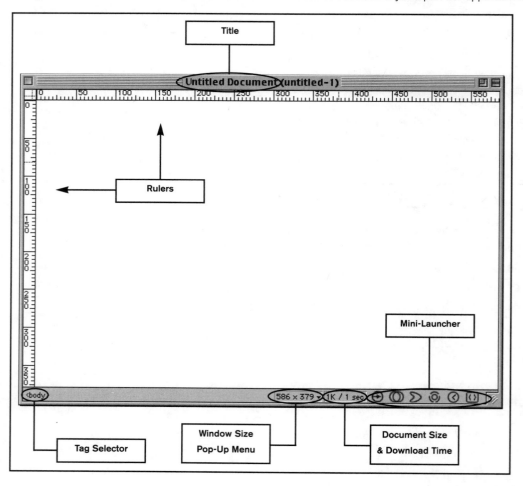

Document Window Features

Feature	Description
Title Bar	The Title Bar contains the name of your Web page (for instance, "My Web Page") and the file name of your Document (for example, **webpage.html**).
Rulers	You can show or hide rulers by selecting **View > Rulers > Show** or **Hide**.
Tag Selector	If you select visual elements on your screen, the Tag Selector highlights the corresponding HTML code. It's a fast and easy way to select different items on your page.
Window Size	The Window Size pop-up menu lets you re-size your window to various preset or custom pixel dimensions.
Document Size & Download Time	The Document Size and Download Time section gives you the approximate size (kilobytes) and download time for the current page.
Mini-Launcher	The Mini-Launcher is a small version of the Launcher toolbar and gives you access to various key features within Dreamweaver.

Preferences

There are many different preferences that you can change to make Dreamweaver 2 your very own custom HTML editor. You can change these settings at any time in your workflow. To access the **Preferences** window, select **Edit > Preferences**. For more information on Dreamweaver Preferences, take a look at the Chapter, *"Preferences Appendix"* on pages 284-299.

Under the **General** category are settings that determine the appearance and operation of Dreamweaver as a whole. For example, you might consider changing the Objects Palette's appearance setting to **Icons** and **Text**, as described earlier in the chapter, until you become more familiar with the icons representing the various Dreamweaver objects.

External Editors

This is a really cool feature! You can specify External Editors for HTML and image editing, if you want to. For instance, you can specify another HTML editor like BBEdit or HomeSite to edit the code that Dreamweaver generates. This book does not cover the use of external HTML editors; they are mostly used by programmers who want to more tightly control the code that Dreamweaver automatically generates. Dreamweaver 2 ships with BBEdit (for Mac) and HomeSite (for Windows), so these will be preset as the default external HTML editors. In addition, you can specify external image editors. This means you can launch Fireworks or any other image-editing applications, from right inside Dreamweaver 2.

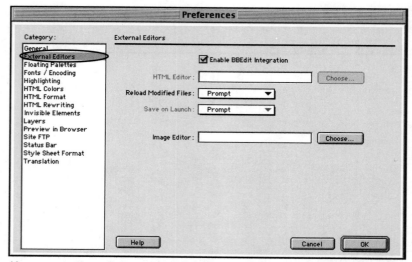

*You can specify an External Editor by choosing **Edit > Preferences** and clicking on the **External Editors** category.*

Preset Window Sizes

One of the pitfalls of Web design is that your page's look will change depending on the size of the monitor that displays it. Dreamweaver has a handy feature—the **Window Sizes** option—to help you design more accurately for a specific monitor size.

You can access the Window Sizes option by selecting **Edit > Preferences** and clicking on the **Status Bar** category. Or you can select the Window Size pop-up menu in the Status Bar.

The Window Sizes menu offers you a variety of preset sizes for the Document window. For example, if you want to design for a 640 x 480 pixel screen, you can select either of the 640 x 480 pixel dimension settings and Dreamweaver will automatically resize your window. No longer do you have to guess how much area you have to design with!

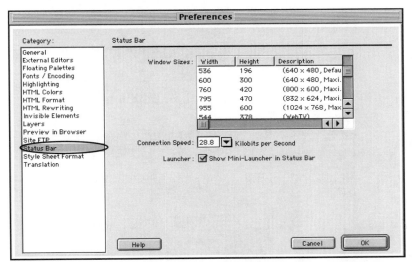

*You can set your own **Window Sizes** settings by choosing **Edit > Preferences** and clicking on the **Status Bar** category.*

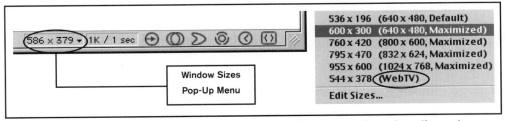

*You can click on the **Window Sizes** menu to access the various default dimensions. If you choose **Edit Sizes,** you can add your own size presets.*

How to Define Your Browser of Choice

Netscape 4.5 was used in all the screen captures for this book, and Netscape 4.6 has been provided for you on the *H•O•T CD-ROM*. You are welcome to use the browser of your choice for the exercises in this book. **Warning:** A few exercise steps will not work in earlier browser versions. To set up your browser preference, follow the steps below.

STEP-BY-STEP

1. Choose **Edit > Preferences…**.

2. Click on **Preview in Browser** under Category.

3. Click on the **Add…**, **Edit…**, or **Remove** buttons to set, change, or remove a browser from the list of choices. **Note:** The Primary Browser defines which browser will launch using the **F12** shortcut key. The Secondary Browser defines which browser can be launched using **Cmd+F12** (Mac) **Ctrl+F12** (Windows).

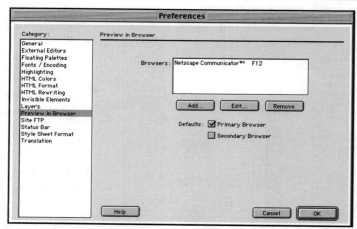

*The Preview in Browser preference sets the primary browser opened with the **F12** shortcut key.*

Note_____

Shortcut Keys

There are lots and lots of shortcut keys in Dreamweaver, and all of them are listed in your manual. Below is a chart which list my favorite ones.

Shortcuts in Dreamweaver

Command	Mac	Windows
New Document	Cmd+N	Ctrl+Shift+N
Line Break	Shift-Enter	Shift-Enter
Page Properties	Cmd+J	Ctrl+J
Select a Word	Double-click	Double-click
Check Spelling	Shift+F7	Shift+F7
Find	Cmd+F	Ctrl+F
Convert Layers to Table	Cmd+Shift+F6	Ctrl+Shift+F6
Convert Tables to Layers	Cmd+F6	Ctrl+F6
Preview in Primary Browser	F12	F12
Preview in Secondary Browser	Cmd+F12	Ctrl+F12
Objects	Cmd+F2	Ctrl+F2
Properties	Cmd+F3	Ctrl+F3
Launcher	Shift+F4	Shift+F4
Library	F6	F6
Styles	F7	F7
Behaviors	F8	F8
Timelines	F9	F9
HTML	F10	F10
Layers	F11	F11
Frames	Cmd+F10	Ctrl+F10
Templates	Cmd+F11	Ctrl+F11

3.Site Control

• **Defining a Site** • **FTP**

• **Relative and Absolute Links**

• **Understanding Paths** • **Site maps**

chap_03 folder

Dreamweaver 2
H•O•T CD-ROM

Those of you who have already built Web pages will likely agree that file management is one of the biggest challenges of this medium. By file management, I mean the organization, folder structure, and naming conventions of all the pages and graphics in your Web site. Few other disciplines require the creation of so many documents at once, because Web pages are usually comprised of numerous text and image files.

To compound the difficulty of managing lots of files, most people build Web sites from their hard drive, and when they're finished they upload these files to a Web server so that the files can be viewed from the WWW. Let's say that you created a folder on your hard drive and called it "HTML" and created another folder called "graphics." If you put your HTML and graphics files inside those two folders, you would have to replicate this exact folder hierarchy when you upload those files to your Web server, or your links to those files would break.

Dreamweaver has a site-management scheme that requires that you keep all your files within one main root folder, so you can easily duplicate the folder hierarchy that's on your hard drive when you upload to a Web server. A root folder is no different than any other kind of folder on your hard drive, except that you have specified to Dreamweaver that this is where all HTML and media files for your site reside. If you think of the root folder as the folder from which all other files stem, just like the roots of a tree, then you will understand its function. A root folder can contain many subfolders, but Dreamweaver cannot keep track of elements unless they are stored inside of the root.

Taking the concept further, let's say that you decided midstream to change the folder hierarchy of your site by adding a folder or changing a folder name. If you were hand-coding the pages, it would be a real pain to make these changes. Dreamweaver makes this process painless, as long as you work within its site-management structure.

By the time you are through these exercises, you will have learned to define a site and a root folder, create a site map, and reorganize files and folders. Not bad for a day's work!

 Warning_____

Site Management!

You might think that Site Management in Dreamweaver is a neat but optional feature, and that you would rather skip it now to return later when you're in the mood. Don't do it! Site Management is actually integral to Dreamweaver 2, and the program kicks up quite a fuss if you don't use it properly. This book will ask that you define a site with each new chapter, because if you have files outside your defined area, you will be constantly plagued by warnings. If you choose to ignore this, you will not be using Dreamweaver 2 properly.

 Note_____

Mac and Windows Differences

For the most part, Dreamweaver has the identical interface for both Mac and Windows platforms. The one case where this is untrue is with Site Management. For this reason, this chapter sometimes contains different directives for the Mac and the Windows user.

Exercise #1_____Defining a Site

This exercise will show you how to define sites in Dreamweaver. You will be working with a folder of HTML and image files from the *H•O•T CD-ROM* that you will transfer to your hard drive. Once you've finished this exercise, Dreamweaver's site-management feature will catalogue all the files inside this folder. This exercise teaches you how to define an existing site from an existing Web site. You would use this identical process if you wanted to use Dreamweaver on a site that you or someone else had created outside Dreamweaver. At the end of the chapter, you'll complete an exercise that will show you how to define a site from an empty folder, which might more likely simulate your approach if you were starting a new site from scratch.

STEP-BY-STEP_____

1. Copy the contents of the **chap_03** folder to your hard drive. For clarity, it's best if you leave this folder named **chap_03**.

The folder contains images and HTML files that are requested within this chapter. It is essential that you copy these folders. Do not work directly off the CD, because you will be asked to add and change files which require that you have the files on your hard drive.

2. Open Dreamweaver and press **F5** to bring up the Site window. On the pop-up menu select **Define Sites....** **Note:** If you've worked in Dreamweaver before, and have already defined other sites, you would click **New**.

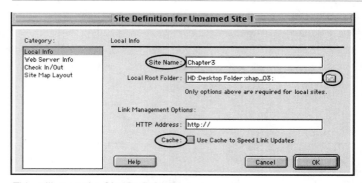

*This will open the **Site Definition** window.*

3. Type **Chapter 3** for the **Site Name**.

This is an internal naming convention so you can use any kind of name you want without worrying about spaces or capitalization. Think of it as your own pet name for your project, just like you give a folder or hard drive a custom name.

4. Click on the small yellow folder icon to the right of the **Local Root Folder** text box. Browse to the **chap_03** folder that you copied to your hard disk and click **OK** (Mac) or **Open > Select** (Windows). Make sure to put a check in the **Use Cache to Speed Link Updates** checkbox. This will increase the speed with which Dreamweaver performs its link-management features.

5. Click **OK**.

A message box will be displayed, indicating that the initial site cache needs to be created. You can choose to not have this message displayed in the future by clicking on the check-box (highly recommended!).

6. Click **OK**. After the site cache has been created, you'll be brought back to the **Define Sites** window.

7. Click **Done**.

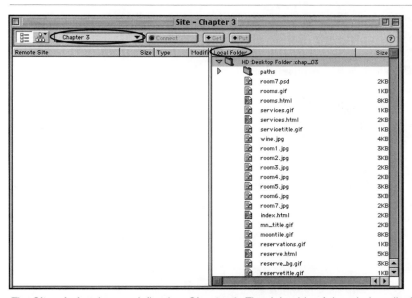

*The **Site window** is now defined as **Chapter 3**. The right side of the window displays the **Local Folder**. This is the folder on your hard disk that contains all of your HTML files and images. The list represents all the files on your hard drive within the **chap_03** folder. The left side of the window displays the **Remote Site** or the **Site Map** information. Nothing is displayed right now because you haven't gotten to that exercise yet. **Note:** If you see locks next to the file names, refer to "Introduction" on page XI.*

Getting Your Pages Online

In order for your site to be seen on the World Wide Web, your files need to be uploaded to a live Web server. Most Web developers and designers build pages on their hard drive before transferring their files to a live Web server. In Dreamweaver, the files on your hard drive are referred to as *local files*, and the files on a live Web server are referred to as *remote files*.

This book directs you to build its exercises on your local hard drive. In order for these exercise files to be viewed from the World Wide Web, they must be transferred to a live Web server. If you have an Internet connection and have purchased space for a Web site, then you would be able to upload these exercises if you wanted to. You can upload your files from Dreamweaver by using the Site Definitions FTP (**F**ile **T**ransfer **P**rotocol) settings.

The information that you need to fill out in the FTP settings of Dreamweaver will be different for every person reading this book. This is one reason FTP is not included as an active exercise, and why uploading these files is optional. To get the proper information for these settings, you need to contact the company hosting your Web site. If you are working on an Intranet, then someone from your networking or data-processing department would be able to supply you with this information.

To access the FTP area within Dreamweaver, press **F5**, and select **Define Sites...** from the pop-up menu. Choose **Chapter 3** and click **Edit...**. Click on **Web Server Info** and choose **FTP** from the pop-up menu.

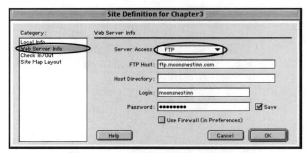

The information shown in the above example of what FTP settings look like is only a sample, and will not work for you. These settings will vary for every person reading this book, and you need to contact your Web hosting company or site administrator to get the proper settings that will work for your remote Web site.

Note _____

What is FTP?

FTP stands for **F**ile **T**ransfer **P**rotocol. This term is usually associated with the process of uploading Web files to a live Web server. You will hear this term used as a noun ("I used an FTP program to upload my files") and as a verb ("I am going to FTP all of my files now!").

It is important to note that you do not have to use Dreamweaver to exchange files with the remote server. You can use other FTP applications as well, such as Fetch (Mac) or WS_FTP (Windows).

Below you will find a handy chart that describes the FTP settings in Dreamweaver.

FTP Settings in Dreamweaver	
Setting	**Description**
FTP Host	This will typically be an address similar to the URL of your Web site. In some cases it may begin with an FTP prefix.
Host Directory	If you have a specific directory on the server where you are supposed to place your files, you would enter that here. This option is not always used.
Login	You will be given a user name to access the remote server. It is important that you enter this information exactly as it is given to you, otherwise you will have problems connecting to the remote server.
Password	In addition to a user name, you will also be given a password to access the remote server. If you don't want to enter the password every time you connect to the remote server, place a check in the Save checkbox and then Dreamweaver will remember your password! By the way, the password entered here is just stored in a text file on your hard drive so anyone can read it. Don't check this if security is a concern at your site.

Exercise #2_____**Relative and Absolute Links**

This exercise will help you understand two different types of links—those that are relative and those that are absolute. Relative links reference files that are relative to your site. All the files that you see in the Local Folder of your Site window are internal files and can be referenced as relative links. If you want to link to an external file, such as someone else's site, you have to use an absolute link. If you don't understand the difference between these two types of links, read on.

STEP-BY-STEP_____

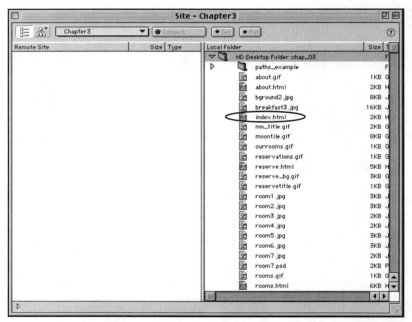

1. Press **F5** to make sure that the Site window is open. Look on the right side of the Site window to the **Local Folder** and double-click on **index.html** to open it. Alternately, you could choose **File > Open** and browse to the **chap_ 03** folder to locate **index.html**.

I suggest that you train yourself to open HTML files from the Site window instead of your hard drive. If you do, it will ensure that you have defined a site and that Dreamweaver's site-management features are being enforced. Believe me, this will save you a lot of pain!

2. Click on the **about the inn (about.gif)** image at the bottom of the screen to select it. **Warning:** Don't double-click the image! If you do, Dreamweaver will give you an error message that you have not yet defined an image editor. If this happens, click **Cancel**. All you need to do is get the image selected (it will have a white bounding box around it, as shown).

3. With the image selected, look at the **Properties Inspector** and notice that this image links to **about.html**. (If your Properties Inspector is smaller than the one shown here, click on the **arrow** at the bottom-right corner to expand it.) The link **about.html** is a **relative** link. It does not have additional information in front of it, such as **http://www.moonsnestinn.com/about.html**. The file does not need that information because the file name is relative to other internal files in the site.

Movie_____

inspector_context.mov

To view a movie that demonstrates how the inspector
changes depending on con-
text, check out the **inspec-
tor_context.mov** located
inside of the **movies** folder
on the *Dreamweaver 2
H•O•T CD-ROM.*

4. Highlight the word **ojai** at the bottom of the **Document** window. **Tip:** You can
double-click on the word to select it!

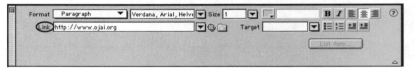

5. In the **Properties Inspector**, notice that this image links to **http://www.ojai. org**.
This is an external link to another site on the Internet. This type of link is referred
to as an **absolute** link. It needs the additional information to specify its location,
because it is not relative to any internal Documents, and it exists on its own
server, separate from the **moons nest inn** site.

6. Save and close the file.

Note_____

Absolute and Relative URLs

The term URL stands for **U**niform **R**esource **L**ocator. In plain English, URLs are the addresses you use when you go to a Web site. Some are simple, such as **http://www.lynda.com**, while others are very complicated and hard to remember, such as **http://www.lynda.com/dw2hot/ lessons/chapterone/introduction**. Regardless of whether a URL is short or long, there are two different types: absolute and relative.

A sample **absolute** URL looks like this:

http://www.lynda.com/index.html

An absolute URL is a complete URL that specifies the exact location of the object on the Web, including the protocol that's being used (in this case, **http**), the host name (in this case, **www.lynda.com**) and the exact path to that location (in this case, **/index.html**). Absolute URLs are always used when you want to link to a site outside your own.

You can use absolute URLs within your own site, but it's not necessary, and most Web publishers opt to use relative URLs instead. If you use relative URLs for internal Documents, it's easier to move them if you change your domain name.

A sample **relative** URL looks like this:

index.html

If I were linking from **pageone.html** of my site to **pagetwo.html** of my site, I wouldn't need to insert the entire **http://www.lynda.com** part anymore. It's actually more flexible to move relative files around your site than to code them with absolute path names.

Exercise #3_____File and Folder Management

From within Dreamweaver's Site window, you can create new folders and files, as well as move them around. When you do this, you're actually adding folders and files to your hard drive, as this exercise will demonstrate. Accessing your hard drive from within Dreamweaver is essential to site-management practices, because Dreamweaver can then keep track of where the files have been moved or added. This exercise will show you how to add folders and files to the **Chapter 3** site.

STEP-BY-STEP_____

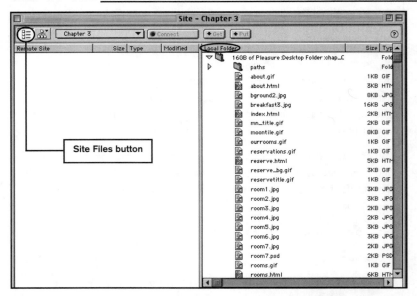

1. Make sure the Site window is open (**F5**) and Click on the **Site Files** button in the upper left corner.

2. Select the folder at the top of the **Local Folder** view.

3. Select **Site > Site Files View > New Folder** (Mac) or **File > New Folder** (Windows). This will add a new folder to the Local Folder and your hard disk.

4. Type **html** for the folder name and press **Return** (Mac) or **Enter** (Windows).

5. Now you need to select the files to be moved into the folder you just created. Here, you'll learn how to select discontinuous files—files that are not adjacent to one another.
- (Mac) **Click** on **about.html**, then **Cmd+Click** on **reserve.html**, **rooms.html**, and **services.html**. (Hold down the **Cmd** key as you click on the three file names).
- (Windows) **Click** on **about.html**, then **Ctrl+Click** on **reserve.html**, **rooms.html**, and **services.html**. (Hold down the **Ctrl** key as you click on the three file names).

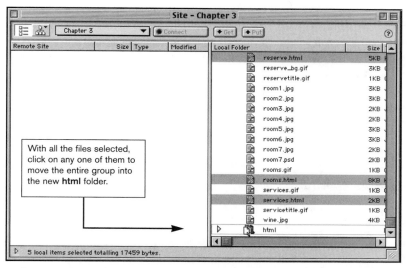

With all the files selected, click on any one of them to move the entire group into the new **html** folder.

Movie_____

movelist.mov

To view a movie that demonstrates how to move the list of files to a different folder, check out the **movelist.mov** located inside of the **movies** folder on the *Dreamweaver 2 H•O•T CD-ROM*.

6. Once you have all four files selected, drag them to the **html** folder that you just created. This will move all four files into this new location.

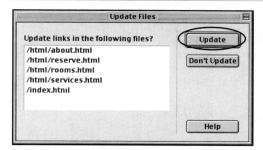

7. When you move the files, Dreamweaver prompts you to update the links. Click the **Update** button. Dreamweaver is listing all the different files that were affected by the files you just moved. Once you click **Update**, these files will be rewritten automatically to reflect the change in file structure.

 Note_____

Use the Site Window!

If you want to add, modify, move, or delete files or folders in your Web site, do it inside Dreamweaver's Site window, as shown in Exercise #3. If you make these folder changes on your hard drive without opening Dreamweaver, you'll have to go in and repair the links manually by relinking each page. If you make your changes inside the Site window, then Dreamweaver will keep track of them and automatically update your pages.

Exercise #4_____Understanding the Path Structure

This next exercise builds on Dreamweaver's Site window features, and shows how path structures are altered if you move files around. A path structure is simply the path to different files in your site. Both relative and absolute URLs can be configured in a variety of different path structures. In this example you will reference files in three distinct ways, each demonstrating the different type of path structures you might encounter.

STEP-BY-STEP_____

In this first example, you will simply insert a file that is within the same folder.

1. Make sure the **Site** window is open (**F5**).

2. Under the **Local Folder** column, double-click on the **paths** folder.

3 Open **path1.html**.

4. Choose **Insert > Image**. Select **moontile.gif**.

*Once you have inserted this image, look at the **Properties Inspector**. Notice that the **Src** is set to **moontile.gif**. As you become more experienced with building Web pages, you will begin to notice that a file name with no slash in front of it means that the file was in the same folder as the HTML that referenced it.*

In this second example, you will insert an image that is inside another folder.

1. Delete the image that you just inserted by selecting it (clicking once on it) and pressing the **Delete** key.

2. Choose **Insert > Image** and open the **images** folder nested inside the **paths** folder to select **moontile2.gif**.

*Once you have inserted this image, look at the **Properties Inspector** again. Notice that the **Src** is now set to **images/moontile2.gif**. The slash means that the file is nested in-side another folder.*

3 Save and close **path1.html**.

In this last example, you will open an HTML Document that is inside a folder and insert an image that is outside a folder.

1. From the **Site** window (**F5**) open **path2.html** from the **html** folder nested within the **paths** folder.

2. Choose **Insert > Image** and navigate outside the **html** folder, into the **images** folder to find **moontile.gif**.

*Once you have inserted this image, look at the **Properties Inspector** again. Notice that the **Src** is now set to **../moontile.gif**. The two dots before the slash indicate that the image was one folder up from the HTML Document that referenced it.*

3. Save and close the file

Note _____

Different Path Notations

When you reference files in HTML, it is necessary to specify exactly where the Document is. Dreamweaver writes the HTML for you, and inserts different path structures depending on where the files are located. Below is a chart to reference how path structures are specified within HTML.

Path Notations in Dreamweaver	
Path Notation	**Description**
document.gif	No slash (/) or dots (..) indicates that the file is inside the same folder as the HTML file.
images/document.gif	The forward slash (/) indicates that the file is inside the images folder, or the file is located one level down from the HTML file.
../images/document.gif	The two dots (..) indicate that the folder is one level up from the HTML file.

Exercise #5_____Creating a Site Map

The site map is a great way to examine the structure of your Web site. It lets you see the different levels and what is contained within those levels. Many people use site maps to show their client how the site looks from a structural viewpoint. It's handy that Dreamweaver can easily create site maps, and even render them as PICT (Mac) or BMP (Windows) files. If you change the structure of the site, the site map will change as well. There is no right or wrong time to make a site map, it is simply a convenience to have this feature available when you want one. This exercise will show you how to create and save a site map.

STEP-BY-STEP_____

1. Press **F5** to open the **Site** window.

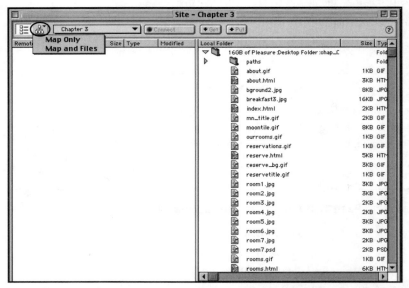

2. Click on the **Site Map** button in the upper-left corner of the Site window. A pull-down menu lets you to choose between two options, **Map Only** or **Map and Files**.

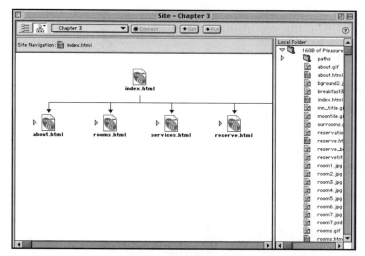

The **Site Map** view, set to **Map and Files**, will open in the left side of the window. The Site Map view is great if you want to see the overall structure of your Web site and how the different pages link to each other.

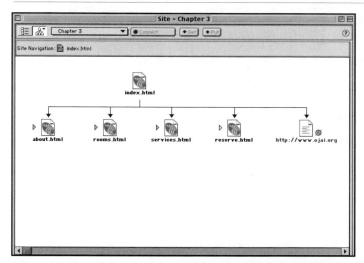

Here in the **Map Only** view, you can see the relative and absolute links displayed side by side. The **absolute** links are in blue and have a small globe to their right. The **relative** links have a small arrow on their left.

---

3. To save this view as an image file:
   • (Mac) select **Site > Site Map View > Save Site Map as PICT**.
   • (Windows) select **File > Save Site Map as…**.

Exercise #6_____Creating a Site from Nothing

So far, you've had a chance to work with Dreamweaver's site-management window by defining a site based on folders and files from the *H•O•T CD-ROM*. What about when you finish this book and go to create your own Web site? You might know how to define a Web site that already exists, but might not know how to go about creating a site from scratch. I wouldn't want that to happen to you, so this next exercise will walk you through the steps of defining a site before you have any content to put in it.

STEP-BY-STEP_____

1. Leave Dreamweaver open, but go to the desktop of your computer. Create a new empty folder on your desktop and name it **website**.

2. There are different directives for defining a site for Mac and Windows users.
   • (Mac) Return to Dreamweaver and choose **Site > Define Sites...** from the top menu. Click **New....**

*Windows users will not find the **Site** menu unless the **Site** window is open.*

   • (Windows) Press **F5** to open the Site window (if it isn't open). Choose **Site > Define Sites...** from the menu bar at the top of the Site window. Click **New**. **Note:** The Site menu item is not available from any other window except the Site window.

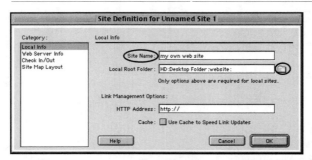

3. Fill in the site name (I chose **my own web site** but you can name it what you want). For the **Local Root Folder**, click on the yellow folder icon and navigate to the empty folder you created on your desktop called website. Click **Select** then **OK**.

4. The message box will be displayed, indicating that the initial site cache needs to be created. Check the box **Don't ask again**, and click **Create**.

5. Click **Done**.

6. This is what your Site window will look like now that you have created a new site based on an empty folder. Notice there's nothing in the Site window? Dreamweaver is doing an accurate job of displaying the contents of an empty folder.

7. You can add files and folders directly from Dreamweaver!
   • (Mac) Choose **Site > Site Files View > New File**. An untitled file will appear.
   • (Windows) Choose **File > New File**. An untitled file will appear.

You can name the file from the Site window, just as you can name an untitled document on your hard drive. If you double-click on the highlighted file, you will see a blank Dreamweaver document appear.

8. Leave Dreamweaver open, but look on the desktop of your computer and open the **website** folder. Lo and behold, there is an HTML document in there! The same HTML file that appeared in the Site window is also on your hard drive.

9. Try moving some other files into this folder. If you return to Dreamweaver, these other files will appear in the Site window. Basically this Site window is a mirror of what exists on your hard drive.

To summarize, Dreamweaver allows you to create files and folders directly from its Site window. Some Web designers create a lot of images first and throw them into a folder and define that as a site inside Dreamweaver. Others might start with an empty folder and build empty HTML files first, and create and add images later. There is no right or wrong way to start a Web site, but Dreamweaver is flexible enough to work from scratch with an empty folder, or to create a site around existing files.

*When using Dreamweaver, the key is to use the **Define Sites** feature for whichever root folder contains or will contain your Web content. If you follow this practice, you will be using Dreamweaver to its fullest potential for helping you ensure that links do not break and all your pages function properly.*

4. Basics

- **File Name Versus Title Name**
- **Significance of index.html**
- **Inserting Images and Text** • **Page Properties**
- **Links** • **META Tags**

chap_04 folder

Dreamweaver 2
H•O•T CD-ROM

If you're the impatient type (as I would frankly characterize myself) this is the chapter you've been waiting for. The following exercises are going to teach you how to create and save a page, insert and align images and text, link images and text, color text links, insert META information, such as Keywords and Descriptions for search engines, and view the HTML that Dreamweaver 2 created. If that seems like a lot to cover, it is and it isn't. Dreamweaver makes most of these operations as simple as accessing a menu or property bar.

The basics of creating a Web page used to involve knowing HTML and making sure every letter of every tag was correct. While Dreamweaver shields you from writing HTML from scratch, it's generating complex code automatically in the background. This chapter will help clarify the relationship between the visual changes on your screen and the HTML code behind them.

Saving a Document in Dreamweaver is similar to saving in any other program. However, it's always a good practice to save before you start inserting elements on a page. That's because Dreamweaver's site-management capabilities depend on the program knowing the name and location of the page as you are building it.

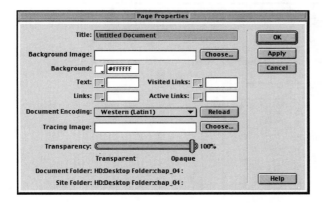

This chapter will introduce you to the Page Properties window of Dreamweaver, which is where the title name and all the colors for your text are set. The handy Color Picker Palette allows you to set any color you want, or choose a color from an image on your page. This feature is new to Dreamweaver 2. It's great for flawlessly matching background colors to image colors!

By the time you are done with this chapter, your Dreamweaver feet will finally be wet and you will be well on your way to learning the interface for creating pages and sites. The exercises here will be your foundation for building more complex pages in future chapters.

Exercise #1_____Defining the Site

With each new chapter, you'll be copying exercises from the *H•O•T CD-ROM* files to your hard drive and defining a new site based on the contents of the new chapter folder. This will familiarize you with setting up Dreamweaver's site-management features, and help you troubleshoot many problems that will kick up if the site is not defined. Normally, if you were working on a single site, you would likely only define your site once. If you switched projects, however, you would need to define a new site. Dreamweaver allows you to manage multiple sites, which is helpful if you have multiple clients or projects for which you plan to use the program. Because each chapter of this book features different files, each chapter is considered a new site.

STEP-BY-STEP_____

1. Copy the contents of the **chap_04** folder to your hard drive.

2. Make sure the **Site** window is open. If it's not, press **F5**.

3. Click on the pop-up menu at the top of the **Site** window and select **Define Sites....**

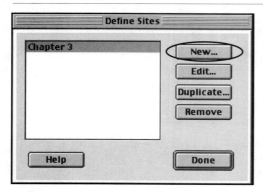

4. Click **New....**

5. Type **Chapter 4** for the **Site Name**.

6. Click on the small yellow folder to select **chap_04** as the **Local Root Folder**.

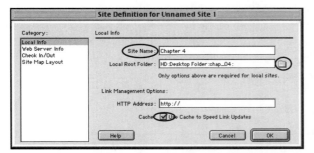

7. Make sure to check the **Use Site Cache to Speed Link Updates** checkbox.

8. Click **OK**.

9. If the **Create Site Cache** dialog box opens, click **Create**. Click **Don't ask again** so that this dialog box doesn't repeatedly appear.

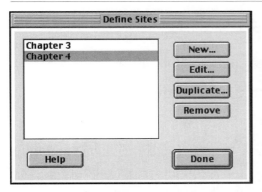

10. When the **Define Sites** window opens, click **Done**.

11. The **Site** window will open. You won't need it right now, so press **F5** to close it.

Exercise #2_____Creating and Saving a Document

This exercise will show you how to create and save a Document in Dreamweaver. You will be naming this Document **index.html**, which has special significance in HTML, and almost always means that it is the beginning page of a site. Additionally, you will learn to set the title of this Document to **Moon's Nest Inn**.

STEP-BY-STEP_____

*A blank Document should be visible. If you don't have one, select **File > New**.*

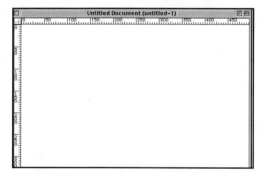

1. Select **Modify > Page Properties....**

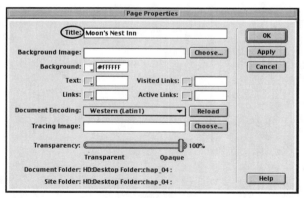

2. Type **Moon's Nest Inn** for the **Title** option. Leave the other options at their default values for now.

3. Click **OK**.

You will be returned to the Document window. The page is blank, but you're going to turn it into a cool and functional Web page in a jiffy.

Before you get started, it is very important that you save your file first. All of the site-management features introduced in the last chapter depend on Dreamweaver knowing the name of your file, so the program constantly notifies you if you are working on an unsaved Document. Besides, no one wants to unexpectedly lose work, and this practice is good insurance against system crashes and/or power outages.

4. Select **File > Save As....**

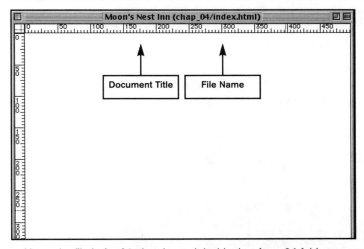

5. Name the file **index.html** and save it inside the **chap_04** folder on your hard disk.

*There are two names in the title bar of your Document window. The first name is the title of the Document (**Moon's Nest Inn**). The title can be different from the file name, as in the example shown above. The second name is the file name (**index.html**) which shows up to the right of the title.*

Note_____

File Names Versus Titles

As you create Web pages with Dreamweaver, you will need to specify various names for your files, folders, sites, etc. This might not seem tricky at first glance, but there are actually two different names associated with HTML files—the file name and the title.

When you save a Document, you will be assigning its file name, which must always end with the **.htm** or **.html** extension. There is another name associated with the Document too, and it is called the *title*. The file **index.html** here, for example, has the *title* of **Moon's Nest Inn**.

It's essential that you pay attention to spaces and capitalization in your file names, but Document titles are much more flexible and should be more descriptive than the file name. When the page is viewed from a Web browser, the title will be much more visible to your end user than your file name. This is also the wording that will appear in people's bookmark list.

*In the above example you will build in this chapter, note that the **title** appears in the browser's title bar, while the **file** name appears in the URL. This is how the page you create will appear to your end users. Titles are also important, because when people use search engines, they are often how your files will be listed.*

Note_____

The Significance of index.html

You just created a Document called **index.html**. What you might not appreciate is that this particular file name has special significance. Most Web servers recognize the **index.html** as the default home page. If you type the URL **http://www.lynda.com**, for example, what you will really see is **http://www.lynda.com/index.html**, even though you didn't type it that way. The web server knows to open the **index.html** file automatically without requiring that the full URL be typed in. Therefore, if you name the opening page of your Web site with the file name **index.html**, the Web server will know to automatically display this file first.

To take this concept one step further, you can have an opening page to each section of your Web site, not just to your home page. There are two definite advantages to this. Not only will visitors to your site be spared having to remember really long URLs and typing **index.html** time and again, but they won't end up looking at a generic index, like the example below.

This is why the file name **index.html** is so significant and it's also why most professional Web developers use it as the root file name, although on some servers a different name is used, such as **default.html**. You may not realize that you are not limited to just one **index.html** on your site. You can have one inside each folder that represents a category for your site, such as Company, Services, Store, and Products.

Name	Last modified	Size	Description
Parent Directory	17-May-1999 17:11	-	
00INDEX	22-Jan-1998 19:42	1k	
CLUTS/	22-Jan-1998 19:43	-	
_message	22-Jan-1998 19:59	1k	
bclut2.aco	22-Jan-1998 19:42	3k	
bclut2.aco.sit.hqx	11-Aug-1998 00:24	1k	
bclut2.zip	30-Apr-1999 14:16	1k	

*If you do not have an **index.html**, browsers will display a general list of your files, such as the above example.*

Exercise #3_____Inserting Images

In this exercise, you will learn to insert images for your page's headline, logo, and navigation bar.

STEP-BY-STEP_____

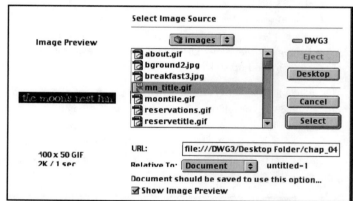

1. Click on the **Insert Image** object in the **Objects Palette. Note:** You could also choose **Insert > Image** from the menu bar or use the shortcut key combination **Opt+Cmd+I** (Mac) or **Alt+Cmd+I** (Windows).

2. Browse to **mn_title.gif** inside the **images** folder. Click **Select**. If you don't see the extension **space.gif**, refer to the *"Introduction,"* pages XII–XIII.

3. Click off the image to deselect it, and press **Return** or **Enter**. The Return key will create a paragraph break, causing a space to form between the headline graphic and the next image.

4. Click on the **Insert Image** object in the Objects Palette. Browse to **moontile.gif** inside the **images** folder. Click **Select**.

5. Click off the image to deselect it, and press **Return** or **Enter** twice. This inserts two paragraph breaks into the formatting of the page.

6. Click on the **Insert Image** object in the Objects Palette and browse to **about.gif** inside the **images** folder. Click **Select**.

7. Don't move your cursor (make sure it's right next to the image that you just inserted). Click on the **Insert Image** object in the Objects Palette and browse to **rooms.gif** inside the **images** folder. Click **Select**.

8. Click on the **Insert Image** object and browse to **services.gif** inside the **images** folder. Click **Select**.

9. Click on the **Insert Image** object and browse to **reservations.gif** inside the **images** folder. Click **Select**.

10. Save your file and leave it open for the next exercise.

This is what your page should look like at this point.

 Tip

Paragraph Versus Line Breaks

You may have noticed that each time you pressed the **Return** or **Enter** key, Dreamweaver skipped down the page two lines. Pressing the **Return** or **Enter** key inserts a single paragraph break. The HTML tag for a paragraph break is **<P>**. This is useful when you want to increase the space between different paragraphs. However, there will be times when you just want to go to one line directly below the one you are working on without introducing extra space. Pressing **Shift +Return** (or **Shift+Enter**), inserts a line break instead. The HTML tag for a line break is **
. Knowing the difference between a **<P> and a **
** will allow you to control the spacing between lines of text.

Exercise #4_____**Inserting Text**

Adding text to your Web page is really simple in Dreamweaver. Just like your favorite word processor, you can simply start typing text on your page and the text will appear. In this exercise, you will add some text at the bottom of your page as an alternative navigation system, which is useful to people who might have their images turned off in their browser settings or be browsing in a non-graphical browser (such as site-impaired audiences).

STEP-BY-STEP_____

1. Click below the images you inserted in the last exercise, and hit **Return** to create a paragraph break. Type **home**, press the **spacebar**, press **Shift+Backslash** to insert a small vertical line (|), and press the **spacebar** again.

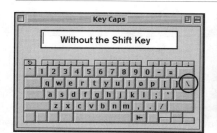 

*Note: The Backslash key is located in different spots on different keyboards. This is what it looks like. A **Shift+Backslash** creates a straight line character, known as a "pipe," which is what you're trying to achieve.*

2. Type **about the inn**, press the **spacebar**, press **Shift+Backslash** to insert a small vertical line, and press the **spacebar** again.

3. Type **our rooms**, press the **spacebar**, press **Shift+Backslash** to insert a small vertical line, and press the **spacebar** again.

4. Type **guest services**, press the **spacebar**, press **Shift+Backslash** to insert a small vertical line, and press the **spacebar** again.

5. Type **reservations**, press the **spacebar**, press **Shift+Backslash** to insert a small vertical line, and press the **spacebar** again.

6. Press **Shift+Return**, to create a line break. This puts your type-insertion cursor on the next line without introducing a two-space paragraph return.

7. Type **want to learn more about ojai?**

8. Save your file.

> home | about the inn | our rooms | guest service | reservations
> want to learn more about ojai?

This is the result you should get at the end of typing in this exercise.

This is what your page should look like now.

Exercise #5_____Centering Images and Text

Now that you have entered in the images and text for your page, it's time to learn how to center them. The next section reviews centering procedures with text and images.

STEP-BY-STEP_____

1. Select **the moon's nest inn** logo from the previous exercise (**mn_title.gif**) at the top of the screen. Choose **Modify > Alignment > Center**.

2. Use your **Shift** key to multiple-select the images: **moontile.gif** (the round in the middle of the page), **about.gif** (about the inn), **ourrooms.gif** (our rooms), **services.gif** (guest services), and **reservations.gif** (reservations). Choose **Modify > Alignment > Center** again.

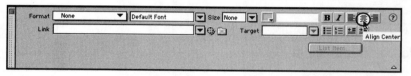

3. There's another way to center text, which you can try. Select the navigation text at the bottom of the screen by dragging the cursor across it to highlight all the words. Click on the **Align Center** button in the **Properties Inspector**. The text at the bottom should snap to the center.

Your page should look like this at the end of the exercise.

4. Save the file and leave it open for the next Exercise #6.

Exercise #6_____Modifying Page Properties

This exercise will walk you through changing the colors of your page using the Page Properties window. The Page Properties control many important attributes of your page, including the Document title (which we looked at in Exercise #2) and the colors you set for your text and links.

STEP-BY-STEP_____

1. Select **Modify > Page Properties...**, or use the shortcut to access Page Properties, **Cmd+J** (Mac) or **Ctrl+J** (Windows).

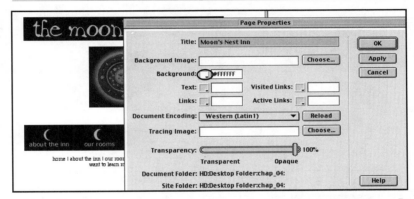

2. Move this window to the side so you can see the **Page Properties** and your Document at the same time.

3. Click on the small box to the right of the word **Background**. This will open the Dreamweaver 2 Color Palette shown on the next page.

 Note_____

What is Browser-Safe Color?

Browser-safe colors are the 216 colors supported by browsers across platforms (Mac and Windows). If you use the browser-safe colors inside the Page Properties settings, you reduce the risk of having your colors shift when people view your Web pages.

Note_____

The Dreamweaver Color Palette

All of colors in the Color Palette are browser-safe, and they're arranged in a manner that shows the darkest colors at the bottom and the lightest colors at the top. You can use the Eye Dropper to select from these colors. To understand all of the Eye Dropper settings, see the chart below.

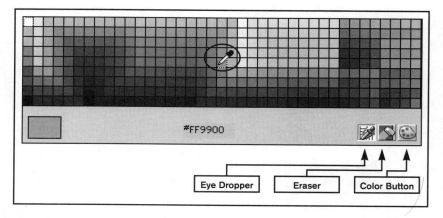

Color Palette Buttons

Eye Dropper	The Eye Dropper allows you to select any color visible on your screen. When you press this button, any color you eye-drop on snaps to the nearest Web-safe color. If you don't press this button, Dreamweaver will pick up the actual color, which may not be browser-safe!
Eraser	The Eraser lets you close the Color Palette without selecting a different color. You would use this if you picked a color and then changed your mind. Think of it as the equivalent of a "Cancel" button.
Color Button	The Color button launches the Apple System Color Picker (Mac) or the Color dialog box (Windows). If you use this button, you increase the odds of not picking a browser-safe color.

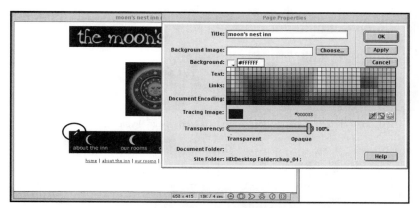

Movie_____

page_properties_eyedropper.mov

To view a movie that demonstrates Step 4, check out the **page_properties_eyedropper.mov** located inside of the **movies** folder on the *Dreamweaver 2 H•O•T CD-ROM*.

4. With your mouse depressed, move the **Eye Dropper** outside of the Page Properties window to let up on the (**about the inn**) image. This will set the Background Color of your page to match the edge of this image. To instantly see the results, click **Apply**. Don't click **OK** yet, because there are still more colors to set in upcoming steps!

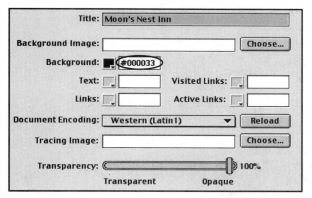

To set other colors, you can insert your own values.

5. Click inside the text box next to the **Text** option. Type **#CCCCFF**. You just colored all your text light blue in this Document. Again, to preview, click **Apply** again. The Apply button is actually accepting your changes, it is not merely a preview. Clicking it is the same as clicking **OK**, except that it does not close the window.

6. Type **#3333FF** for the **Links** option. All the text in this Document that contains a link will be bright blue. Type **#6666FF** for the **Visited Links** option. After someone has visited a link, it will turn blue, letting you know that that link has already been viewed.

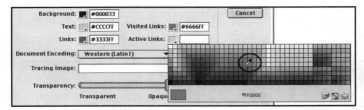

7. You could also choose a color by sight, instead of typing in a hexadecimal value. Click the box to the right of the words **Active Links**, and the Color Palette will open. Select a red color. This will set the active link color to red. The only time an Active Link color shows is when the mouse is depressed on the link. Click **OK**.

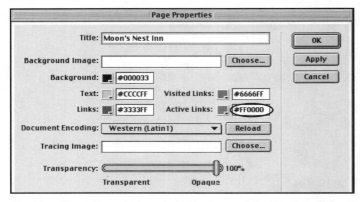

The Page Properties window should look something like this. **Note:** *You might have a different red for* **Active Links** *than shown here, since you selected this color by sight, not numeric value.*

This is what the results of this exercise should look like.

8. Save the Document and leave it open for the next exercise.

Note_____

The Page Properties Window

The Page Properties window does more than just set the colors of the links and your Document title. See the chart below for an explanation of all its features.

Page Properties	
Property	**Description**
Title	The title of your page is what will appear in the title bar of the Web browser and when your page is bookmarked. This name can contain as many characters as you want, including special characters, such as %(#*$!.
Background Image	If you want a Background Image for your Web page, you would specify it here. A Background Image can be any GIF or JPEG file. If the image is smaller than the Web browser window, then it will repeat (tile).
Background	This sets the Background Color. The values can be in hexadecimal format or by name (i.e., red, white, etc.).
Text	This sets the default text color. It can be overwritten for specific areas of text.
Links	This sets the link color. This option can be over ridden for specific links.
Visited Links	This sets the Visited Link color. A Visited Link color specifies how the link will appear after a visitor has clicked on it.
Active Link	This sets the Active Link color. The Active Link color specifies how the link will appear while someone clicks on it.
Document Encoding	This specifies the language for the characters and fonts used in the Document.
Tracing Image	Tracing Images are used as guides to set up the layout of your page. A Tracing Image can be any GIF, JPEG, or PNG file. You will learn to work with a Tracing Image in Chapter 5, *"Layout."*
Transparency	This sets the transparency level of your Tracing Image.

Exercise #7_____Creating Links with Images and Text

The ability to link to pages and sites is what makes the Web dynamic. This chapter will show you how to set up links using Dreamweaver's Properties Inspector.

STEP-BY-STEP_____

1. Select the **moontile.gif** image in the center of the screen.

2. Click on the small yellow folder next to the **Link** option in the Properties Inspector. **Note:** If your Properties Inspector window is smaller than what is shown here, click on the arrow at the bottom right corner to expand it.

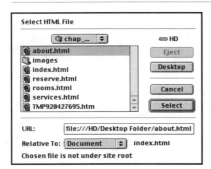

3. Browse to **about.html** and click **Select**. Congratulations, you have just created your first relative image link. Why was it relative? Because it linked to a Document within this site, not to an external Web site.

4. Highlight the **about.gif** (**about the inn**) image at the bottom of the screen.

5. Click on the small yellow folder next to the **Link** option in the Properties Inspector.

6. Browse once again to **about.html**. Click **Select**. Now **moontile.gif** and **about.gif** are linked to **about.html**.

7. Now repeat this process for the remaining navigation icons. Highlight **rooms.gif (our rooms)** image and link it to **rooms.html**. Click **Select**. Highlight the **services.gif (guest services)** image and link it to **services.html**. Click **Select**. Highlight the **reservations.gif (reservations)** image and link it to **reserve.html**. Click **Select**.

*You have just successfully added links to all the images on this page! If you want to preview the links, press **F12** to view this page in a browser and then click on any of the images. They should take you to the pages you linked to.*

Next, you will create some links using text. The process is almost identical, except you will be selecting text instead of images.

8. Highlight the word **home** at the bottom of the page.

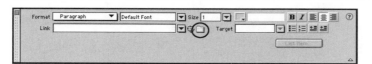

9. Click on the small yellow folder next to the **Link** option in the Properties Inspector.

10. Browse to **index.html**. Click **Select**.

11. Repeat this process for each word in the text navigation at the bottom of the screen. You can select each word easily by double-clicking on it. Once selected, link the **about** text to **about.html**, the **our rooms** text to **rooms.html**, the **guest services** text to **services.html**, and the **reservations** text to **reserve.html**.

*As you create the text links, you will notice the color of the text will change. That's because you set the **Links** color option in the **Page Properties** to light blue and Dreamweaver is previewing that setting for you.*

12. Highlight the word **ojai** at the bottom of the page.

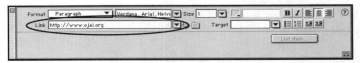

13. Type **http://www.ojai.org** into the **Link** option in the Properties Inspector. Congratulations, you just created your first absolute link. It's an absolute link because it begins with an **http** header and includes the full address.

14. Select **File > Save**. You don't want to lose any of your work!

15. If you want to preview all of your links, press **F12** to launch a browser and try them out.

Exercise #8_____Meta Tags

One of the big challenges aside from building a Web site is letting the search engines know that your site exists. There are two steps to getting your site listed: the first is to list it with all the various search engines out there, and the other is to insert META tags into your HTML so the search engines can find you on their own and correctly index your site. Many search engines send robots (also called spiders) out to search the Web for content. When you insert certain META tags into your Document, you make it much easier for the search-engine robots to understand how to categorize your site. This exercise will show you how to enter META tags with specific attributes, so you can make your Web page more search-engine friendly.

STEP-BY-STEP_____

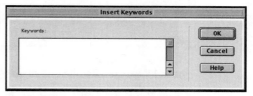

1. Click on the arrow at the top of the Objects Palette. This will reveal a small pop-up menu which contains the words **Common**, **Forms**, **Head**, and **Invisibles**. You are going to work with the **Head** option, because it contains the **META** elements. Select the **Head** option.

2. Click the **Insert Keywords** object. A dialog box will be displayed for you to enter in the keywords for your page.

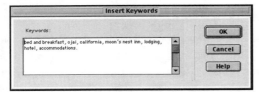

3. Type **bed and breakfast, ojai, california, moon's nest inn, lodging, hotel, accommodations**. Basically, you're listing words that someone might use in a search engine to bring up your site.

4. Click **OK**.

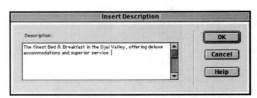

5. Click on the **Insert Description** button in the **Head Objects Palette**. A dialog box will appear for you to enter the description of your Web page.

6. Type **The finest Bed & Breakfast in the Ojai Valley, offering deluxe accommodations and superior service.**

7. Click **OK**.

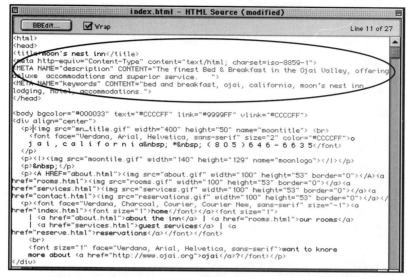

8. Press **F10** to view the HTML in this Document. See the **META** information inside the **HEAD** tag? Visitors to your site won't be able to see the **META** tag information because it's only visible inside your HTML. It's a part of authoring the page that has nothing to do with appearance—and everything to do with helping the search engines find your site.

9. Save and leave this Document open for the next exercise.

 Note_____

Keywords and Descriptions

Keywords are **META** tag values that specify certain words to help Internet search engines index your site. Many search engines limit the number of keywords you can use. Choose your words wisely and use no more than 10-15 keywords that best describe your site's contents.

Descriptions are **META** tag values that also help various search engines index your site. Some search engines will actually use in their directory the very descriptions you specify to describe your site. Again, some search engines limit the number of characters indexed, so keep it short and simple! If you would like more information on **META** tags, be sure to check out these URLs.

Web Developer—META Tag Resources
http://www.webdeveloper.com/html/html_metatag_res.html

The META Tag Builder
http://vancouver-webpages.com/META/mk-metas.html

Exercise #9_____Looking at the HTML

You briefly looked at raw HTML code in the last exercise. This next exercise will help you understand the relationship between the images and text on your page, and the HTML code that Dreamweaver generated.

STEP-BY-STEP_____

1. You can view the HTML generated in Dreamweaver by clicking on the **HTML** button in the Launcher or by pressing **F10**.

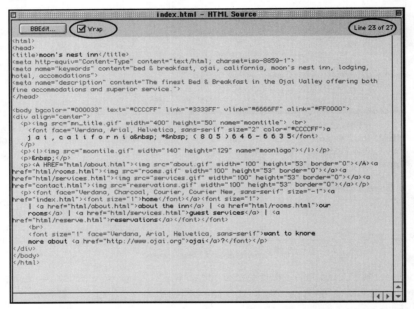

*The HTML Source window is pretty self-explanatory in Dreamweaver 2. However, there are a couple of options you should know about that definitely make it easier for you to view code. The **Wrap** checkbox causes the text to wrap to the next line based upon the size of the HTML Source window. This eliminates the need to scroll to the right to view all the code. Just as handy is the **Line Indicator** in the upper-right corner, which displays which line of code your cursor is on. This is helpful when you are troubleshooting errors in specific lines of your code.*

2. Make sure there is a check in the **Wrap** checkbox. This will cause the text to wrap to the next line based on the size of the HTML Source window.

3. Press **F10** to close the window.

4. Select the **moontile.gif** image in the middle of the page by clicking on it.

```
<html>
<head>
<title>Moon's Nest Inn</title>
<meta http-equiv="Content-Type" content="text/html; charset=iso-8859-1">
<meta name="keywords" content="bed & breakfast, ojai, california, moon's nest inn, lodging, hotel
accomodations">
<meta name="description" content="The finest Bed & Breakfast in the Ojai Valley offering both fin
accommodations and superior service.">
</head>

<body bgcolor="#000033" text="#CCCCFF" link="#3333FF" vlink="#6666FF" alink="#FF0000">
<p align="center"><img src="images/mn_title.gif" width="400" height="50"> </p>
<p align="center"><a href="about.html"><img src="images/moontile.gif" width="140" height="129"
border="0"></a>
</p>
<p> </p>
<p align="center"><a href="about.html"><img src="images/about.gif" width="100" height="53"
border="0"></a><img src="images/rooms.gif" width="100" height="53"><img src="images/services.gif"
width="100" height="53"><img src="images/reservations.gif" width="100" height="53"></p>
<p align="center"><a href="#">home</a> | <a href="#">about the inn</a> | <a href="#">our
 rooms</a> | <a href="#">guest service</a> | <a href="#">reservations</a><br>
 want to learn more about <a href="#">ojai</a>?</p>
</body>
</html>
```

5. Press **F10** to return to the HTML Source window. Notice that the HTML code for the image is highlighted. This is very helpful when you want to look at specific HTML code in your page! You can actually teach yourself HTML by deconstructing your code in this way.

5.Layout

- **Tracing Images • Layers**
- **Converting Layers to Tables**
- **Converting Tables to Layers**

chap_05 folder

Dreamweaver 2
H•O•T CD-ROM

In traditional layout programs, such as Adobe PageMaker and QuarkXPress, most people take for granted that they can move blocks of text and images around almost anywhere on the screen. Unfortunately, standard HTML doesn't have any tags for easily positioning elements. This has caused considerable frustration among Web-page designers. There is good news—Dreamweaver 2 has built-in functions that give you the freedom of absolute positioning while still conforming to strict HTML guidelines.

This chapter will cover Dreamweaver's key features that allow you to position elements anywhere on your Web page: Tracing Images, Layers, and Convert Layers to Tables.

What is a Tracing Image? Let's say that you have been in Photoshop, Fireworks, Illustrator, or any drawing or painting program of your choice, and you've mocked up a wonderful Web page. Don't you just wish you could take that mock-up and put it up on the Web? Dreamweaver's Tracing Image option allows you to place any GIF, JPEG, or PNG into a Tracing Layer on your page, which can then be used as an alignment reference for your HTML elements.

So far, you've been putting artwork and text directly on your page. With that method, you can right, left, or center align elements, and that's the end of the story. This frustrates most people because it would be a lot nicer if you could stick that artwork or text anywhere you wanted on the page and have it stay there. Layers are your savior, as they can be positioned freely on your page! Rather than simply placing artwork and text on a page, like you have been doing so far, you can put your content into Layers and move it anywhere you want.

If Layers are so flexible and let you move your images and text around so easily, why doesn't everyone use them? There's a little problem, in that they are not backwards compatible with older browsers. If you're targeting an audience who uses a 3.0 browser or earlier, or an AOL browser, Layers aren't going to work for you.

There's more good news. Once you've designed a freeform layout using Layers, Dreamweaver allows you to then convert your Layers to HTML Tables so that the Web page is compatible with older versions of Netscape Navigator and Internet Explorer.

Tables were originally developed to insert data into HTML pages, but many people use them for layout by turning off the borders and making them invisible. This trick allows you to use Tables like you would a grid in page layout. You can put images and text into an invisible Table, and the rows and columns and cells hold the objects in place. The bummer about Tables is that they're not intuitive to work with, and the code for creating them can get quite complex. Besides, when you are designing, it's best to be able to change your mind and nudge something up, down, left, or right at whim. You can do that easily with Layers.

Dreamweaver again offers a great solution. You can go back and forth freely between converting Layers to Tables and Tables to Layers so that you can really fine-tune your layout without worrying about writing complex code. With Dreamweaver 2, you can finally focus more of your energy on design, and less on HTML workarounds for layout. Life is good!

Exercise #1_____Applying a Tracing Image

In this exercise, you will learn how to apply a Tracing Image to your Web page as well as how to change its transparency and position on the page. You'll work with a Tracing Image that was supplied on the *H•O•T CD-ROM*. If you were to create your own Tracing Image, you would create a mock-up of your Web page in a graphics application of your choice, such as Photoshop, Fireworks, Illustrator, or whatever, and save it as a GIF, JPEG, or PNG. You would then specify this mock-up as a Tracing Image, so that you could use it in Dreamweaver as your guide to recreate your page design.

The Tracing Image is visible only in Dreamweaver. Visitors to your site cannot see it. Keep in mind that when you are viewing the Tracing Image in Dreamweaver while building your page, you cannot see the Background Image or Background Color that you are setting, unless you lower the Tracing Image transparency setting.

STEP-BY-STEP_____

1. Copy the **chap_05** folder to your hard disk. Click **F5** to access the **Site** window. Define the site as Chapter 5. If you do not remember how to do this, revisit Exercise #1 in Chapter 3, *"Site Control."*

2. From the Site window, double-click on **index.html** to open it. This page is blank, but it won't be for long!

3. Select **Modify > Page Properties**. The shortcut keys for this are **Cmd+J** (Mac) and **Ctrl+J** (Windows).

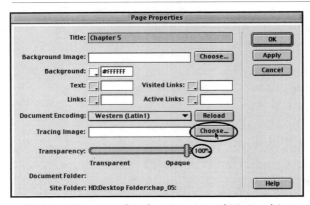

4. Click the **Choose...** (Mac) or **Browse...** (Windows) button next to the **Tracing Image** option.

*Note: For this exercise, make sure the **Transparency Slider** is at 100%. This will enable your **Tracing Image** to be visible when you insert it.*

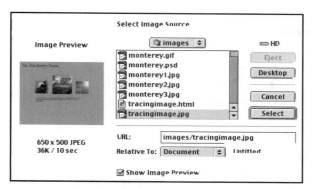

5. Browse to **tracingimage.jpg** inside the **images** folder.

6. Click **Select**, and then **OK** in the **Page Properties** window.

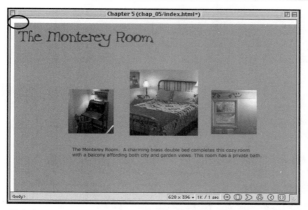

*This is what your page should look like with the **Tracing Image** applied. It was inserted at 100% opacity in the **Page Properties** window, which makes it opaque. **Note:** The white border you see to the left of the **Tracing Image** is an offset created by Dreamweaver to emulate a Web browser. For an explanation of this feature, see the note on the next page.*

7. Press **F12** to preview this page in the Web browser (if you haven't defined a browser yet, this is explained in Chapter 2, *"Interface"*). When you do this, notice that the page appears as a blank screen. This is supposed to happen! The Tracing Image only appears in Dreamweaver, and it will not be visible to your end-user.

 Warning_____

Trouble With Transparency!

Occasionally Dreamweaver will not allow you to insert a **Tracing Image** when your **Transparency Slider** is set to 50%. You can troubleshoot this problem by dragging the slider up or down the scale in any direction.

Note_____

Browser Offset

The white space you see above the Tracing Image is the result of an offset that Dreamweaver created. You can control this off-set by selecting **View > Tracing Image > Adjust Position**.

Why would Dreamweaver introduce such an offset? The program is emulating what would happen on a Web browser. For some dumb reason, browsers don't display images flush top and left, but that's exactly how they display Background Images—flush top and left. This means that any image which is in the foreground (meaning it is not a Background Image) will always be displayed with this offset. While Dreamweaver allows you to get rid of the offset, the offset is intentionally there to show you how the fore-ground artwork will align in a Web browser.

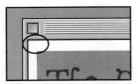

Dreamweaver offsets Tracing Images from the top-left corner to emulate an offset that exists in Web browsers. You can get rid of this offset if you like. I usually leave the offset alone, since it is representative of what will happen in a browser anyway.

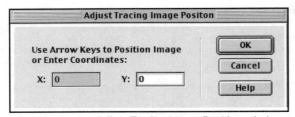

*You can use the Adjust Tracing Image Position window to fix the offset. Choose **View > Tracing Image > Adjust Position**, and enter **X:0** and **Y:0**.*

8. Select **Modify > Page Properties** to access the **Tracing Image** settings again.

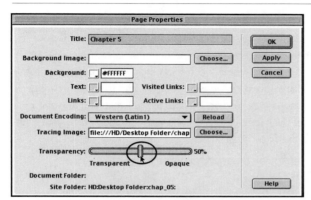

9. Drag the **Transparency Slider** down to **50%** and click **OK**.

With the transparency reduced, it's much easier to use the Tracing Image as a guide without competing with foreground images and text.

10. Select **File > Save** and leave this file open for the next exercise in which you'll add images to match this layout.

Note_____

Tracing Images, Background Colors, and Images

Once you apply a Tracing Image to your page, it will hide the Background Color and Background Image while you are editing the Document inside Dreamweaver. However, if you view the page that contains the Tracing Image from a browser, the Background Color and/or Background Image will be visible and the Tracing Image will not. In other words, Tracing Images are only visible to you while you're working in Dreamweaver. This is a good thing, because you don't want people seeing your blueprint, you want them to see the final results.

*The **Tracing Image** is an internal function of Dreamweaver to help you follow a preconceived layout. When you preview the file at the top, your browser will not display the image. In this case there is no placed artwork, so the browser window remains empty.*

Note_____

Tracing Images, Layers, and Tables

The following chart outlines the concepts behind Tracing Images, Layers and Tables, which you will learn about in the following exercise.

Tracing Images, Layers, and Tables	
Item	**Definition**
Tracing Image	Consider this the blueprint you follow to build your pages.
Layer	This is where you put your text and images so you can move them around freely. The con to using Layers is that they only work on 4.0 browsers and above.
Table	Tables work on almost all browsers, from version 2.0 and above. Tables can hold images and text in place, but they are not intuitive when it comes to design. It's ultimately the best of both worlds to design with Layers and convert to Tables.

Exercise #2_____Adding Layers

In this exercise, you will learn how to create Layers on your page and insert images and text inside them. Then—presto, you'll be able to move everything around. Ahh, the beauty of Layers!

STEP-BY-STEP_____

 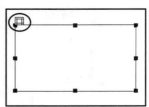

1. Select **Insert > Layer**. This will insert an empty Layer in your Document, in the form of a rectangle on the top left of your screen.

2. Click on the white **Layer Selection Handle**. This will cause eight resizing handles to appear around the Layer.

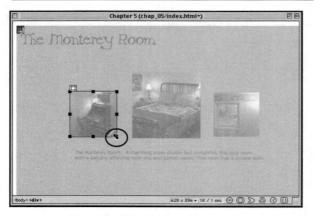

3. Using the **Layer Selection Handle**, move the Layer so its upper-left corner aligns with the photo of the **desk** that is visible in the Tracing Image. Using the bottom-right **resizing handle**, resize the Layer so that it fits around the edge of desk image.

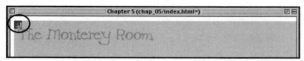

Notice the blue thingie in the upper-left corner? It's called an Invisible Element in Dreamweaver. It's blue here because it's selected. If you click off the Layer to deselect it, you'll see it turn yellow. For more on Invisible Elements, see the note on the next page.

4. Click **inside** the Layer. You should see a blinking I-beam cursor inside the Layer.

5. Select **Insert > Image**.

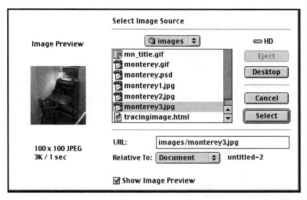

6. Browse to **monterey3.jpg**. inside the **images** folder. Click **Select**.

An image is now inside the Layer. Notice how that image is darker while the Tracing Image is screened back? That's because you set the opacity to 50% in the last exercise. This makes it easy to decipher between the layout and the final artwork, doesn't it?

Note_____

Invisible Element Markers

When you create a Layer in Dreamweaver, a small yellow icon appears at the top of your page. This is referred to as an Invisible Element. Each time you create a Layer, a yellow marker will be inserted. By selecting these markers, you can easily select the associated Layers.

You'll see these markers in the **index.html** Document after you have completed Exercise #2. If you find that these markers get in your way, select **View > Invisibles Elements** to hide/show them all. You can turn off Invisible Elements permanently if you want, by choosing **Edit > Preferences > Invisible Elements**.

*This is what an **Invisible Element** looks like in Dreamweaver.*

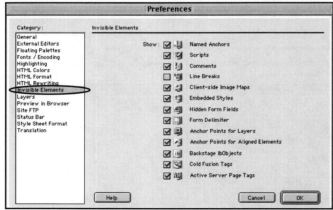

*I rarely use Invisible Elements and prefer to turn them off. You can turn them on or off permanently in Dreamweaver's **Preferences**, under **Edit**.*

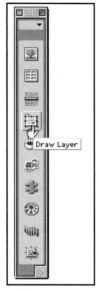

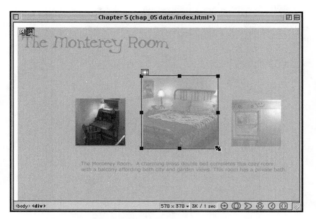

7. Click on the **Draw Layer** object in the Objects Palette.

8. With this tool selected, draw a Layer around the large center image of the **bed**. You've just inserted a Layer by using the Objects Palette instead of the Insert menu. Either way works fine, and you have now been exposed to both.

9. Click inside this Layer and click the **Insert Image** object in the Objects Palette.

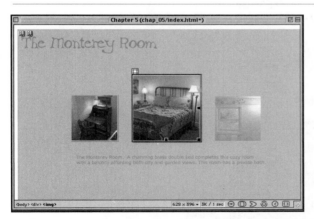

10. Browse to **monterey1.jpg** inside the **images** folder. Click **Select**.

11. Draw another Layer around the small image of the **window**. You can use either the Objects Palette or the Insert menu to accomplish this.

12. Choose **Insert > Image**, browse to **monterey2.jpg** inside the **images** folder. Click **Select**.

13. Draw another Layer around the words **The Monterey Room** at the upper left-hand corner of the page. If you have trouble aligning the image, select it using the selection handle and use the arrow keys on your keyboard to nudge it into place.

14. Click inside the second Layer and choose **Insert > Image** and browse to **monterey.gif** inside the **images** folder. Click **Select**.

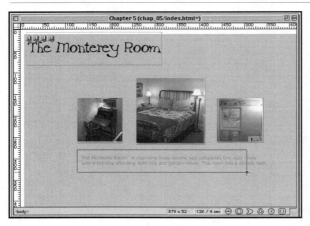

15. So far you have inserted images into Layers. Inserting text is just as simple. Draw another Layer around the three lines of text at the bottom of the screen.

16. Click inside the Layer and type **The Monterey Room. A charming brass double bed completes this cozy room with a balcony affording both city and mountain views. This room has a private bath.** For the purpose of this exercise, don't worry about matching the type of the original layout. You'll learn more about type in Chapter 7, *"Type."*

17. Save the file, and leave it open for the next exercise.

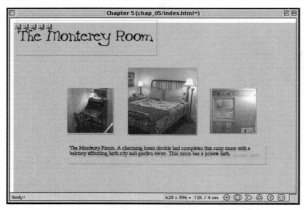

This is what your page looks like now. Most likely your text won't perfectly match the Tracing Image. That's alright—the Tracing Image is there as a guide only.

Exercise #3_____Converting Layers to Tables

You've just positioned artwork precisely to match a specific layout. As you may recall from the introduction to this chapter, Layers only display on version 4.0+ browsers. People in earlier browsers will
see the content of the Layers all jumbled up along the left side of your page, which of course is not
cool at all! I'm guessing that you want the luxury of freely positioning artwork with Layers but still
want people with older browsers to view your site. This exercise will show you how to convert
Layers to standard HTML Tables so anybody can see your perfect layout, no matter their browser.

STEP-BY-STEP_____

1. Make sure that you still have **index.html** open.

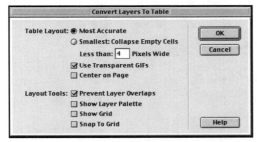

2. Select **Modify > Layout > Convert Layers to Table….** The Convert Layers to Table dialog box will open. The shortcut key is **Shift+Cmd+F6** (Mac) **Shift+Ctrl+F6** (Windows).

3. Click the **Table Layout: Most Accurate**. Click the **Prevent Layer Overlaps** checkbox.
Click **OK**. This setting is required since Layers can overlay but Tables cannot.

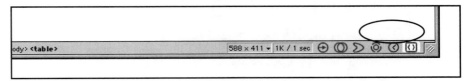

*Note: When you convert your Layers to Tables, by default Dreamweaver will set the Table
borders to 0, shown above in the **Properties Inspector** window. Why? Because you do
not want to advertise that you are using Tables. The 0 gives you an* Invisible Border *creating the illusion of floating Background Images and text on your Web page.*

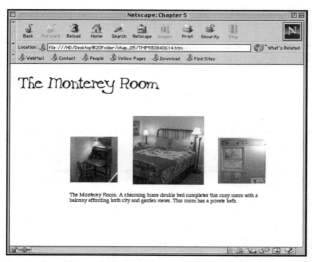

4. Preview the results in the browser by clicking **F12**. Notice that in the browser you can't tell if Layers or Tables were used. Converting Tables to Layers affects the compatibility of the HTML Document, not the appearance.

5. Save the file and leave it open for the next exercise.

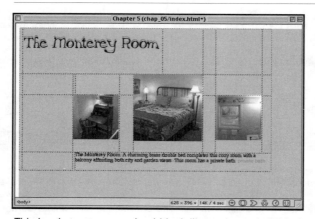

This is what your page should look like at the end of this exercise in Dreamweaver.

Tip_____

Convert Layers to Table Options

The Convert Layers to Table dialog box has several options to help you control how your Layers are converted. The chart below explains how these features work.

Convert Layers to Table Descriptions	
Most Accurate	This option (default) creates a Table cell for each Layer and creates all the cells necessary to maintain the Layer structure. The term "cell" refers to one of the rectangles within a Table. More information about Tables and cells can be found in Chapter 6, *"Tables."*
Smallest: Collapse Empty Cells	This option sets the edges of the Layers to align if they are within a certain pixel range. This typically results in fewer columns and rows. This can be a good thing, because fewer columns and rows equate to faster downloading, or it can be a bad thing, because it can potentially disrupt your layout's appearance. I recommend experimenting to see which suits your needs best.
Use Transparent GIFs	This option inserts transparent GIFs in each of the empty cells. This helps maintain the table structure across browsers. Tables can collapse in some browsers if they contain no content, and transparent GIFs can fill in as content, though they are invisible.
Center on Page	This option centers the Table on the page.
Prevent Layer Overlaps	Table cells cannot overlap. This option prevents you from overlapping your Layers by warning you about which Layers, if any, overlap.
Show Layer Palette	This opens the Layers Palette, which allows you to rename or reorder your Layers. This exercise didn't require that you view the Layers Palette, but you'll get a chance to learn about this in Chapter 13, *"DHTML."*
Show Grid	If it's not already visible, this will turn on the grid for the page.
Snap To Grid	This snaps the Layer to the nearest snapping point on the grid. This can be useful for aligning objects.

Exercise #4_____Converting Tables to Layers

In Chapter 6, *"Tables,"* you'll learn how to create Tables in Dreamweaver. In the meantime, you'll have to trust me when I tell you that creating Tables for layout purposes is a lot less easy than using Layers. Dreamweaver gives you the freedom to control your layout and browser compatibility by converting Layers to Tables. This powerful feature can be reversed as well, allowing you to convert Tables back to Layers. If you've ever hand-coded HTML Tables, you will no longer have to fuss with editing individual cells and rows of Tables because you can go freely between Layers and Tables. This back-and-forth control is extremely useful and once you get the hang of it, it will save you countless hours modifying the layout of your pages.

In this exercise, you will convert the Table version of your page back to Layers, make modifications to the layout, and then convert it back to Tables for browser compatibility. You will turn the Tracing Image off and be encouraged to modify the layout of the page however you want. By the end of this exercise, you should definitely appreciate how powerful these features are in helping you create and modify the layout of your pages.

STEP-BY-STEP_____

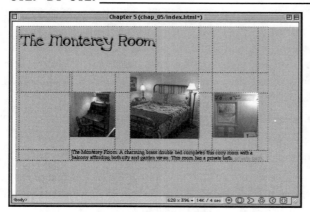

1. Return to Dreamweaver. The **index.html** file should still be open. If not, open it!

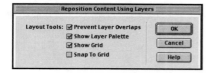

2. Select **Modify > Layout > Reposition Content Using Layers....**

3. Uncheck the **Snap To Grid** option. This gives you the most freedom and won't force your Layers to snap to the nearest grid point.

4. Click **OK**.

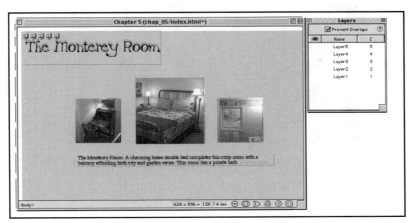

*Your Table is converted into Layers and the grid is turned on to help with the layout of your page. If you want to change the layout, you'll find that it's much easier to do so with Layers than Tables! If the grid bothers you, turn it off by choosing **View > Grid > Show.***

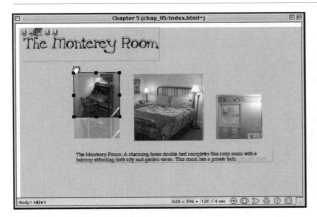

5. Click on the Layer with the **desk** image.

6. Click and drag this Layer up so that the top of it aligns with the top of the **bed** image.

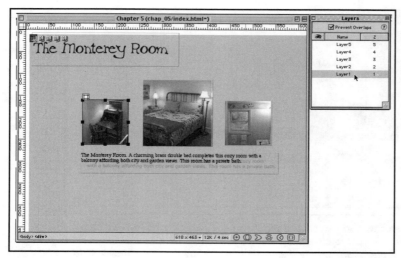

Note: *When you click and drag the desk image notice that the Layer becomes highlighted in the Layers Palette.*

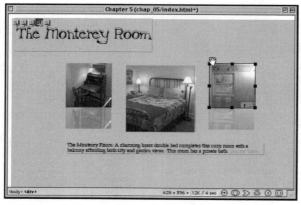

7. Click on the Layer with the image of the window.

8. Click and drag this Layer up so that top of it aligns with the top of the image of the **bed**.

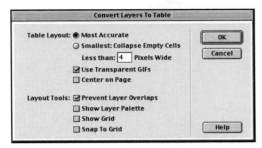

9. Select **Modify > Layout > Convert Layers to Table....**

10. Click **OK.**

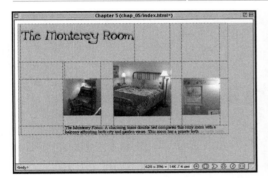
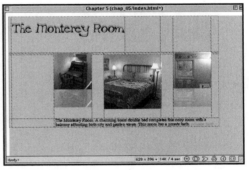

Old Layout   **New Layout**

You can start to see how easy it is to change the layout of your pages by converting back and forth between Layers and Tables.

6. Tables

- **Creating, Sorting, and Modifying a Table**
- **Using Tables to Align Images & Text**
- **Assembling Seamless Images**
- **Combining Pixels and Percentages**

chap_06 folder

Dreamweaver 2
H•O•T CD-ROM

HTML Tables were introduced back in Netscape 1.2 as a way to deal with charts and data. If you've never heard the term "Tables" before, they are commonly used in financial or data-based spreadsheets and are defined by columns and rows. The HTML engineers who created Tables for the Web did not predict that developers would one day use Tables to align images, not just to display text and numbers. This chapter focuses on both uses for Tables: as a formatting device for data and as a layout device for custom positioning of images.

This chapter will show you how to create custom Tables, insert rows and columns, come up with color schemes, and handle formatting and sorting tasks. You will also learn how to use Tables to align and position images. All said and done, Tables are a critical component to your Web-design tool-box, and Dreamweaver gives you great control over mastering them.

Note_____

What is a Table?

A Table, as you'll learn in this chapter, is a highly versatile feature in HTML. It can be useful for organizing data or positioning images. What does a Table look like under the hood of Dreamweaver? It is comprised of a combination of HTML tags.

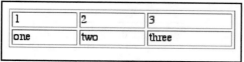

1	2	3
one	two	three

A Table in the browser.

```
<TABLE WIDTH="75%" BORDER="1">
  <TR>
    <TD>1</TD>
    <TD>2</TD>
    <TD>3</TD>
  </TR>
  <TR>
    <TD>one</TD>
    <TD>two</TD>
    <TD>three</TD>
  </TR>
</TABLE>
```

*Here's the HTML for the Table above. Tables always begin with a **TABLE** tag. The **WIDTH** and **BORDER** elements are attributes of the **TABLE** tag. **<TR>** stands for Table Row, and **<TD>** stands for Table Data.*

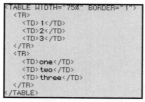

Anatomy of a Table

A Table contains rows, columns and cells. If these terms are unfamiliar to you, this diagram should help!

Exercise #1_____Changing the Border of a Table

This first exercise helps you build your Table-formatting skills on a premade Table. It also alerts you to a common HTML problem relating to empty Table cells. You see, even if a Table cell is empty, you've got to put something in it to hold the Table formatting. That "something" can be a single-pixel transparent GIF. You'll learn how to add this in a few moments, once you get going with this exercise.

STEP-BY-STEP_____

1. Define your site for Chapter 6. Copy **chap_06** to your hard drive and press **F5** to define it. If you need a refresher on this process, visit Chapter 3, *"Site Control."*

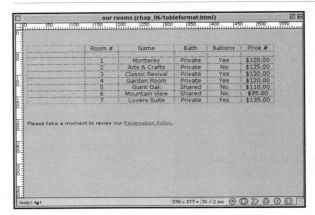

2. Open the file **tableformat.html**. The dotted lines that you see around each cell are just formatting guides, and will not show up inside the browser.

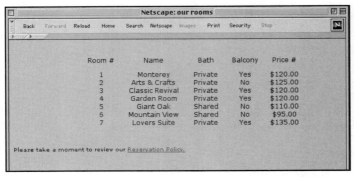

3. Click **F12** to preview this file in your Web browser. Notice how the dotted lines don't appear in the browser? Dreamweaver uses a default setting of "1" for Table borders. In this file, that setting was changed to "0" in order to make the border disappear. Next you'll learn how to control the weight of the lines with the border property.

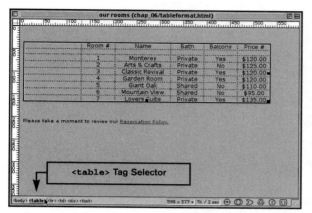

4. Return to Dreamweaver and select the entire Table. You can do this by using the tag selector at the bottom left of the Document window. Click your mouse anywhere inside the Table. You should see the word **<table>** appear as a tag selector. Click on the **<table>** element in the tag selector and the entire Table should become selected.

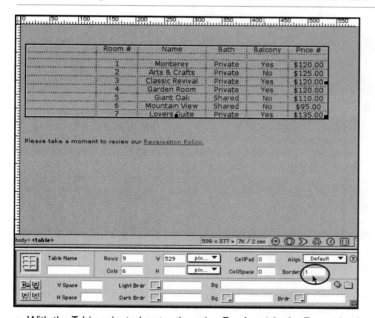

5. With the Table selected, enter the value **Border: 1** in the Properties Inspector.

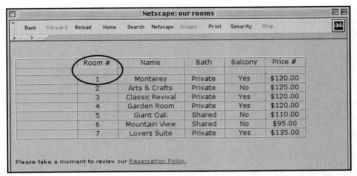

6. Click **F12** to preview the results. See how the border value affected the appearance? This is one of the many controls that you have over the appearance of Tables.

You might also notice that Netscape displays the cell underneath Room # in a different way than the other Table cells. See how in every other row there is content, but the one row without content looks different? That's because it is empty.

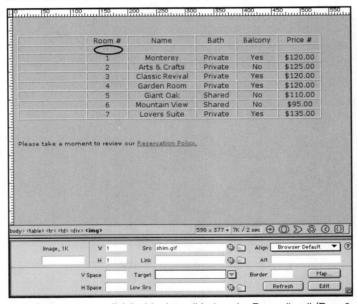

7. In Dreamweaver, click inside the cell below the Room # cell (Row 2, Column 2). Choose **Insert > Image** and browse to **shim.gif**. Be careful to deselect the image (click off the graphic) after you insert it. If you hit **Return** or **Enter** with it selected, it will disappear!

The file that you just inserted (shim.gif) contains a single-pixel transparent GIF, which is invisible to your end user. By placing it inside the empty Table cell, you fool the browser into thinking there is content, even though your audience will never see that content. The sole purpose for inserting the graphic is to fix the appearance of the empty Table cell.

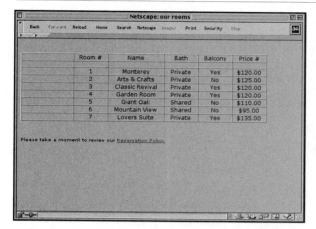

8. Choose **File > Save** to save the changes to the border. Click **F12** to preview the results. See, no more funky pixels, Mom! The empty cell looks like every other cell, which is just the way it should! No one will ever be the wiser that the solution to this problem was a transparent GIF. Return to Dreamweaver and leave this Document open for Exercise 2.

 Note_____

What is a Transparent GIF?

The GIF file format supports a feature called "transparency," which is a term for a mask. Transparency makes it possible to specify areas in a GIF graphic to disappear in a Web browser. A single-pixel transparent GIF is a graphic that only contains a single pixel which has been instructed to disappear. You can create transparent GIF files in Fireworks, Photoshop, ImageReady or a host of other graphics applications. Methods for making them vary in each program, so consult the user manual of whichever graphics application you own. If you like, you can store the file shim.gif for Web projects other than this book, and that way you will always have a single-pixel transparent GIF on hand. **Note:** The name "shim" is a term used in carpentry to hold things in place. You may name your single-pixel transparent GIF anything you like—shim was just a name chosen for this exercise.

Exercise #2_____Sorting the Table

Dreamweaver is the first HTML editor I've seen that can sort the content of Tables both alphabetically and numerically. Before this feature existed, if you wanted to sort a Table, you had to copy and paste each row or Column manually. Thankfully, sorting Table content in Dreamweaver is only a simple dialog box away.

STEP-BY-STEP_____

1. Return to Dreamweaver and make sure that the Document **tableformat.html** is still open. If not, go ahead and open it again.

2. Make sure that the Table is selected and choose **Commands > Sort Table**.

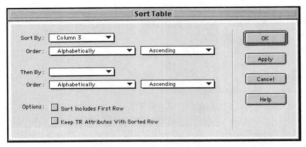

3. Change the settings to **Sort By: Column 3, Order: Alphabetically Ascending**. Click **OK**.

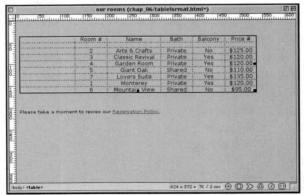

Notice that the file has been sorted differently than when you first opened it? The third column is now in alphabetical order. You can affect Table content through this kind of command. Try doing this manually, and you'll appreciate this feature fast.

4. Save the file and keep it open for the next exercise.

Note_____

The Sort Table Window

The Sort Table window has a variety of options to modify. See the chart below for an explanation of all its features.

Sorting Features	
Feature	**Description**
Sort By	Use this option to select which column you would like to sort.
Order	Use these two pull-down menus to choose Alphabetically or Numerically and Ascending or Descending.
Then By	Use this option if you want to sort multiple columns in your Table.
Sort Includes First Row	If this box is checked, the first row in your Table will be sorted. This option is off by default because most often the first row is used as a header for the Table.
Keep TR Attributes With Sorted Row	If this box is checked and a row is moved around due to sorting, all the attributes for that row will also move (i.e. color, font, etc.). **<TR>** stands for Table Row in HTML.

Exercise #3_____Changing the Color Scheme

Now that you know how to change the order of a Table's text, the time has come to work on color formatting. This next exercise will show off Dreamweaver's color-picking features for Tables. As it often does, Dreamweaver offers a variety of ways to get the job done. When it comes to coloring your Tables, you may use Dreamweaver's automatic color features or set whatever custom colors you desire.

STEP-BY-STEP_____

1. Make sure that the Table is selected and choose **Commands > Format Table**.

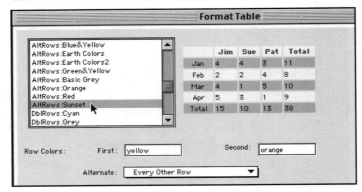

2. Scroll through the list of choices and try clicking on some of them. See how the representation of the Table in the middle changes colors? These color combinations are part of Dreamweaver, and can be applied to any Table. Choose **AltRows: Sunset** and click **OK**.

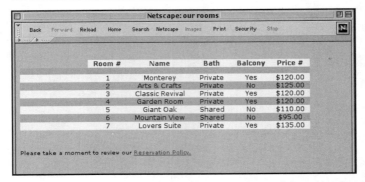

3. Click **F12** to preview the results. Notice how the top left row is missing color information? You can correct this, by once again inserting **shim.gif** in the offending cell.

4. Return to Dreamweaver. Click inside the top left cell. Choose **Insert > Image** and browse to **shim.gif**. There's that teeny single pixel again, so teeny yet so capable because when you preview in your browser, the mistake is corrected.

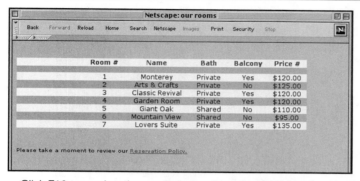

5. Click **F12** to preview the results in your browser, the Table should appear as it does in this image, nice and colorful all the way to its top left corner.

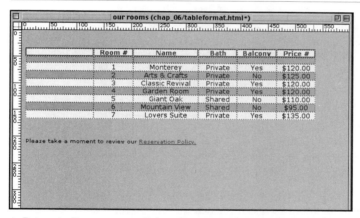

6. Return to Dreamweaver. Select the top row by clicking and dragging (position your mouse in the left-hand or right-hand corner of the row—until it becomes an arrow—and click once, to select the whole row).

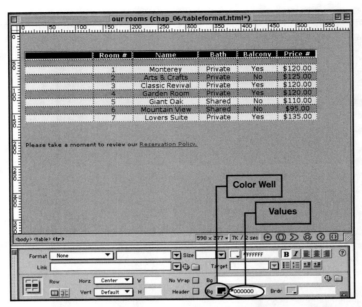

7. With the top row selected, go to the Properties Inspector. Change the **text** color and **Bg** color (Bg as in background), as shown above. You can enter the values or click on the color well to the left of the values to select colors from the built-in Dreamweaver Color Palette.

8. Save your changes and close this Document. Congrats, you've just combined automatic color features and custom color settings in one Table.

 Note _____

Alternative to Transparent GIFs

This exercise showed you how to insert transparent GIF files to correct empty Table cells, but there's another way to do this as well. If you change your Objects Palette to show Invisibles, you can insert a non-breaking space **<nbsp>** tag into an empty Table, and the Table will render correctly. The advantage to transparent GIF files is the fact that their **WIDTH** and **HEIGHT** attributes can be stretched to move Table cells around (as you'll learn first-hand in Exercise #5). If all you want to do is insert content, and don't care about changing the shape of an empty Table cell, the non-breaking space tag will work just as well as a single-pixel transparent GIF.

Exercise #4_____Creating and Modifying a Table

This exercise will show you how to create your own Table from scratch and how to modify it. You will learn to work with a combination of the **Insert Table** object, the **Modify > Table** menu, and the Properties Inspector. You won't be building a finished page yet. Instead, you'll have a chance to explore many of the different Table options first.

STEP-BY-STEP_____

1. If an Untitled Document isn't already open, choose **File > New**. Save this file into the **chap_06** folder and name it **firsttable.html**. Choose **Modify > Page Properties** and enter **Title: My First Table**. Click **OK**.

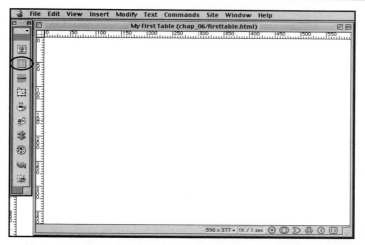

2. Click on the **Insert Table** button in the Objects Palette or choose **Insert > Table**.

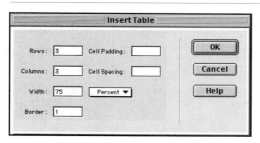

3. The above dialog box will appear. Without changing any of these default settings just yet, click **OK**.

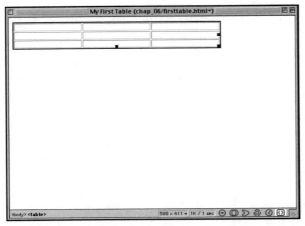

This results in a Table that is three rows high and three columns wide (Dreamweaver's default settings when inserting a Table).

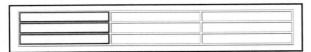

4. Select the left column, by clicking your mouse inside of the top left cell and dragging down to the bottom of the row while leaving the mouse depressed.

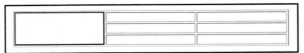

5. Choose **Modify > Table > Merge Cells** (the shortcut key for this is **M**). This will result in a Table with three columns, with the left column using only one cell and the other two columns containing three rows of cells.

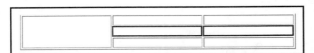

6. Select the left middle cell, by clicking your mouse inside and dragging over to the right middle cell while leaving your mouse depressed.

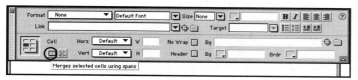

 Movie _____

tag_selector.mov

To get a visual explanation of Step 8 from Exercise #4, watch the movie **tag_selec-tor.mov** located inside of the **movies** folder on the *Dreamweaver 2 H•O•T CD-ROM*.

7. Click on the **Merge Cell** button on the Properties Inspector. This achieves the same effect as the Modify menu did in Step 5. As with many things in Dreamweaver, there are multiple ways to accomplish the same task. I prefer to use the Properties Inspector to merge cells, though you may prefer to use the Modify menu method.

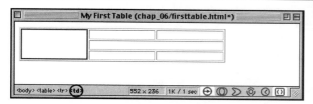

8. Just as you can merge rows and columns, you can also add and delete them. Selecting rows and columns can be tricky at times. For example, to select the column on the far left, you will find that you can no longer click and drag inside it because now it is only a single cell. Instead, put your cursor inside the cell and click on the **<td>** element on the tag selector (**<td>** stands for Table Data).

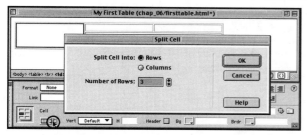

9. Click on the **Split Cell** button on the Properties Inspector. This brings up the Split Cell dialog box. Enter **3** (it might already be entered) and click **OK**.

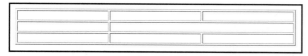

10. You just added back to this Table the three rows that you deleted in Step 5. See how flexible this Table editor is?

11. To delete the left column completely, select the left column again and choose **Edit > Cut Cmd+X** (Mac) or **Ctrl+X** (Windows). You can delete rows or columns by selecting them and cutting them out at any time. **Note:** Sometimes, and I'm not sure why, Cut will not work and hitting your Delete key will.

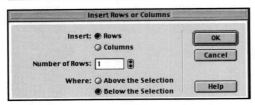

12. You can add a new row by clicking inside the lower right cell and choosing **Modify > Table > Insert Rows or Columns....** In this instance, I chose to insert **Rows** and told it to go **Below the Selection**.

13. Here are the results of that action. You could have inserted Above the Selection instead or chosen a column instead of a row. Dreamweaver offers a lot of flexibility when it comes to formatting Tables, which you'll likely find useful for the variety of Table tasks which will arise over the course of your future Web-design projects. Save and close the file.

Note_____

Contextual Table Menus

Time and again, Dreamweaver lets you accomplish the same task in many different ways. For example, Exercise #4 showed you how to merge and split cells using the **Modify > Table** menu or the Properties Inspector. Wouldn't you know there is a third way? You could select the column as you did in Step 8 and **Ctrl+Click** (Mac) or use your right mouse button (Windows) to access a contextual menu, which in this case is a handy list of everything you'd ever want to do to a Table.

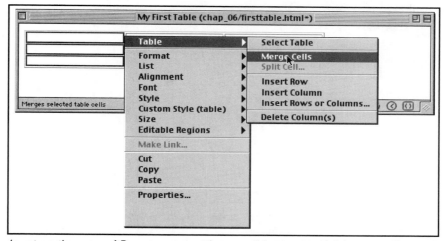

*In yet another case of Dreamweaver putting everything you need right at your finger-tips, this comprehensive menu pops up via **Ctrl+Click** (Mac) or the right mouse button (Windows). You can use any of three ways to access this same information (Properties Inspector, Modify menu or contextual menu) depending on your preference.*

Exercise #5_____**Aligning Images and Text with Tables**

Many people use Tables to align images and text because Tables offer the ability to position artwork freely on a page. This next exercise will show you how to work with a page layout and modify the alignment through adjusting the height and width of Table rows and columns.

STEP-BY-STEP_____

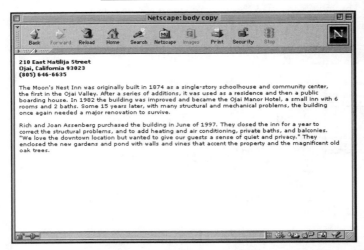

1. Open the file **bodycopy.html**. Click **F12**. This is a text file that has no Table formatting. See how the width of the text within the Document extends to the width of the browser? This is default alignment behavior, and the problem with it is that it can create very wide layouts on large monitors.

Most design experts agree that column widths should be limited in order to make reading text easier. In order to create a more narrow column, you will need to learn how to create a Table with fixed pixels.

2. Create a new Document by choosing **File > New**. Save the Document to your **chap_06** folder and name it **align.html**.

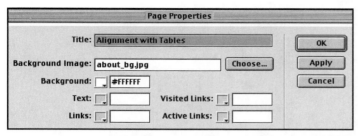

3. Choose **Modify > Page Properties**, **Cmd+J** (Mac) or **Ctrl+J** (Windows) and give it the Title name **Alignment with Tables**. Click on the **Choose...** button below the **Title:** field to place a Background Image. Select **about_bg.jpg**. Click **OK**.

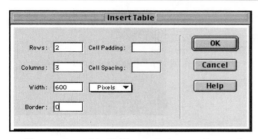

4. Choose **Insert > Table**, and change the settings to **Rows: 2, Columns: 3, Width: 600 Pixels** (make sure you change this to Pixels, not Percent), **Border: 0**. Click **OK**.

 Note_____

Fixed Pixels Versus Percentages in Tables

Values can be created using two types of Tables: percentages or pixels. So far, this chapter has worked with percentage-based Tables. A percentage-based Table will stretch with the width of the browser, meaning that its size will vary depending on the shape of the browser window. If you specify that a Table uses a width of 75%, for example, the Table will stretch to fill three-fourths of the horizontal space regardless of the browser window size. This can be a great thing in some cases, but not in others. When you want to restrict the size of a Table regardless of the browser window size, pixel-based Tables are the way to go. When you want the Table to stretch to the size of the browser window, percentage-based Tables are best. To complicate matters, it's possible to nest a pixel-based Table inside a percentage-based Table or vice versa. By the time you've finished the exercises in this chapter, you should have some concrete examples as to why and when to choose which type of Table, and how to combine the two for more complex Table formatting.

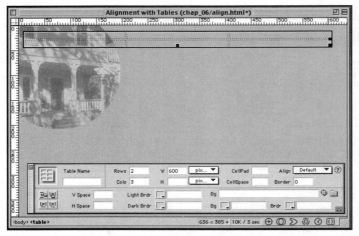

The result of those settings should look like this. You're laying the framework for a fixed-pixel Table that is suitable for aligning objects.

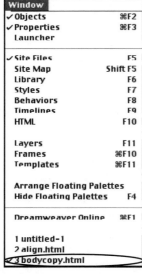

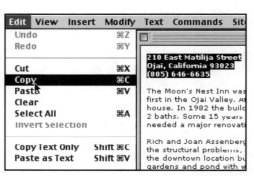

5. Choose **Window > bodycopy.html** (at the bottom of the menu). The Window menu lists all the open Documents. If for some reason **bodycopy.html** is not open, go ahead and open it from the Site window (**F5**).

6. Select and **Copy** the text that contains the address information.

7. Choose **Window > align.html** to bring forth the other open Document. Click inside column 2, row 1 and **Paste**. You can alternatively go back and forth between these two Documents by clicking on them on the screen if you have a large enough monitor.

8. Switch back to the text-only Document by choosing **Window > bodycopy.html**. Select and **Copy** the first paragraph. Switch back to the Document with the Table in it by choosing **Window > align.html** and click inside column 1, row 2 and **Paste**.

9. Switch between the two Documents using the Window menu to **Copy** and **Paste** the second paragraph into the Table, as shown above. You can close the **bodycopy.html** Document now, because you're finished with copying and pasting.

Notice that row 2, column 2 does not align with row 2, column 3? This is an example of default Table formatting, which vertically centers the text in a Table cell unless otherwise instructed. In order to fix this, you'll need to adjust the Table-alignment settings. The next step will show you how.

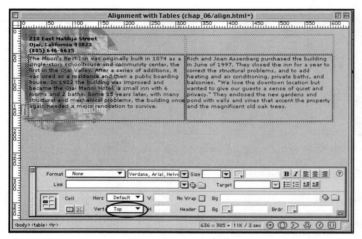

10. Select the entire second row by clicking inside the first column on the left and dragging your mouse across all the columns in the second row. Change the Properties Inspector's **Vert** setting to **Top**. As you can see, this corrects the irregular alignment, but it also collapses the empty cell on the far left.

Empty cells in Dreamweaver and in browsers are certainly problematic, aren't they? The only solution is to insert a transparent GIF again, which you'll do in the following step.

11. If your rulers aren't visible choose **View > Rulers > Show**. The visible ruler helps you see the page's pixel dimensions.

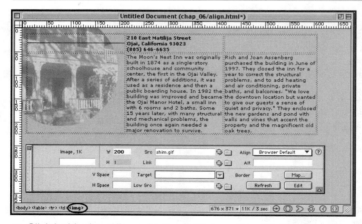

12. Click inside the collapsed left cell. Choose **Insert > Image** and browse to **shim.gif**. The **shim.gif** will be selected, and you should see its settings inside the Properties Inspector. Hint: If the **shim.gif** accidentally gets deselected, click inside its Table cell and select the **<img>** element in the tag selector to reselect it. Enter 200 for the width setting (**W**). This should stretch the single-pixel GIF to hold the left-hand cell's dimension open.

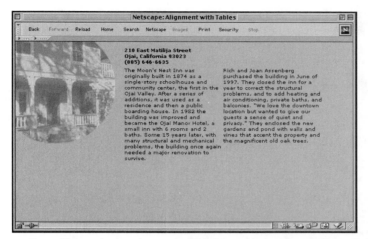

13. Press **F12** to preview the results. This layout is starting to look good, but the space between the Table cells feels a little cramped, doesn't it? Return to Dreamweaver and select the Table by clicking anywhere inside it and choosing the **<table>** element inside the tag selector.

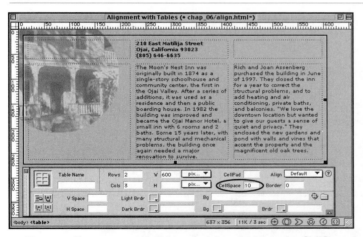

14. Return to Dreamweaver and insert a value of 10 into the **CellSpace** setting on the Properties Inspector. As you can see, **CellSpace** controls the amount of space between cells. Click **F12** to preview the results.

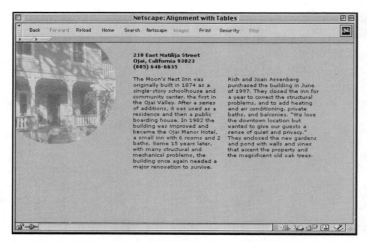

*The results of changing the **CellSpace** attribute. Want to experiment further with this file? Try changing the dimensions of the **shim.gif**, the **CellSpacing** or **CellPadding** settings. You are in total control over the alignment of this page. By leaving the rulers turned on, you can get a better idea of what values to enter into the settings.*

15. Close and save all the open Documents before you begin the next exercise.

 Note_____

Using Rulers

Rulers in Dreamweaver are helpful for getting a sense of scale. You can access rulers by choosing **View > Rulers > Show**.

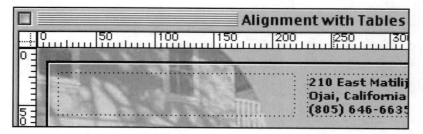

Note_____

CellPad Versus CellSpace

Using CellPad and CellSpace settings alters the amount of space between Table cells. CellPad adds room inside the Table cell, whereas CellSpace adds to the border width. When used with Table borders set to 0, CellSpace and/or CellPad achieve the identical result, by interjecting more space between the data and the edge of each cell.

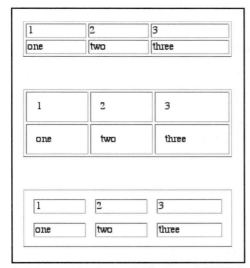

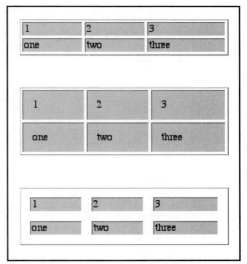

In this example, the top Table uses no CellPad or CellSpace, the middle Table uses a CellPad setting of 10, and the bottom Table uses a CellSpace setting of 10.

With colored Table cells, the differences between CellPad (middle) and CellSpace (bottom) are much more noticeable.

Exercise #6_____**Percentage-Based Table Alignment**

In the last exercise, you worked with a Table that was fixed at 600 pixels. When you want to control your alignment precisely, fixed pixels are the way to go. There's another way to achieve alignment with Tables that is based on percentages. This next exercise will use percentage-based Tables to ensure that the page elements will be centered on any size browser window.

STEP-BY-STEP_____

1. Create a new Document, and name it **center.html**. **Save** it into the **chap_06** folder.

2. Choose **Modify > Page Properties** and give it the Title name **Centered Page**. Click **OK**.

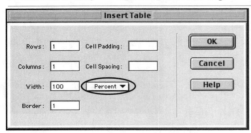

3. Choose **Insert > Table** and enter the following settings, **Rows: 1, Columns: 1, Width: 100 Percent**. For this exercise to work, it's imperative that the **Width** be set to **Percent** and not **Pixels**. Click **OK**.

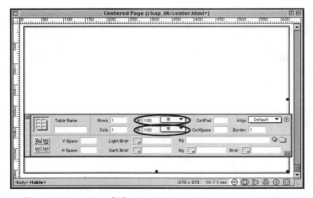

4. The width setting (**W**) should already be set to **100%** on the Properties Inspector. Select the **<table>** tag and change the height setting (**H**) in the Properties Inspector to **100%**. If you stretch the Document window by clicking and dragging on the bottom right corner, you will notice that the Table will scale to fit the browser window regardless of its size.

Note: *If you press* ***F12*** *to preview this page right now, you can move the browser window size around and you'll see the Table stretch there too. What's happening? You specified that the width and height of this Table would fill 100 percent of the browser's shape, regardless of its size. This is critical to the success of this exercise, because you are now going to align an image to this Table, and the image will be aligned in relationship to the size of the browser, regardless of its shape.*

5. Click inside the giant Table cell or select the `<td>` (table data) element in the tag selector. Choose **Insert > Image**, browse to **tilelogo4.jpg** and select it.

6. Select the image and choose **Modify > Alignment > Center**. The image will pop into the center of the large Table.

7. Click **F12** to preview and try stretching the browser to different positions. No matter how you set the browser window, this image will always be perfectly centered!

This is the power of percentage-based Table alignment. You could center an image to a pixel-based Table, but because the Table wouldn't stretch to the size of the browser window, the image would center to the Table's shape, not the browser's shape.

8. To finish the effect, return to Dreamweaver. Select the Table by clicking inside it and highlighting the **<table>** tag selector. Change the Properties Inspector to the Table setting **Border: 0**. This will turn off the border.

9. Choose **Modify > Page Properties** and enter the value **#000033** into the Background setting and click **OK**.

10. Click **F12** to see the results. People who view this page will never know you used a Table, yet the image will always be centered.

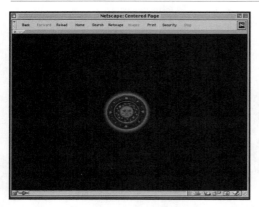

What's so great about hiding the Table from them? Because you've just created a layout that is centered regardless of the size or shape of the browser window, and people who view this page won't be distracted by a Table border at the edge of the browser screen.

11. Return to Dreamweaver. Save and close this file.

Exercise #7_____Seamless Image Assembly

If you've looked around the Web much, you've probably noticed that Tables are sometimes used to assemble multiple images so that they look like a single image. Why would anyone want to do this? Tables can ensure that artwork stays aligned and grouped, whereas HTML without Tables can be subject to movement depending on the size of the browser window. The exercise will show you how to reassemble multiple images into a pixel-based Table so that they won't be misaligned.

STEP-BY-STEP_____

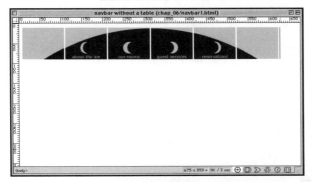

1. Open the file **navbar1.html**. Notice the gaps between each of the images? This can be the result of putting images next to each other without a Table.

2. Press **F12** to preview this Document and make your browser window smaller. Notice how the row of images gets disrupted? By placing them inside a Table, they will become grouped, and won't be able to move around like this.

3. Return to Dreamweaver. Click once on each image (don't double-click!), you'll see its dimensions inside the Properties Inspector. You have six images which are 100 pixels wide each. If you add that number together, it's 600. That's important, because you will be creating a 600-pixel wide Table in order to assemble these as one seamless-looking image.

4. Position your cursor after the last image and hit the return key, so your insertion cursor appears below the images on the screen and on the left.

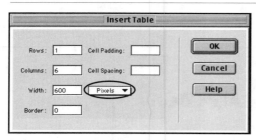

5. Choose **Insert > Table** and change the settings to **Rows: 1, Columns: 6, Width: 600 Pixels** (not Percent!), **Border: 0**.

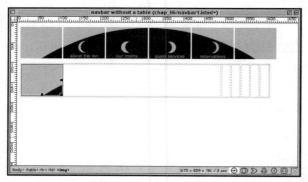

6. Click inside the far-left cell, and choose **Insert > Image**. Browse to **navbar1.gif** and click **Select**. The Table format is messed up, but the image is now inside the appropriate cell.

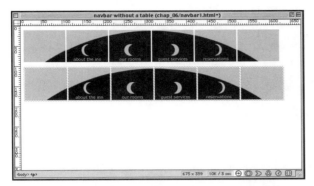

7. Once you insert all the other images into the appropriate cells, the Table should appear like this. The names of the files, from left to right are: **navbar1gif**, **navbar2.gif**, **navbar3.gif**, **navbar4.gif**, **navbar5.gif**, and **navbar6.gif**. The results should look like this.

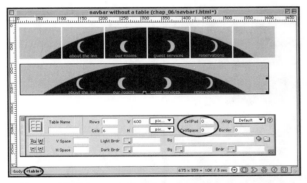

8. To get rid of the rest of gaps between the cells, select the entire Table by clicking inside any cell and selecting the **<table>** tag selector. Once you've selected it, change the settings on the Properties Inspector to read **CellPad 0**, and **CellSpace 0**. The Table will come together seamlessly.

9. Press **F12** to preview your seamless table. Now that is what a navigation bar ought to look like!

10. Save this file, but leave it open for the next exercise.

Exercise #8_____Combining Pixels and Percentages

This next exercise will show you how to combine a pixel-accurate Table, like the one you just created in Exercise #7, with a percentage-based Table like you created in Exercise #6. Why would this be important? Let's say that you had a navigation bar, like the one you just built, that you wanted to be center justified regardless of whether it was seen on a small or large monitor. Combining the last two techniques lets you do just that.

STEP-BY-STEP_____

1. Create a new Document and save it as **navbar2.html** inside the **chap_06** folder.

2. Choose **Insert > Table** and change the settings to **Rows: 1, Columns: 1, Width: 100 Percent** (not Pixels!), **Border: 0**. With the Table selected, change the height (**H**) on the Properties Inspector to **100%**. You are creating the same kind of Table that you made in Exercise #6.

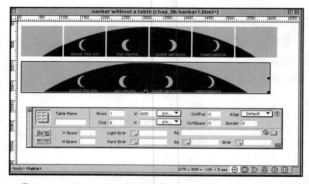

3. Return to the **navbar1.html** Document (use the Window menu and look at the bottom to locate it) and select the Table. Remember, you can click anywhere in the Table to use the tag selector in order to select it. With the Table selected, choose **Edit > Copy**.

4. Now switch over to the **navbar2.html** Document, and click inside the centered Table. Choose **Edit > Paste**.

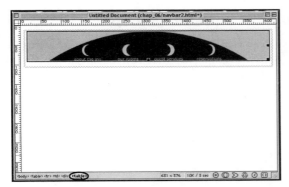

5. Select the Table that you just pasted. Again, if you click inside it you can use the **<table>** tag selector to select it. Notice there are two **<table>** tag selectors now? That's because you've got one Table nested inside another.

6. With the nested (navigation bar) Table selected, change the **Align** setting to **Center** inside the Properties Inspector.

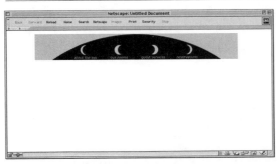

7. Preview in the browser (**F12**) and you should see that the navigation bar remains centered regardless of how wide you drag your browser window out. Congratulations again, you've just made a nested Table using a combination of pixels and percentages. Sounds impressive, but even better than that—it's useful!

8. Save and close the file.

Exercise #9_____Working with Imagemaps

In Exercise #7, you learned how to seamlessly piece together four images into a Table. An alternative to piecing together individual images would have been to take a single image and make it an imagemap. An imagemap contains invisible coordinates that allow HTML to assign multiple links to a single image. With imagemaps, you can specify multiple regions of a single image and have each of those areas link to different URLs.

STEP-BY-STEP_____

1. Open the **imagemap.html** file.

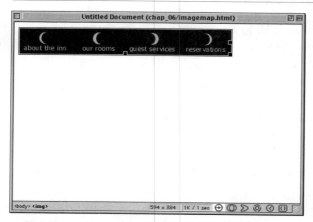

2. Click once on the **navbar.gif** so that it is selected.

3. Click on the **Map** button in the Properties Inspector. This will open the **Image Map Editor**. You will use this window to create, edit, and delete your image maps.

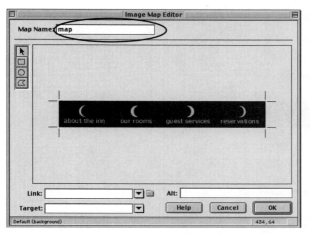

4. At the top, type in **Map Name: map**. Giving an imagemap a name is required, and it can be any name you want as long as it has no spaces. I usually use the word "map" because it let's me know what I was referring to in the name. Each imagemap on your page must have a unique name. Be sure to stay away from upper case, spaces, and special characters.

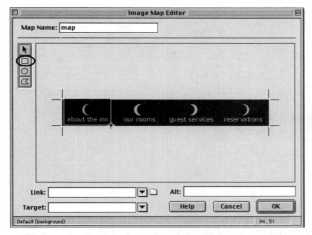

5. Click on the **Rectangle** tool and draw a box around the **moon** and **about the inn**. The area you are drawing is the area that will contain a link. The shapes are also known as "hotspots."

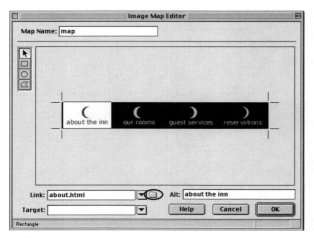

6. The area of the shape you just created is now highlighted. At the bottom, next to the **Link** field click on the small yellow folder. Browse to and select **about.html**.

7. Type in **Alt: about the inn**. This is what the user will see if they hold their mouse over this area of the image map for a few seconds.

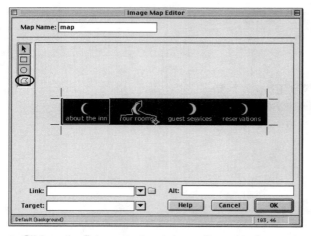

8. Click on the Polygon tool and draw a line around **our rooms** and the **moon** image above it. Each time you click it will add another point and let you draw from that new point. When you are finished drawing your shape, double-click.

By using the Polygon tool, you can draw much tighter image maps over your image. This will create a linked region that better matches the shape of the artwork.

9. At the bottom, type in **Link: http://www.moonsnestinn.com** as an **external link**. External links must contain the entire URL with all the http header information. Internal links can be accessed through the yellow folder icon.

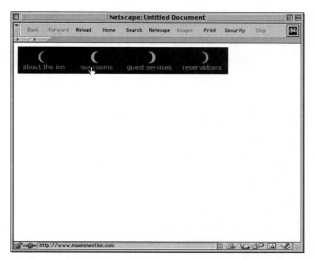

10. Click **OK**.

11. Press **F12** to see what this looks like in a browser window. Move your mouse over the different areas of the image. Notice how your cursor turns into a little hand, indicating an active link?

12. Press **F10** to view the HTML code for the image map you just created. Dreamweaver inserted all the coordinate information for where you drew the shapes around the images. Who would want to figure out all of these X and Y coordinates? That's what people had to do before programs like Dreamweaver were invented.

13. Save and close the file.

7.Type

• Creating and Formatting Text • Font Lists • Aligning Text
• Using the <PRE> Tag • Ordered, Unordered, and Definition Lists
• Color Schemes • Formatting Text in Tables
• Character Entities • Blockquotes and Non-Breaking Spaces

chap_07 folder

Dreamweaver 2
H•O•T CD-ROM

Most professional typographers cringe when they look at Web pages because type on the Web, for lack of a better expression, sucks. It sucks for many reasons. It sucks because Web browsers default to Times Roman and most sites use the default font. It sucks because type appears differently on Macs, Windows, and UNIX platforms. It sucks because browsers rely on whichever fonts are installed in end-users' systems, so you can't freely use any font you want. It mostly sucks because your choices for formatting type are limited, and that's guaranteed to frustrate the best of us.

Aside from all that, Dreamweaver gives you many hooks and handles into making the best of this sucky situation. This chapter will cover how to set font styles (such as bold, italics and underlined), font sizes, font colors and font faces (such as Times Roman, Helvetica, Arial, etc.). It will also cover making lists, such as bullet lists, definition lists and unordered lists. If you haven't heard those terms before, they, too, will be explained later. In the end, your Web-based type education should be quite complete!

A Word about FONT FACE

The **FONT FACE** element in HTML allows you to specify a typeface other than the end-user's default font. You can apply the attribute in Dreamweaver by creating Font Sets, which are described in Exercise #1. The caveat is that the typeface must be installed in your end-user's system, or the browser will not be able to display it. It is therefore helpful to know which fonts ship in the systems of Macintosh and Windows machines. Below is a chart that lists them both for you.

System Fonts	
Default System 8.6 Macintosh	**Default Windows 98 Fonts**
Arial	Arial
Arial Black	**Arial Black**
CAPITALS	Arial Narrow
Charcoal	**Arial Rounded MT Bold**
Chicago	Book Antiqua
Comic Sans MS	Bookman Old Style
Courier	Century Gothic
Courier New	Copperplate Gothic
Gadget	Comic Sans
Geneva	Courier
Georgia	**Courier New**
Helvetica	**Franklin Gothic Medium**
Impact	Garamond
Minion Web	**GOUDY STOUT**
Monaco	*Harlow Solid Italic*
Monotype.com	**Helvetica**
New York	Helvetica Narrow
Palatino	**Impact**
Sand	LUCINDA CONSOLE
Techno	*Lucinda Handwriting*
Textile	*Lucinda Sans*
Times	Lucinda Sans Unicode
Times New Roman	MATTISSE
Trebuchet MS	Matura MT Script
Verdana	New Century Schoolbook
	News Gothic MT
	OCR A Extended
	Palatino
	STENCIL
	Tahoma
	Tempus Sans
	Times New Roman
	Trebuchet MS
	TW CEN MT
	Verdana
	ZapfChancery

Tip_____

HTML Default Text Size

It might come as a surprise that HTML text uses different sizing conventions than traditional print type sizes. Actually, all HTML text has a default size of 3, with a total range from 0 to 7. If you have no idea what a default size of 3 looks like, see the picture below.

To change HTML text to a size other than the default of 3, you can either specify a number from 1 through 7, or + or −1 through + or -7 relative to the **BASEFONT** size (which is 3). For example, if you want some HTML text to be size 6, specify the font size to be 6 or +3. Either setting produces an HTML type at size 6. Some browsers let you set the **BASEFONT** for a page by using **BASEFONT SIZE** = "4." You can specify any size you want, using one of the several above-mentioned methods.

```
FONT SIZE None
FONT SIZE 1
FONT SIZE 2
FONT SIZE 3
FONT SIZE 4
FONT SIZE 5
FONT SIZE 6
FONT SIZE +1
FONT SIZE +2
FONT SIZE +3
FONT SIZE +4
FONT SIZE +5
FONT SIZE +6
FONT SIZE +7
FONT SIZE -1
FONT SIZE -2
FONT SIZE -3
FONT SIZE -4
FONT SIZE -5
FONT SIZE -6
```

*Above is a handy list of the **FONT SIZE** settings in Dreamweaver. The top example (None) is the equivalent of **FONT SIZE** 3. Notice how the type does not really look different in **FONT SIZE** +4 through +7, or **FONT SIZE** -2 through -6? There is not a huge dynamic range between these settings.*

Exercise #1_____Creating and Formatting HTML Text

In this exercise you will learn how to add HTML text to a Web page. In addition, you will also learn how to format this text by modifying the typeface, size, style, and other attributes. As you will see, creating and formatting HTML text with Dreamweaver 2 is just as easy as working with any word-processing application.

STEP-BY-STEP_____

1. Define your site for Chapter 7. Copy **chap_07** to your hard drive and press **F5** to define it. If you need a refresher on this, visit Chapter 3 *"Site Control."* Browse to **text1.html** and open it.

2. Type **About the Inn** and press **Return** or **Enter**.

3. Type **Our Rooms** and press **Return** or **Enter**.

4. Type **Guest Services** and press **Return** or **Enter**.

5. Type **Reservations** and press **Return** or **Enter**.

6. Select the words **About the Inn**.

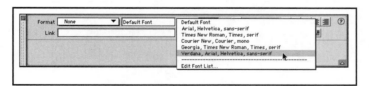

7. In the **Properties Inspector**, select the **Verdana, Arial, Helvetica, sans-serif** option in the **Font List** pop-up menu. This is will change your text to Verdana if you have that font installed. If not, it will display in the next font in the list.

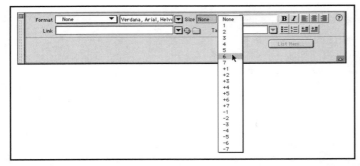

8. In the Properties Inspector, select the **Size** pop-up menu and choose the value **6**. This will change the size of your type.

9. Go to the **Size** pop-up menu again and select **+3**. Notice how the type size stays at 6. That's because all HTML text has a basefont size of 3, from which you add or subtract to make your type larger or smaller.

10. Select the words **Our Rooms**.

11. From the Properties Inspector, select the **Color** pop-up menu.

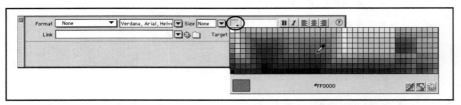

12. Select a bright red color. Your text color is now red. This setting will override any text color that you specify under **Modify > Page Properties**.

13. Select the words **Guest Services**.

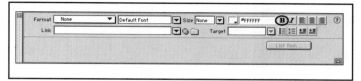

14. Click the **Bold** button in the Properties Inspector. This will make the selected text bold.

15. Click the **Italic** button in the Properties Inspector. This will make the selected text italic.

16. Select the word **Reservations**.

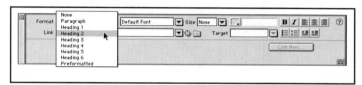

17. From the **Format** pop-up menu, select **Heading 2**. For more information about the topic of Headings, see the tip on the next page.

At the end of this exercise your page should look like this.

18. Save and close the file.

Note_____

Headings

HTML text can also be formatted using Headings. The Heading tags looks like this: **<H1>**. They range from 1 to 6 and change the size of the HTML text. Here's a tricky thing that you might want to remember: The smaller the number next to the H, the bigger the text will be. For example, **<H1>** would produce the largest text while **<H6>** would produce the smallest text. Generally, the (**<H1>-<H6>**) tags insert a line break before and after without requiring additional code. Heading tags can be useful for formatting large areas of text.

Why might you use a Heading tag instead of a **FONT SIZE** element? If your Web page is accessed by an end-user who is sight-impaired, he or she might not "see" your Web page, but will instead have a reading device "read" it aloud. Heading tags can be "read" by HTML readers as headlines, whereas large type are given the same emphasis as body copy. You might not imagine that your site has much of a sight-impaired audence, and perhaps don't think this information need apply to your site-design strategy. Many Web-design and HTML authorities, myself included, believe there will come a day where the Federal Disabilities Act will apply to Web pages, and all of us will have to give consideration to our sight-impaired audiences. My advice is to use Heading tags instead of large font sizes for headlines.

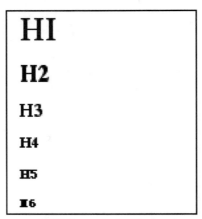

Here's what the range of HTML text looks like in a browser.

Exercise #2_____**Font Lists**

In this exercise you will learn how to add and modify the Font Lists that come with Dreamweaver 2. By specifying a font (or fonts) using the Font Lists, you ensure that the HTML text on your page is viewed as you intended. You will learn how to modify what typefaces are in the existing Font Lists and how to create your own custom Font List. This knowledge will let you break out of the Times Roman mold a little bit, which is a welcome thing in the bland Web-type landscape we all see every day. At the end of this exercise is a helpful note, explaining just how a Font List works.

STEP-BY-STEP_____

1. Open **text2.html**.

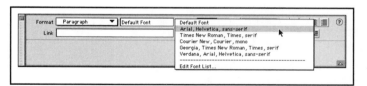

2. Select the words **This is the Arial, Helvetica, sans-serif Font List.**

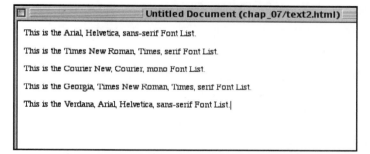

3. From the **Font List** pop-up menu, select **Arial, Helvetica, sans-serif.**

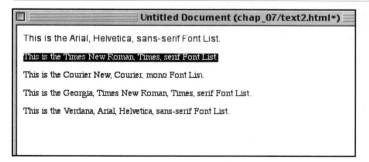

4. Select the words **This is the Times New Roman, Times, serif Font List.**

5. From the **Font List** pop-up menu, select **Times New Roman, Times, serif**. This will change your text to Times New Roman if you have that font installed; if you do not, it will go to the next font.

6. Select the words **This is the Courier New, Courier, mono Font List**.

7. From the **Font List** pop-up menu, select **Courier New, Courier, mono**. This will change your text to Courier New if you have that font installed; if you don't, it will go to the next font.

8. Select the words **This is the Georgia, Times New Roman, Times, serif Font List**.

9. From the **Font List** pop-up menu, select **Georgia, Times New Roman, Times serif**. This will change your text to Georgia if you have that font installed; if you don't, it will go to the next font.

10. Select the words **This is the Verdana, Arial, sans-serif Font List**.

11. From the **Font List** pop-up menu, select **Verdana, Arial, sans-serif**. This will change your text to Verdana if you have that font installed; if you don't, it will go to the next font.

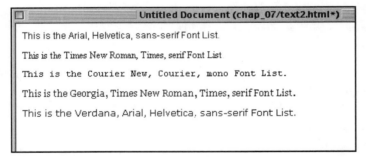

This is what your page should look like now.

12. Click off the text to deselect it, and hit **Return** or **Enter** below the last sentence on the page, type **This is my very own Font List**.

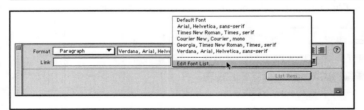

13. From the **Font List** pop-up menu, select **Edit Font List....**

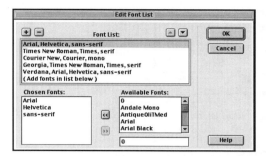

14. Select **Arial, Helvetica, sans-serif** at the top of the **Edit Font List** window.

15. Select **Arial** under the **Chosen Fonts** option. Click the >> button to remove Arial from this Font List.

16. Select **Arial Black**, or any other font, under the **Available Fonts** option.

17. Click the << button to add this to the current Font List. You have just modified the order in which the fonts will be used for this Font List.

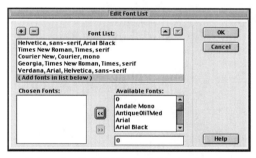

18. Select the (**Add fonts in list below**) option.

19. Select **Arial Black** under the **Available Fonts** option and press the << button to add this to your list.

20. Select **Verdana** under the **Available Fonts** option and press the << button to add this to your list.

21. Click **OK** to add your new list to the Font List.

22. Select the words in the Dreamweaver Document, **This is my very own Font List**.

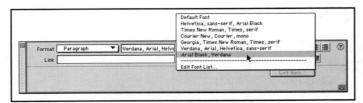

23. From the **Font List** pop-up menu, select **Arial Black** and **Verdana**. This will change your text to Arial Black if you have that font installed; if you don't, it will go to the next font.

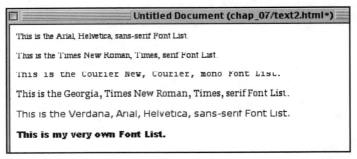

This is what your screen should look like now. This exercise gives you a great idea about how these Font Lists will display on your computer system. It might appear differently on other people's browsers, because they might have different fonts installed in their systems than you do.

24. Save and close the file.

 Note

How Font Lists Work

Font Lists are a very useful way of ensuring that the HTML text on your Web page is viewed the way you intended. A Web browser will search for each font in the list until it finds one that is installed on the end-user's system. Once it finds a font in the list, it will use that font to display the HTML text on your Web page. For example, if your Font List was Arial, Helvetica, sans-serif, the browser would try to use Arial first to display text. If the user did not have Arial installed, the browser would then try to use Helvetica. If it could not find Helvetica, it would then use the first sans-serif font it found. The goal of Font Lists is to create sets of fonts that have similar structure and characteristics, so that there is minimal change from viewer to viewer.

Note_____

Type Size Between Mac and Windows

Unfortunately for all of us well-intentioned Web publishers, HTML type appears much larger on Windows than it does on the Mac. While the Mac and Windows both display images at 72 dpi (dots per inch), Windows displays type at 96 dpi while the Mac displays type at 72 dpi. This deceptively small technical difference results in much larger type on Windows.

Macintosh

Windows 98

The images above illustrate the difference in size between the two platforms. Pretty scary, huh? There is no solution to this, except to turn to Style Sheets (see Chapter 8, *"Style Sheets"*) to size your text by using pixels, but that only works on 4.0 and later browsers.

To compensate, I often make type smaller at -1 or -2 on my Mac, but it only results in a better-looking Windows version and a worse-looking Mac version. Ugh! The theory goes that there are more Windows users than Mac users, so I've taken the tack to make the type on my pages look acceptable on Windows, and slightly small on Macs.

One other solution to the size-difference issue is to use images of text instead of HTML text. Since images display at 72 dpi on either Mac or Windows, the type will look identical on either platform. The downside is that images are larger in file size than HTML text, and are not searchable by search engines. It's always one gotcha or another, right?

Exercise #3_____Aligning Text

In this exercise you will learn how to align text on the page. Unfortunately, HTML does not give you much control aligning text. You have three basic options, Left Align, Center Align, and Right Align. You do have some extra options when you align text next to images, which you will also explore in this exercise.

STEP-BY-STEP_____

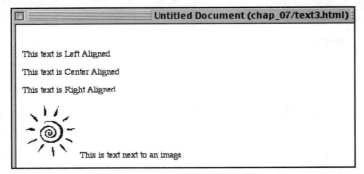

1. Open **text3.html**.

2. Select the words **This text is Center Aligned**.

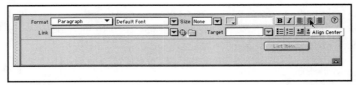

3. In the **Properties Inspector**, click the **Align Center** button. This will center your text on the page. **Note:** The centering of the text is relative to the size of the browser window.

4. Select the words **This text is Right Aligned**.

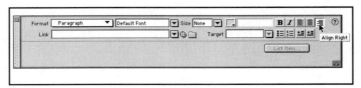

5. In the Properties Inspector, click the **Align Right** button. This will place your text on the right edge of the page.

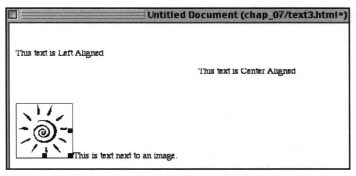

6. Highlight the **burst.gif** image. Notice when you select an image to align with type, you have different alignment options available in the Properties Inspector?

7. From the **Align** pop-up menu in the Properties Inspector, select the **Top** option. Notice that the text moves to the top of the image.

8. Save and close the file.

 Note

Aligning Text and Images

Dreamweaver offers a lot of alignment options for text and images. Below is chart defining all of the alignment terms, so now you will know what you are requesting when you select one!

Dreamweaver Alignment Features	
Alignment	**Description**
Browser Default	Varies between browsers, but usually uses the Baseline option.
Baseline	Aligns text to the bottom of the image.
Bottom	Aligns text to the bottom of the image.
Absolute Bottom	Aligns text, including descenders (i.e., j), to the bottom of the image.
Top	Aligns the tallest character to the top of the image.
Text Top	Aligns the tallest character to the top of the image.
Middle	Aligns the baseline of the text to the middle of the image.
Absolute Middle	Aligns the middle of the text to the middle of the image.
Left	Left-aligns the image and wraps text to the right.
Right	Right-aligns the image and wraps text to the left.

Exercise #4_____Using the PRE Tag

HTML text is kind of weird in that it only allows you to insert a single space between characters. If you wanted to insert more than one space, you could use the **<PRE>** tag (which stands for "preformatted"). This exercise will show off the **<PRE>** tag, and another use for a Tracing Image, to which you were introduced in Chapter 5, *"Layout."*

STEP-BY-STEP_____

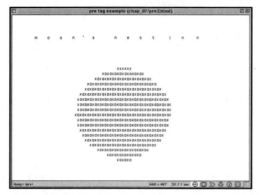

1. Open **pre2.html**. Notice the unusual formatting of the text?

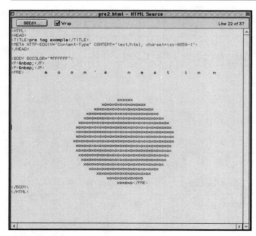

2. Press **F10** to view the HTML. Hey, what's going on here? It almost looks identical to the page in the Document window, does it not? You have just discovered the wonders of the **<PRE>** tag, which allows for more spaces than any other text-formatting tag.

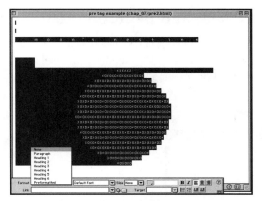

3. Press **F10** again, to make the HTML window disappear so you can see the Document window more easily. Select all the text on the screen **Cmd+A** (Mac) or **Ctrl+A** (Windows) and change the Properties Inspector's **Format** pop-up menu to **None**. See all the text collapse to the left-hand side? There is no tag like the **<PRE>** tag – it's the only tag in HTML that allows you to put any number of spaces between text characters without retagging.

4. Want to try this on your own? Choose **File > New** to make a new blank page. Save it as **pre3.html** into the **chap_07** folder. I realize it might seem strange to save an empty Document, but Dreamweaver kicks up quite a fuss if you don't save files before you start adding content.

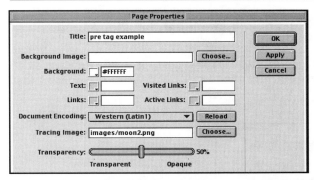

5. Choose **Modify > Page Properties** to access the **Page Properties** window. Enter the **Title: pre tag example**. To the right of the **Tracing Image:** cell click **Choose...** and load **moon2.png** located in the **images** folder. Change the Transparency slider to **50%**. Click **OK** to return to the screen.

6. The **Tracing Image** of the circle shape should appear in your page. Change the Properties Inspector's **Format** option to **Preformatted**. Use the spacebar to space over to where the circle is and start typing **x's** and **o's** to follow the contour of the shape. The Tracing Image will act as a Template guide for the circle, and the Preformatted option accepts all the spaces in the Document.

7. Choose **F12** to preview in your browser. You won't see the Tracing Image, but you will see your x's and o's. Save and close this Document to move on to the next exercise.

Exercise #5_____Ordered, Unordered, and Definition Lists

In this exercise you will learn how to create a variety of lists, an Ordered List, Unordered List, and Definition List. These are HTML terms that refer to whether the list is formatted with a bullet, an indent, or a roman numeral. These lists can be generated from existing text or from scratch.

STEP-BY-STEP_____

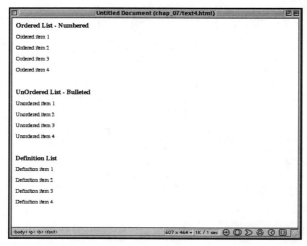

1. Open **text4.html**.

2. Select the four lines of text under the **Ordered List—Numbered** section (i.e., Ordered item 1, Ordered item 2, Ordered item 3, Ordered item 4).

3. Select **Text > List > Ordered List**.

> # Ordered List - Numbered
>
> 1. Ordered item 1
> 2. Ordered item 2
> 3. Ordered item 3
> 4. Ordered item 4

*This is what an **Ordered List** looks like.*

4. Select the four lines of text under the **UnOrdered List—Bulleted** section (i.e., Unordered item 1, Unordered item 2, Unordered item 3, Unordered item 4).

5. Select **Text > List > Unordered List**.

UnOrdered List - Bulleted

- Unordered item 1
- Unordered item 2
- Unordered item 3
- Unordered item 4

*This is what an **Unordered List** looks like.*

6. Select the four lines of text under the **Definition List** section (i.e., Definition item 1, Definition item 2, Definition item 3, Definition item 4).

7. Select **Text > List > Definition List**.

Definition List

Definition item 1
    Definition item 2
Definition item 3
    Definition item 4

*This is what a **Definition List** looks like.*

8. Save the file and close it. You'll find that knowing how to set up these different types of lists will come in very handy as you create your own Web pages and sites.

Exercise #6_____Color Schemes

Color Schemes are preset groups of colors that Dreamweaver provides for your background, text, links, active links, and visited links colors. You can apply a Color Scheme to a page at any time. They are useful when you are not sure what colors to use. Why is this exercise in the Type section? Because Color Schemes affect the color of type and links on your page, that's why!

STEP-BY-STEP_____

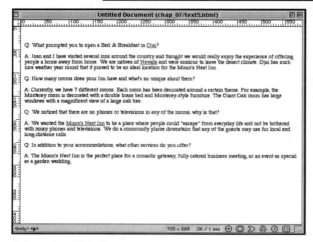

1. Open **text5.html**.

2. Select **Commands > Set Color Scheme**.

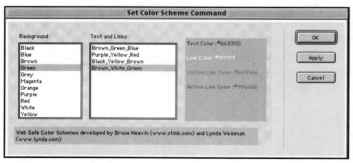

3. Select **Green** under the **Background** option. Select **Brown, White, Green** under the **Text and Links** option. Click **OK**.

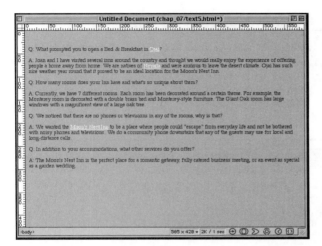

*This is what the page looks like with the **Color Scheme** applied. If you don't like it, go ahead and choose another!*

4. Select **Commands > Set Color Scheme** again. Pick a different combination of colors and click **Apply**. Knock yourself out! (In other words, enjoy yourself.)

5. When you're done having fun with colors, save and close the file.

Exercise #7_____ **Formatting Text in Tables**

In this exercise you will learn to change a Table's type, style, color, alignment, and more. In the old days, which weren't so long ago, you would have had to edit each individual cell, one at a time, and it could have taken hours to edit a large Table. Not anymore! With Dreamweaver 2, you can do it with a few deft clicks and drags. Praise the Dreamweaver engineers who figured this one out!

STEP-BY-STEP_____

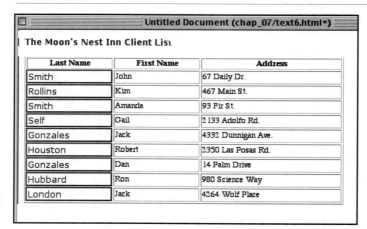

1. Open the **text6.html** file.

2. Highlight **cell 1** (Smith) in **row 2** and drag down to the last cell (London).

3. From the **Font List** pop-up menu in the **Properties Inspector**, select the **Verdana, Arial, Helvetica, sans-serif** option. All the text in the selected column will update before your eyes. If you've ever hand-coded this sort of thing, you will be gasping in delight right now.

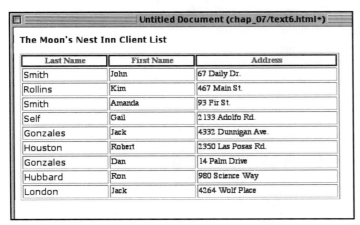

The Moon's Nest Inn Client List

Last Name	First Name	Address
Smith	John	67 Daily Dr.
Rollins	Kim	467 Main St.
Smith	Amanda	93 Fir St.
Self	Gail	2133 Adolfo Rd.
Gonzales	Jack	4332 Dunnigan Ave.
Houston	Robert	2350 Las Posas Rd.
Gonzales	Dan	14 Palm Drive
Hubbard	Ron	980 Science Way
London	Jack	4264 Wolf Place

4. Highlight **cell 1** (Last Name) in **row 1** and drag across to **cell 3** (Address).

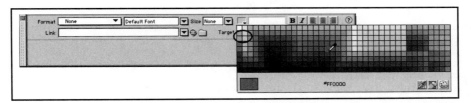

5. Using the Properties Inspector, change the text color to a bright red.

6. Press **F10** to see the HTML. Look at all those **FONT** tags! Aren't you glad you didn't have to insert each one by hand?

7. Save and close the file.

Exercise #8_____Character Entities

Character Entities are text elements such as the © Copyright symbol, ® Registered symbol, and the ™ Trademark symbol. These symbols are very common and can be found on most Web pages. Common though they may be, figuring out how to create them can be a bear. Luckily, this exercise will teach you how to create these symbols!

STEP-BY-STEP_____

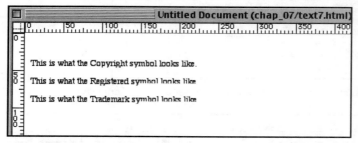

1. Open **text7.html**.

2. Click to the left of the capital **C** in Copyright.

3. Press **Option+G** (Mac) or **Alt+0169** (Windows). The Copyright symbol will be inserted. If you are using Windows, make sure you use the keypad (not the keyboard) for all these exercises — otherwise they won't work.

4. Click to the left of the capital **R** in Registered.

5. Press **Option+R** (Mac) or **Alt+0174** (Windows). The Registered symbol will be inserted.

6. Click to the left of the capital **T** in Trademark.

7. Press **Option+2** (Mac) or **Alt+0153** (Windows). The Trademark symbol will be inserted.

Untitled Document (chap_07/text7.html*

This is what the ©Copyright symbol looks like.

This is what the ®Registered symbol looks like.

This is what the ™Trademark symbol looks like.

This is what your page should look like. You've now added entity creation to your growing list of new Dreamweaver skills!

8. Save and close the file.

 Note

Macintosh and Windows Character Entities

The chart below outlines some of the more frequently used Character Entities, the Macintosh and Windows keyboard shortcuts, and the HTML code for each. **Note:** If you are using Windows, you must use the keypad (not the keyboard) to enter the numbers or this will not work!

Character Entities in Dreamweaver

Entity	Macintosh	Windows	HTML
©	Option+G	Alt+0169	©
®	Option+R	Alt+0174	®
™	Option+2	Alt+0153	™

Exercise #9_____**Blockquotes**

On the surface, it looks like you have rather limited control over HTML text. How much can you really do with left, center, and right alignment? What if you want to indent a margin or something really wild like that? You can use the **<BLOCKQUOTE>** tag, that's what! This handy tag allows you to indent your text from both sides of the page, which can be very useful when you're setting up outlines and quotations.

In this exercise, you will learn how to use the **<BLOCKQUOTE>** tag to indent and align text on the page. You will also learn about the Non-Breaking Space tag, and the difference between a Line Break tag and a Paragraph Break tag. So, roll up those sleeves and get started now, before you faint from too many exercises in this chapter!

STEP-BY-STEP_____

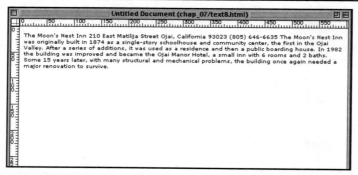

1. Open **text8.html**.

2. Click to the right of the word **Inn** in the first sentence.

3. Press **Shift+Return** (Mac) or **Shift+Enter** (Windows). This will insert a line break, which will force the text to the very next line.

4. Click to the right of the word **Street** in the second sentence.

5. Press **Shift+Return** (Mac) or **Shift+Enter** (Windows).

6. Click to the right of the number **5** in the first sentence.

7. Press **Return** (Mac) or **Enter** (Windows). This will insert a paragraph break and insert a blank line between the two bodies of text.

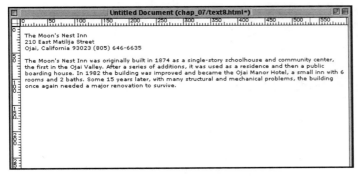

This is what your page should look like at this point.

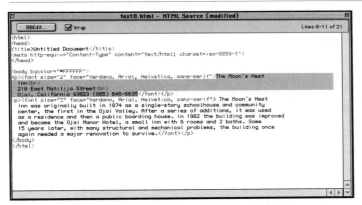

8. Press **F10** to see the HTML code. Notice the **
** and **<P>** tags!

9. Press **F10** to close the HTML window. Select the entire second paragraph of text by clicking and dragging over it.

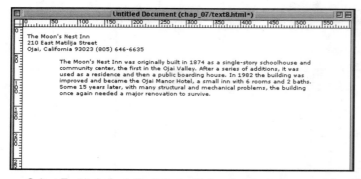

10. Select **Text > Indent**. Do it again. Notice that each time you select this option your text is indented from both sides! **Warning:** This is very cool but press **F12** and preview in a browser. Now, stretch the screen and then squish the screen. Yup, things start to fall apart. There is nothing you can do about that, except to put all this text in a fixed-percentage Table, which you learned how to do in Chapter 6, *"Tables."*

11. With the text still selected, select **Text > Outdent**. The text will be outdented on both sides of the page.

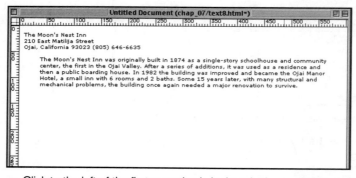

12. Click to the left of the first parenthesis in the telephone number at the top.

13. Press the **spacebar**. Nothing happens, right? That's because HTML only allows for one space between characters. Don't worry, you're going to learn the work-around for this dilemma next.

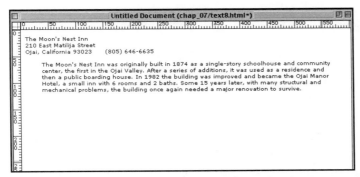

14. Press **Option+Spacebar** (Mac) or **Ctrl+Shift+Spacebar** (Windows) to insert a non-breaking space. This tag lets you insert as many spaces between text as you want. The image above shows what your page should look like after adding 5 non-breaking spaces.

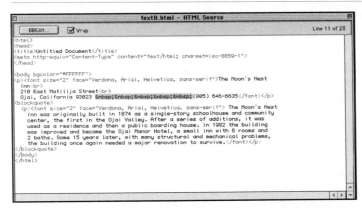

This is what the HTML for the page should look like. Notice the ** ** *code for each of the non-breaking spaces you added.*

15. Save and close the file. Take a nap, or go to the next chapter ;-).

8.Style Sheets

- **Redefining the Style of HTML Tags**
- **Making Classes • Linking to a Style Sheet**
- **Converting Style Sheets to HTML**
- **Browser Sniffing**

chap_08 folder

Dreamweaver 2
H•O•T CD-ROM

Cascading **S**tyle **S**heets offer a more flexible and accurate way to define the appearance of your text and formatting than standard HTML. If, for example, you wanted all the text in your Document to be blue and all the headlines to be green, with standard HTML you would have to go through the elements on the page one by one and assign those colors to the text. Using Style Sheets, you can redefine all the body elements in the entire Document to turn blue with just one instruction, and then perform the same single step for the headlines to turn green.

The Style Sheets specification also offers more control over type than standard HTML. With Styles, you can specify the amount of space between lines of type (also called the line height in Dreamweaver), the size of the type in pixels instead of points, and specific fonts for specific page elements. Anyone yearning for more control over typography is going to be drawn to using Styles as opposed to the type tags discussed in Chapter 7, *"Type."*

There is a dark side to Styles, however. It is only supported by Netscape 4.0, 4.5, and Explorer 4 and 5. If someone looked at your Styles-based page with an older browser, they wouldn't see any formatting whatsoever beyond the default colors, sizes, fonts, and positions. Dreamweaver has a great solution to this, however. It's the only program I know of that can convert Styles to HTML tags automatically. Dreamweaver offers the best of both worlds, it allows you to design with Styles and convert to backwards-compatible HTML. Ya gotta love it!

This chapter offers exercises in setting up Styles and Style Sheets. Style Sheets are collections of rules which define the Styles of a Document. You will get a chance to redefine the Styles of HTML tags, create custom Styles called classes which can be repeatedly applied to tags, link to an external Style Sheet, and convert everything you did to HTML.

Many Web developers think highly of Style Sheets, yet they do not use them as often as you would think. Until the support for them is more consistent, using Style Sheets is a challenging decision you will have to make. You could create two Documents: one with Style Sheets and one without. Using a Dreamweaver Behavior, you could deliver the Style Sheet to the people with current browsers and an HTML page to those who have older browsers. This chapter will show you how to do this, too.

Exercise #1_____Redefining HTML Styles with Style Sheets

As you'll soon learn, there are multiple ways to implement Styles in Dreamweaver. In this exercise, you'll learn how to assign font attributes—such as color and size—by redefining HTML tags using the Styles feature.

STEP-BY-STEP_____

1. Copy the contents of the **chap_08** folder to your hard drive. Press **F5** to define the site for this chapter. Click on the **Define Sites** pop-up menu inside the Site window and click **New**. Name this site Chapter 8 and use the yellow folder icon to browse to the **chap_08** folder on your hard drive. Once it appears in the Site window, open **interview.html**.

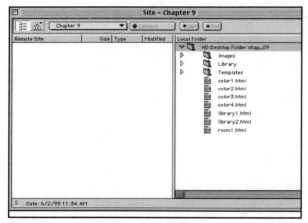

2. Press **F10** to look at the HTML code for this Document. Notice that it uses a combination of **<H3>** and **<H4>** tags as delineators between the formatting of the interview questions? Press **F10** to toggle off the HTML window.

3. Click the **Styles** button in the **Launcher**, or press **F7**.

4. The Styles window will appear. Click on the **Style Sheet...** button at the bottom.

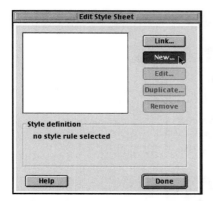

5. Click on the **New...** button in the Edit Style Sheets window.

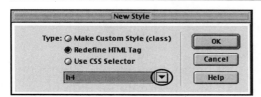

6. Select the **Redefine HTML Tag**, then click on the arrow next to the text box and select **h4** as the tag. Click **OK**. A Style definition window will appear.

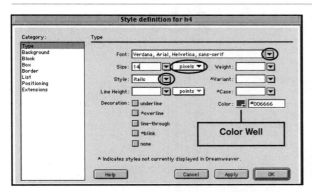

7. Choose **Font: Verdana, Arial, Helvetica, sans-serif** and **Size: 14**. Change the setting from points to **pixels**. Click **Apply** and you will begin to see the type change on the page. Choose **Style: italic** (you can click on the arrow to select it). Change the **Color:** to a **light blue** (you can press down on the color well to select your own color, or type the value #006666). Click **OK** to finalize these settings, then click **Done** in the Edit Style Sheet dialog box.

Note: For the Font setting I prefer to use pixels because it results in better consistency between the Mac and Windows platforms than points. Unfortunately, as discussed in Chapter 7, "Type," Windows renders type at 96 dpi, while Macs render type at 72 dpi. Setting the type to pixels eliminates this problem, but only for 4.0+ browsers.

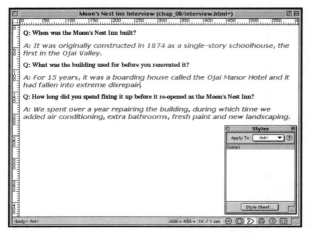

This is what the results of your labor look like so far.

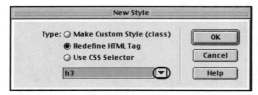

8. Now it's time to reformat the questions. Click on **Style Sheet...** in the **Styles** window. If it isn't on your screen, press **F7** to bring it forth. Select **New**, check **Redefine HTML Tag** (if it isn't already checked) and use the arrow to select **h3**. Finally, click **OK**. This will bring up the Style definition window.

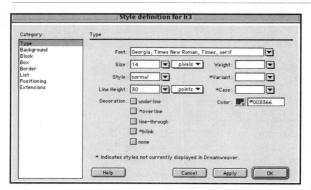

9. Enter **Font: Georgia, Times New Roman, Times, serif**. Enter **Size: 14**. Remember to change points to **pixels**. Select **Style: normal** and **Line Height: 30 points**. Click **Apply**. Notice how the space between the lines of type just increased? Ya just can't do that in vanilla HTML, folks! Change **Color:** to a **dark blue** by using the color well or typing in the value **#003366**, as shown above. Click **OK**, and then **Done** in the Edit Style Sheet dialog box.

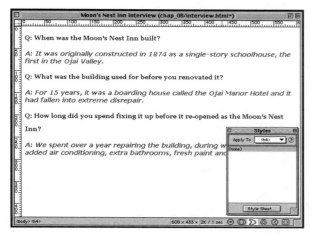

Your screen should look something like this.

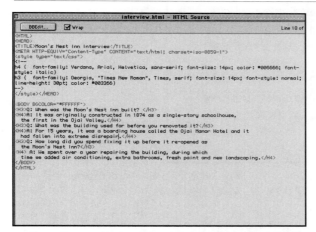

10. Press **F10** to check out the code. Notice all the Style Sheet information that was added to the **<HEAD>** of the document? Pretty darn cool of Dreamweaver to write all of that for you, wasn't it? **Save** this document as **interview2.html** and leave it open.

11. I encourage you to click on the **Style Sheet...** button again, and to select either **h3** or **h4** and click **Edit....** Make some changes and try some other settings. Knock yourself out, have some fun! When you're finished, close the document. Whether you save your changes is up to you, because this book won't require this file again.

So what was the point of all this, you might ask? Styles offer a different method to format your Documents. They ensure consistency and can save a lot of time by formatting global changes. As you'll soon see, redefining HTML is just one way in which to applied Styles. The next exercises will show you how to make changes that are local (apply to individual text characters or words instead of entire tags).

Exercise #2_____Defining a Custom Class

You just learned to redefine the default formatting of a HTML tag with Style Sheets. Now it's time to move on to make your own custom class. A Style Sheet Class is a set of specifications that can be applied to any tag on the page. Why would you use a class instead of redefining the formatting of an HTML tag, like you did in the last exercise? Perhaps there's a set of Styles, like a particular color and text size, that you would like to apply randomly without it being automatically applied to every instance of a particular HTML tag. For example, maybe you don't want all the **<H3>** tags to automatically be green—and perhaps you want some **<H4>** tags to be green, as well.

Rather than redefining an existing HTML tags like you did in the last exercise, a class is a way to apply the same Style to different tags on your page. In other words, a class can be applied to any tag at any time. If this sounds confusing, try the exercise and it will likely make more sense.

STEP-BY-STEP_____

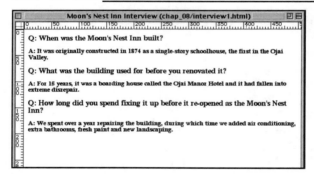

1. Open **interview1.html**. It should look just like it did at the beginning of Exercise #1, since it is an identical file at this point. It is very important that it does not contain any Style Sheet information as of yet!

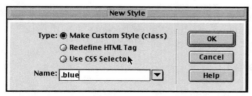

2. Press **F7** to bring forth the Style window if it's not visible. Click on **Style Sheet...** to bring up the Edit Style Sheet window, and then click **New...** to open the New Style window. Check **Make Custom Style (class)** and set **Name:** to **.blue**. Make sure you put a period before the name .blue, it's important because all classes have this period. Click **OK**.

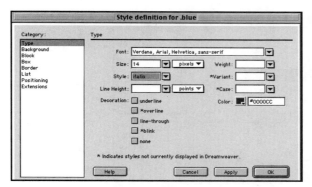

3. Fill out the Style information however you like, but make sure to set **Color:** to a blue! **Note:** Clicking Apply will have no effect in this instance, because you aren't redefining an existing tag. Therefore, click **OK** once you're finished, because you can always re-edit the class. Click **Done** in the Edit Style Sheet window that appears next.

Your Styles window should now contain the word blue in it. **Note:** *It won't contain a period here in front of the word blue, even though you needed to specify one. Why? Beats me! It's an interface inconsistency.*

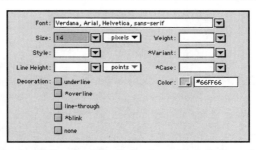

4. Create a **.green** class by following Steps 2 and 3 and setting **Color:** to green. I don't want to be a nag, but remember to put that period in front of the class name **.green**!

5. Click **Done** in the Edit Style Sheet window that appears next.

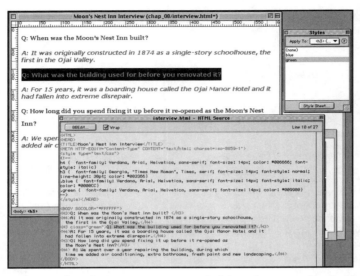

6. Select a line of type on your page, and click on the **green** class inside the Styles window. If you leave the HTML window open, as shown here, you can watch Dreamweaver construct the Style code before your eyes. Classes can be applied to lines of text or even individual words or characters. Go ahead and select different bits of type on your page and click on the **blue** or **green** class to see what happens. Congrats! You've just created a class and applied it to a Document.

7. Save the results into your **chap_08** folder as **interviewclass.html**. Close the Document.

 Note _____

Internal, Inline and External Style Sheets

There are three types of Style Sheets: internal, inline, and external. In Exercise #1, you created an Internal Style Sheet that was applied to all the **H3** and **H4** tags in the Document. An Internal Style Sheet is global to the entire Document, yet it is limited to whatever Document it was contained within. In Exercise #2, you created an Inline Style Sheet when you defined a Custom Class. Inline Styles may be applied selectively to elements within a Document. Remember how in Exercise 2 you applied Styles to specific lines of text, individual words or characters? This is called an "inline" style sheet because it doesn't appear to the entire page. An External Style Sheet is an external Document to which you can link. For example, I could take a regular HTML page and link it to an External Style Sheet and it would take on all the style properties of that Document. This chapter will teach you how to make styles in all three of these ways. You'll find that any of these three choices will be appropriate at different times.

Exercise #3_____Using Selectors to Group Tags

In the last two exercises you learned how to apply Styles to redefine a tag or as a Custom Class on selective text. What about the if you want to apply a single Style to multiple HTML tags? Let's say you wanted to reformat both the **H3 and H4** tags at the same time? Selectors are the answer, as they allow you to apply Styles to multiple HTML tags at once.

STEP-BY-STEP_____

1. Open **interview3.html**.

2. Press **F7** if the Styles window isn't visible and click on the **Style Sheet...** button. Click **New...** and choose **Use CSS Selector** in the New Style window. Enter the value, as shown above, **h3 h4**. Note that there is a space between the two tags. **Warning:** Do not use commas between these values, they will not work! Click **OK**.

3. In the Edit Style Sheet window, set **Color:** to a blue and click **OK**. Click **Done**.

4. Press **F10** to view the code. Type a comma between **h3** and **h4**, as shown above. Dreamweaver doesn't support this feature, so you have to go right into the code to make it work.

While I wish Dreamweaver did directly support a Selector in this fashion, it is commendable that you can edit the code directly and Dreamweaver will still honor it. Many other HTML editors won't let you enter code that the editor doesn't generate.

5. Press **F10** to close the HTML window, the text will turn blue!

6. Save and close the file.

This exercise showed how you can apply a single Style to two HTML tags using a selector, pretty tricky stuff

Exercise #4_____Affecting Links with Selectors

In standard HTML, the default appearance of a link is that it is formatted with an underline. One of the common things that people use Style Sheets for is to turn off the underlines of links. I'm not sure if I think this is a good idea or not because many people rely on the visual cue of under-lined text to know that it is truly a link. Regardless, some of you may want to do it anyway, so this exercise will show you how. Not only that, you'll get to use the CSS Selector feature again! Woo hoo!

STEP-BY-STEP_____

1. Open **interviewlink.html**. As you can see by the underlined text, this Document contains a link.

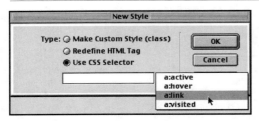

2. Press **F7** if the Styles window is not visible, and click on the **Style Sheet...** button. Click **New...**, and choose **Use CSS Selector** and **a:link** in the New Style window. This allows you to define the **<a>** (anchor) tag's link properties. Click **OK**.

3 This will open the Style Definition window. Choose **Decoration: none**, and click **OK**. The term Decoration refers to how the link is displayed. In this case, because an underline is not wanted, the Decoration is set to **none**. This will return you to the Edit Style Sheet window. Click **Done**.

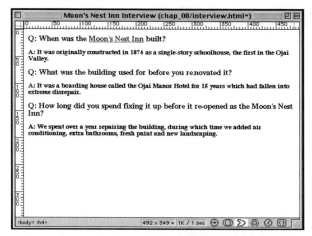

4. You will be returned to the Document window and nothing will look different. That is because this feature does not preview in Dreamweaver, it must instead be viewed inside a web browser.

5. Press **F12**, and you'll see that the link is there, but it isn't underlined.

Note: This can only be seen from a 4.0+ browser. If you have an earlier browser, you will not be able to see it even though you created it. Such is life in the not-so-fair world of never-ending browser incompatibility.

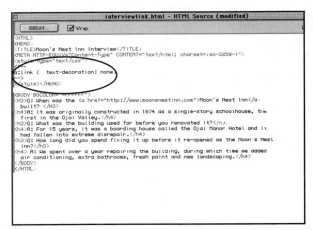

6. Return to Dreamweaver and press **F10** to view the HTML code. Notice the Style Selector information was added! I don't know about you, but I sure like that I don't have to hand-code this sort of thing.

7. Save and close this file.

 Note_____

Changing the Appearance of Links with Selectors

You might have noticed that the pop-up menu for CSS Selectors had four entries: a:active, a:hover, a:link, and a:visited. Exercise #4 showed you how a:link affected the attributes for links, but what do the other entries stand for? The selection a:active affects the Active Link, which is the appearance when the mouse is depressed on a link. The selection a:hover affects the appearance of the link when your mouse rolls over it. You could, for example, have the text color change upon rollover. Note that a:hover is only honored by Explorer, not Netscape. The a:visited selection alters the appearance of a Visited Link, or, in plain English, a link that has already been clicked on.

Tip_____

Redefine HTML, Custom Class, or Selector?

Now that you've completed exercises creating Styles based on redefining HTML, a
Custom Class, and a Selector, you might be wondering when to use which type of
Style. The following chart should help you make sense of it all (I hope!).

Creating Styles in Dreamweaver	
When to Use?	**For What Purpose?**
Redefine HTML Tag	When you want to change the appearance of content based on a certain tag. For example, everything with an **H1** tag could be made to look consistent.
Create a Custom Class	When you want to change the appearance of your Document and have it not be dependent on a tag. Let's say you wanted to make certain words green, regardless of whether they were in a headline or in body copy.
Selector	Selectors can change the appearance of multiple HTML tags all at once. Use this when you want to make appearance changes based on tags, but on more than one at one time. Dreamweaver also includes the a: Selectors as a way to change the appearance of linked text (turning off the underline, for example).

Exercise #5_____Linking to a Style Sheet

You might not have realized this, but so far you've been creating Internal Style Sheets. Internal Style Sheets apply only to the Document in which they reside. It's also possible to create External Style Sheets, so that different pages in your Web site can all share the same set of Style Sheet information. In the linked Style Sheet scenario, the Style information is in the external Document, and it is only referenced by the internal Document. External Style Sheets are very powerful, because you can base all the Style information in one Document, and if you make a change you only have to change it there, instead of in each individual Document that references it. This exercise will show you how to create an External Style Sheet, and then how to link to it once it's created.

STEP-BY-STEP_____

1. Choose **File > New** and immediately save the empty Document as **style.html**.

2. Press **F7** to bring up the Styles window if it's not visible, and click on the **Style Sheet...** button. In the Edit Style Sheet window, click **New....**

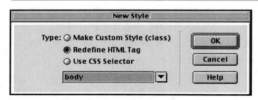

3. Click **Redefine HTML Tag** and select **body** from the pop-up menu (it might pop up automatically). Click **OK**.

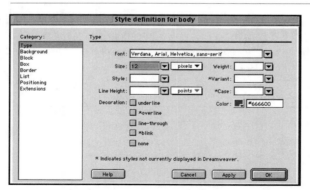

4. Choose **Font: Verdana, Arial, Helvetica, sans-serif**, set **Size: 12 pixels,** and make **Color: green**. Click **OK**.

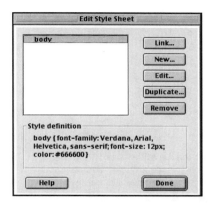

5. In the Edit Style Sheet window, click **New...** again. You're going to add another Style to this External Style Sheet.

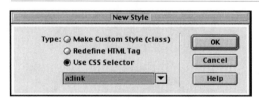

6. Choose **Use CSS Selector** and **a:link**, and click **OK**.

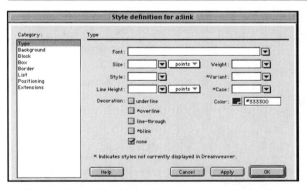

7. Choose **Decoration: None** (because an underline is not wanted). Click **OK**. Click **Done** in the Edit Style Sheet window.

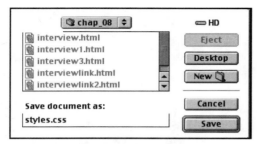

8. Choose **File > Export > Export CSS Styles**. Name the file **styles.css**. In the future, if decide to create you own Style Sheets, you could name this file anything you like (as long as it's all lowercase and has no spaces), but you always have to give it a **.css** extension instead of an **.html** extension for it to work properly. Click **Save**.

9. Close the Untitled Document and do not save the changes. The style sheet information was saved when you chose to **Export CSS Styles**.

10. Open the file **interviewlink2.html**. Press **F7** if the Styles window is not visible. Next, click on the **Style Sheet...** button. Click **Link...** and then click on **Choose...** (Mac) or **Browse...** (Windows). Navigate to **styles.css** and click **Select**. Click **OK**.

11. You should see the **styles.css** (link) listing inside the Edit Style Sheet. Click **Done**.

12. The type on your screen should look green, and when you preview this in a browser by pressing **F12**, the links should not be underlined. Save and close all the open Documents. You could link numerous Documents to the **.css** file if you wanted to. This completes your education for the day in External Style Sheet linking.

Exercise #6_____From CSS to HTML

Now that you've successfully created Internal, Inline and External Style Sheets, you ought to be feeling pretty proud. You may be feeling so good, in fact, that you might have forgotten that Style Sheets still aren't widely supported by browsers. What's a conscientious Web designer to do? Dreamweaver has a great solution—you can convert the CSS to HTML! The only caveat is that HTML doesn't support certain things, such as links with no underlines, or font sizes in pixels. Bear with me for a moment, and you'll see where I'm going with all this.

STEP-BY-STEP_____

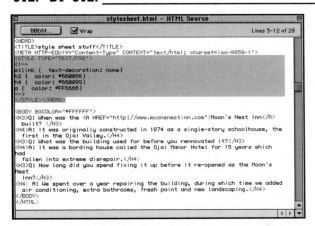

1. Open **stylesheet.html**. Press **F10**, and you'll see Style Sheet information in the Document.

2. Choose **File > Convert > 3. 0 Browser Compatible....**

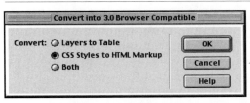

3. Click on **CSS Styles to HTML Markup** in the Convert into 3.0 Browser Compatible window and click **OK**. This will create a separate Untitled Document.

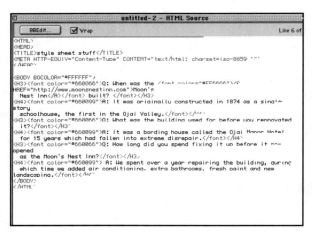

4. Press **F10** to look at the HTML. Look ma, no Style information, just HTML code! Press **F10** to close the HTML window.

5. Save this file as **stylesheet2.html**. You should now have two Documents: **stylesheet.html** and **stylesheet2.html** in your **chap_08** folder.

Why did Dreamweaver create another Document for you? Because you might want to have two pages on hand: one to deliver to your 4.0 browser audience, and another for your audience that can't see the Style Sheets.

You'll see how to serve two different pages in the next exercise called "Browser Sniffing."

6. Close both files.

Exercise #7_____**Browser Sniffing**

Browser sniffing is one of my favorite terms in Web design, for no other reason except that it's so incredibly silly. Aside from that, however, it does have a valuable purpose, which is to sniff out whether your end-user has a 4.0 browser or not. This exercise will show you how to leverage **stylesheet.html** and **stylesheet2.html** by letting the browser-sniffing JavaScript decide which version of the page to display.

STEP-BY-STEP_____

1. Go to the Site window (press **F5** if you can't see it) and open **stylesheet.html**.

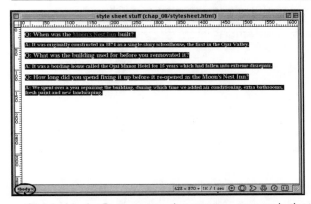

2. Click inside the Document so that **<body>** appears in the tag selector. Click on **<body>** in the tag selector so you can apply a Behavior to this element. Behaviors have to be applied to specific HTML tags, and this is the recommended method for doing so!

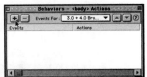

3. Next, you'll want to open the Behaviors window. Either click on the **Behavior** button in the Launcher, choose **Window > Behaviors**, or press **F8**.

4. Set Events For: 3.0 + 4.0 Browsers, and Press the **plus** button. A pop-up menu will appear. Select **Check Browser**.

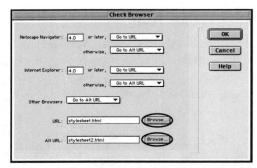

5. Click the top Browse button to select **URL: stylesheet.html**, and click the bottom Browse button to select Alt **URL: stylesheet2.html**. Click **OK**.

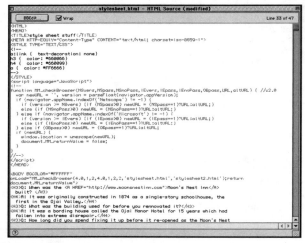

6. Check out the HTML by pressing **F10**. Look at all that JavaScript you just created. You're quite the stud these days! Beyond the mere studliness of it all, however, lies a script that will show two different versions of your site to the appropriate audience. See the next note for important caveats to this achievement!

7. Save and close the file.

Note_____

JavaScript Versus CGI or Server Browser Sniffers

While I think it's incredibly cool that Dreamweaver writes JavaScript browser sniffers so easily, it is my duty to warn you of its limitations. JavaScript
itself only works on 3.0 browsers and beyond, and Internet Explorer 3.0
didn't support it well at all (in fact, some JavaScript which is compatible
with 4.0 browsers gives error messages to the user on older versions!).
Not only that, but many people turn off JavaScript in their browsers because they don't want to be bothered with it. This means that a Java-
Script-based browser sniffer can't correctly sniff 100% of the time. If the
user doesn't have JavaScript or has disabled it, then they'll always see the
dumbed-down version of the page. It is much safer to use a server-side
technology, such as CGI (Common Gateway Interface) scripts, PHP3, ASP
or the Web server itself to perform browser detection, because all are
completely browser independent! Trouble is, mere mortals like me do not
know how to write CGI or PHP scripts, and Dreamweaver doesn't generate 'em automatically either. To utilize a server-based browser sniffer, you'll
either need to hook up with a programmer, or download one of the many
free CGI scripts.

Browser Detection CGI Scripts
http://www.citro.net/scripts/more.shtml#browse
http://www.wirewd.com/wpt/tool/redir.html

9. **Templates/Libraries**

- **Creating and Modifying Templates**
- **Setting Up Templates So Others Can Use Them**
- **Locking Template Content**
- **Creating and Modifying Library Items**

chap_09 folder

Dreamweaver 2
H•O•T CD-ROM

Two of the biggest challenges that face Web designers are making pages look consistent and updating changes throughout a site. Templates and Library Items offer a means to create consistent pages and page elements, and have the added benefit that if changed, they automatically update the pages on which they have been applied.

Templates are useful for entire page designs. They can lock in colors, fonts, tables, or images, while leaving other parts of the Document editable. When you create a Template, you use it by requesting a copy of it. Instead of creating a new, Untitled Document, you would request a new page based on a Template that you designed.

Library Items are useful for page-design elements, such as a navigation bar or copyright notice. They are little pieces of HTML or text that can be dropped anywhere within a page. You will soon learn the differences between these two Dreamweaver features by following the hands-on exercises in this chapter.

Tip_____

Templates and Library Folders

You might have noticed that there were two folders inside the **chap_09** folder, called Templates and Library. Because this folder was prepared for you on the CD-ROM, you might wonder how those two folders got there, Dreamweaver automatically creates these folders for you on any site that uses Templates or Libraries. If you don't use Templates or Library Items, Dreamweaver will not put these folders in your directory structure.

These folders (Templates and Library) do not need to be uploaded to your Web site if you publish it to the WWW. They are for internal purposes only. If Dreamweaver sees that these folders are present in your directory structure, it knows to insert any new Template or Library elements that you create into each folder (Template or Library) without you having to do so.

 Note_____

Templates, Library Items and HTML

Dreamweaver's Template format (**.dwt**) and Library format (**.lib**) are internal file-naming conventions only. These files do not mean anything to other HTML editors, nor are they meant to be viewed on the Web inside a browser. Templates and Libraries are used internally by Dreamweaver, and function only in Dreamweaver. If you base an HTML page on a Template, it is an HTML page on anyone's browser, the same as any other HTML page. It will be regarded differently in Dreamweaver only, in that it will be updated if the original Template or Library Item is changed.

Exercise #1_____Templates in Action

The best way to understand Templates in Dreamweaver is to observe them in action. For this first exercise, you will get to modify an existing Template, which will show you how quickly they can up-date across multiple pages in your site. You will also see how, with just a few clicks, you can use Templates to change your Color Scheme across several pages.

STEP-BY-STEP_____

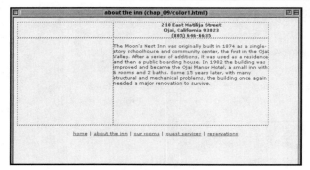

1. Define your site for **Chapter 9**. If you do not remember how to do this, revisit Exercise #1 in Chapter 3, *"Site Control."*

2. Open **color1.html**. This file and several others including (**color2. html, color3. html**, and **color4.html**) inside of the **chap_09** folder have a Template called **summer** already applied to them. If you want, go ahead and open these other files and notice that they all share the same color scheme.

3. When you are working with Templates in Dreamweaver, you will typically want to have the Templates window open. Select **Window > Templates** to open it.

4. To modify a Template, you must first open it. Highlight the **summer** Template in the Tem-plates window and then click on the **Open** button. This will open the Template so you can start editing it.

It's easy to tell when you are editing a Template because the Title bar will display **<<Template>>**, *the Template file name, and a* **.dwt** *extension.*

5. To change the Color Scheme of this Template you will use some of the preset Color Schemes that ship with Dreamweaver. Select **Commands > Set Color Scheme**. Select **Background: Green** and **Text and Links: Brown, White, Green**. Click **OK**.

6. Close this file and save your changes.

7. Once you close and save the modified Template, you will be notified that you have modified a Template and asked if you want to update all the files in your site that use this Template. Because you want to apply the new Color Scheme to all four pages, click **Yes**. If you are presented with the Update Templates dialog box, click **Update**.

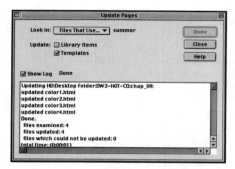

8. Once you click **Update**, Dreamweaver will scan your site to determine if any files are using this Template. If it locates any files that are, it will update them. In this case, there are four such files. A dialog box will list which files were updated. Once you are finished reviewing this screen, click **Close**.

Note: *If you have **color1.html** open while performing this operation, the Templates will be updated...but if you try to close the file and don't save changes you'll lose them.*

 Note

Saving and Updating Templates

As you work with saving and updating Templates, one of two dialog boxes will prompt you to update the files in your site that are using that Template. While the dialog boxes look very different, they both do the same thing. Here are what the two look like:

Each asks if you would like to update the files in your site that use the Template you have modified. If you select **Yes** or **Update**, the files will be automatically updated. If you select **No** or **Don't Update**, the files will not be updated. So, don't be alarmed if you get one of these or the other as you go through this chapter.

If you open each of the four files, you will see that each now has the new Color Scheme. Imagine how much time this could save you if you had hundreds or thousands of pages that share the same Color Scheme!

Working with Templates is an excellent technique to ensure design consistency. The only caveat is that you must work from a Template file to begin with. How do you do that? Check out the next exercise, to find out.

9. Close all the files. You will learn how to make a Template from scratch in the next exercise.

 Tip

Templates and Page Properties

Once a Template has been applied to a page, you can no longer edit any of the Page Properties options, with the exception of the page title. Therefore, the only way to change the Color Scheme is by opening and editing the Template itself, as you just did in Exercise #1.

Exercise #2_____Creating a New Template

In this next exercise, you are going to create a new Template from an existing Document and then make parts of your Template editable and non-editable. Once you have this skill under your belt, you will understand Templates' capabilities and limitations much more clearly.

STEP-BY-STEP_____

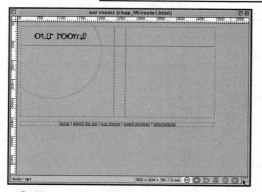

1. Open **room1.html**. This Document was created for you, but the following steps would also work on a Document of your own creation.

2. Once you have created the basic layout of your Document, the next step is to save the Document as a Template. **Select File > Save As Template....**

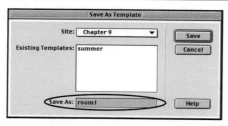

3. When the Save As Template dialog box opens, name this Template **room1**. You can see that your other Template, **summer**, is already listed in this box. Click **Save**.

*Again, you now know that you are now working with a Template because the Title bar displays **<<Template>>** and the file name with a **.dwt** extension.*

Now that you have created your Template, you need to decide which areas you want to be able to modify and which areas you want to lock. By default the entire Document is designated as non-editable. This means that if you were to close the file now, it would be impossible for others or yourself to modify it later.

4. Click inside of the large cell directly under the image **our rooms**. Select **Modify > Templates > New Editable Region....** This designates this area as an editable region so that you or other members of your design team can enter the description of the room here.

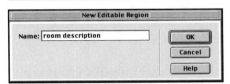

5. When the New Editable Region dialog box appears, enter **room description**, and click **OK**.

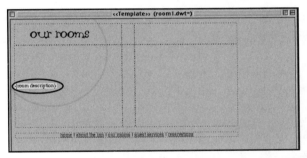

*Notice that the name you entered appears in that cell, surrounded by curly braces. This indicates that this area of the Template is editable—it will let you or other members of your team enter information inside this cell. By naming this region **room description**, you can help others know what information should be entered there.*

6. Click inside the large cell on the far right. Select **Modify > Templates > New Editable Region....** Enter **room image** and click **OK**.

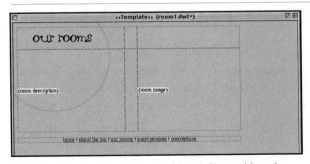

This is what your Template should look like at this point.

7. Now that you have designated the necessary areas as editable, go ahead and close this file. When prompted, make sure that you save your changes.

8. Select **File > New From Template...**.

9. Highlight **room1** from the list and click **Select**. This will create a new Document based on the **room1** Template.

10. Choose **File > Save As...**, and then save the file as **montereyroom.html** into your **chap_09** folder.

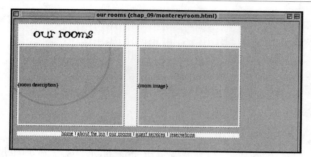

This what the page will look like with a Template applied to it. The highlighted areas are non-editable. The two areas you designated as editable are not highlighted and are ready to be edited.

 Tip_____

Detaching a Template

There may come a time when you want to modify sections of a page that has a Template applied to it. Because some areas are locked, this is impossible to do with the Template still applied to the page. By selecting **Modify > Templates > Detach from...**, you can detach the Template from the page and make the entire Document editable.

11. Highlight the text **room description** and its surrounding curly braces, press **Delete** to make sure that the brackets disappear, and type **The Monterey Room. A charming brass double bed completes this cozy room with a balcony affording both city and mountain views. This room has a private bath**.

12. Highlight the text **room image** on the right and its surrounding curly braces, press **Delete** to make sure the curly braces disappear, then click the **Insert Image** button in the Objects palette.

13. Browse to the **images** folder to locate **monterey1.jpg**. Click **Select**. This will insert the image into this editable region.

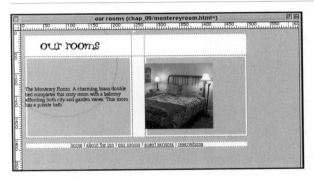

14. Keep this file open.

 Tip_____

Highlighting Preferences

You can modify your Document's highlighting colors in Dreamweaver's Preferences section. By selecting **Edit > Preferences...** and then selecting **Highlighting** under **Category**, you can set the highlighting colors to any color you want.

Exercise #3_____Modifying a Template

Now that that you have created your first Template, you are ready to learn how to update it. In this exercise, you are going to change the alignment of the text and image in your layout, causing the text to move to the bottom and the image to move to the center. Then, all you have to do is sit back and watch Dreamweaver update all the pages in your site that use this Template!

STEP-BY-STEP_____

1. Make sure that **montereyroom.html** from the previous exercise is open. Before you can modify a Template, you must open it from the Template window. Highlight the **room1** Template in the Templates window then, click the **Open** button.

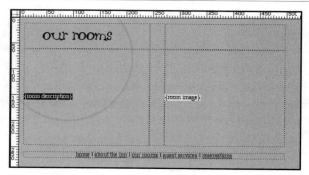

2. The actual Template file will be open for you to edit. Highlight the text **room description**.

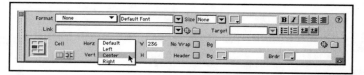

3. In the Properties Inspector, click the **Horz** pop-up menu and select **Center**. This will move the text to the center of the cell.

4. Highlight the **text room** image.

5. Again, in the Properties Inspector's **Horz** pop-up menu, select **Center**. This will move the text to the center of the cell.

6. Go ahead and close this file. When prompted, make sure that you save your changes. A dialog box will appear asking if you wish to update the files in your site which use this Template. Click **Yes**. If you get the Update Templates dialog box, click **Update**. Close the Update Templates dialog box.

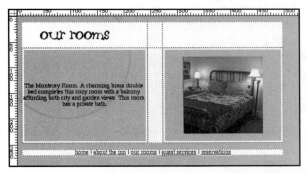

7. This is what the **montereyroom.html** will look like with the revised Template applied to it. **Note:** Templates used in this fashion are only helpful if the pages share the same layout and the same editable-region names.

8. Close all open files and move on to the next exercise.

 Warning_____

Template Warning!

Once a Template has been applied to a page, you can no longer edit any information in the **<HEAD>** tag. This means you can't add any JavaScript, Styles, Behaviors, or anything else that would be contained within a **<HEAD>** tag. If you do need to add this type of code to a page that's based on a Template, you need to break the Template by selecting **Modify > Templates > Detach from....** This would remove its link to the original Template and allow you to edit anything within the **<HEAD>** element. The downside to this, of course, is that if you made changes to the Template, this unlinked copy would not be able to refer to it.

Exercise #4_____Library Items in Action

Library Items and Templates are somewhat similar in function. Both are used to apply changes to multiple pages with ease. The difference is that Templates affect the entire page design, while Library Items are used for individual page elements. You are going to start this section by working with an existing Library Item. This will demonstrate just how cool these things are and how much time they can save you!

STEP-BY-STEP_____

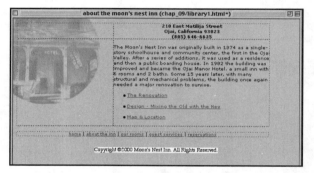

1. Open **library1.html**. At the bottom of this page, you will see a line of text that is high lighted in yellow. This is an indication that this text is a Library Item.

2. In order to modify the Library Item, you need to open the Library window. **Select Window > Library** or **(F6)** if it's not already open with the Templates window. You will see that one Library Item already exists. This is the one that you will modify.

3. Highlight the **copyright** Library Item by clicking on it, and click the **Open** button in the Library window.

*Just as with Templates, it's easy to tell when you are editing Library Items. The Title bar displays **<<Library Item>>** and the file name with a **.lbi** extension.*

4. Highlight the text **1999** and type **2000**. Of course, this is assuming that your computer will be working after the year 2000! Just kidding ;-).

5. Close this file. If you are prompted, make sure that you save your changes.

6. When you are asked to update the pages in your site that use this Library Item, click **Yes**. If you get the Update Library dialog box, click **Update**.

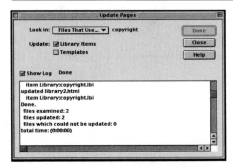

7. The Update Pages dialog box will appear. Just like Templates, this dialog box gives you all the details of how many and which files were updated in your site. Click **Close** when you are finished reviewing this screen.

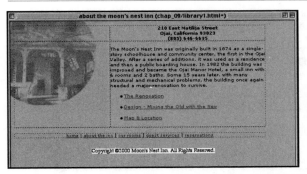

This is what your page should look like with the updated Library Item. Can you imagine how long it would take to update this text on a hundred pages? Library Items can offer incredible time savings.

8. You can now close this file because you won't need it for the next exercise.

Exercise #5_____Creating a Library Item

Now that you understand how efficient Library Items can be, it's time to create your own. In this exercise, you will create a simple text navigation bar for them. You will then apply it to several pages by simply dragging it onto a page! Life is so good sometimes.

STEP-BY-STEP_____

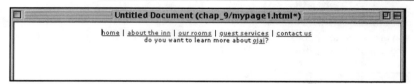

1. Open **library2.html**. This is a just a simple file with text navigation already created.

2. Make sure the Library window is open. If it's not, select **Window > Library** (F6).

3. Highlight both lines of text. In the Library window, click on the **Create** button. Your new Library Item will instantly appear in the window. It needs a name, so type **textnav**.

4. Now that you have created your Library Item, you can apply it to a page. Create a new blank Document by selecting **File > New**. Then select **File > Save** and save this file inside the **chap_09** folder as **mypage1.html**.

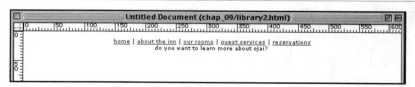

5. In the Library window, highlight the **textnav** item and click the **Add to Page** button. Pow! The Library Item is applied to the page. Notice that it did not retain the center alignment you had applied when it was created. Go ahead and center align both lines of text.

6. Save your file and leave it open.

Exercise 6_____Modifying a Library Item

Now that you know how to create Library Items, you are going to modify the one you just created and then watch Dreamweaver quickly update your page. Can you imagine how joyous you would be if this were a change that needed to be made over hundreds or thousands of pages?

STEP-BY-STEP_____

1. Highlight the **textnav** item in the Library window and click the **Open** button. This will open the Library Item for editing.

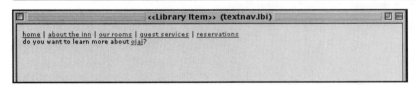

2. Highlight the word **reservations** and type **contact us**. This should replace the type, but maintain the link.

3. Close this file and when you are prompted, make sure you save and update your changes. If you get the Update Templates dialog box, click **Update**. Close the **Update Pages** dialog box when are done reviewing it.

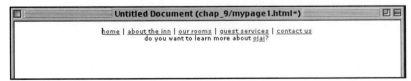

This is what your page should look like with the new Library Item applied to it.

10.Frames

- **The Pros and Cons of Frames • Coloring Frames**
- **Setting Borders and Scrollbars • Links and Targets**
- **Fitting Background Images to Frames**

chap_10 folder

Dreamweaver 2
H•O•T CD-ROM

So far in this book, you've learned to insert text, Tables, and images into individual HTML pages. The concept of Frames is a little more challenging since, in effect, a "Frame" is an HTML page inside another HTML page. Why would anyone want to put an HTML page inside another HTML page? So that one part of a page can update independently from another.

Let's say that you've created an image that belonged at the bottom of an HTML page. If your site contained 100 pages, and you wanted to put that same image at the bottom of all of them, you would need to insert that image 100 times into each of those 100 individual pages.

Frames allow you to reuse a single HTML page by nesting it inside another HTML Document (otherwise known as a Frameset). My husband Bruce, who helps me teach classes at our training center, came up with a wonderful metaphor for teaching Frames: Imagine a TV dinner. You've got your peas and carrots, an entrée and, if you are really lucky, a dessert. Don't forget though about the tray that holds all these food items together! A Frameset, if you will, is the TV-dinner tray that holds together multiple HTML Documents.

If I were to build a Frameset that contained two Frames, a left Frame for my Web navigation element and a right Frame for my content, my audience would see only two Frames. What's hidden is that my audience would be working with three Documents—a Frameset (think TV-dinner tray) and two Frames (the content HTML page and the navigation HTML page). Every time you come to a page that contains Frames, it always includes a Frameset that holds the Frames in place. If this sounds confusing at all, welcome to Frames! Conceptually, they can be a bit of a brain twister.

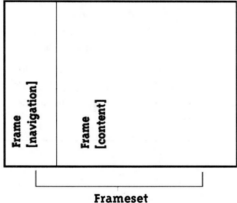

Frameset

I promise that the exercises in this chapter will help you unravel these concepts. You'll learn that Frames are controversial creatures, and that they are either loved or hated by most people. I'll do my best to fill you in on the pros and cons of using Frames, as well as a variety of techniques for using them effectively and creatively. In the end, you will have the honor of deciding if they are right or wrong for your site. Hey, I just teach this stuff!

Frames: A Love-or-Hate Proposition

First, a word from our sponsor (me). Frames are controversial—most people either love or hate them. You may want to consider the pros and cons before you use them in your site. Here are two charts to help you if you're weighing the decision to use or not use Frames.

Love Frames?	
Pro	**Explanation**
Good Workflow	It's easier to update a single page than hundreds, right? If you put a navigation element (all your links) into a Frame of a Frameset, and then your site's navigation changes, you only have to update that one page.
Fixed Navigation	The entire page doesn't have to reload each time a link is clicked, only sections of the page. This means that you can anchor a navigation page so it doesn't have to be reloaded with each new page click and always stays consistent throughout your site.
Special Effects	Frames let you do cool special effects, such as putting a single background into multiple Frames for aesthetic purposes. You'll learn this technique in this very chapter!

Hate Frames?

Con	Explanation
Confusing	If not well implemented, Frames can create confusing navigation for your audience. However, this chapter will teach you how to implement Frames well, of course!
Printing Hassles	It is not possible to print an entire Frameset. That would be like printing three or more HTML pages at once. Your end-user can print individual Frames, but Frames are often transparent to the end user and this can prove challenging. My suggestion? If you think people are going to print a page from your site, don't put it in a Frameset.
Bookmark Hassles	The only part of a framed page that can be bookmarked easily is the Frameset. Let's say I have 20 pages that load into a single Frameset. If my end user wanted to bookmark page 11, they could not. They could only book mark the first page that loads into the Frameset. I have no remedy for this problem, except to say that you should make it very clear from that first page how to get to Frame 11 by adding a simple navigation path to it.
Hidden Security Issues	At my Web site, we once made the mistake of placing a secure order form into an insecure Frameset. Some of our customers complained because they couldn't see the lock symbol at the bottom left of their browser that ensures a page is secure. We eventually took the secure page out of the Frameset so our customers would feel more confident buying from us. You will learn how to change in and out of Framesets in Exercise #3.
Too Boxy!	Frames divide an already small amount of screen real estate into smaller regions, which causes a boxy effect. You'll learn how to make Framesets without unsightly scrollbars and borders. That will help eliminate the ugly boxy effect.

Exercise #1_____Saving Your First Frameset

This chapter is going to gradually build your Frames-making skills. This first exercise will show you how to save a set of Frames properly. Sound simple? Unfortunately, Frames are much harder than anything you've learned so far. By taking you slowly through the process, my hope is that you'll get through these um… interesting hurdles without hitches.

STEP-BY-STEP_____

1. Define your site for Chapter 10. Copy **chap_10** to your hard drive and press **F5** to define it. If you need a refresher on this process, revisit Chapter 3, *"Site Control."*

2. If a blank Untitled Document is not on your screen, choose **File > New** (Mac) or **File > New File** (Windows). You may be surprised by the following advice, given my past warnings, but… don't save this just yet. Why? Because saving now will cause Dreamweaver to believe that this is a single HTML page (which it is not!). You are going to divide this into a Frameset and Frames before you save.

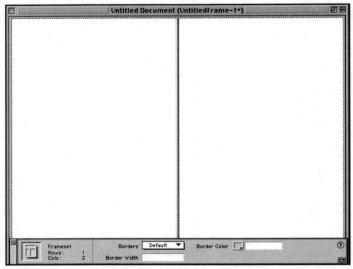

3. Choose **Modify > Frameset > Split Frame Left**. This puts a vertical Frame divider through your page. What's more, it switches you from looking at one page to looking at three: the Frameset, the left Frame, and the right Frame.

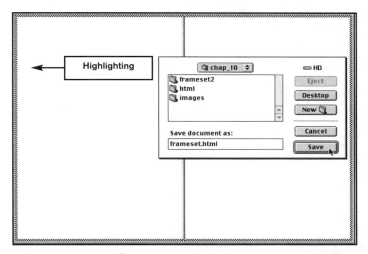

Movie_____

saving frames.mov

To view a demonstration of exercise #1, establishing and saving frames, check out **saving_frames.mov** located inside of the **movies** folder on the *Dreamweaver 2 H•O•T CD-ROM*.

4. Learning to save a Frameset properly is a huge step toward making successful Frames, so listen up! Choose **File > Save All**. And **don't** click Save just yet! Notice the highlighting around the periphery of the page? This is the ONLY visual feedback Dreamweaver will give you that shows you what you are saving. What does that highlighting mean? That you're saving the entire Frameset (remember that good 'ole TV-dinner tray metaphor?). Give this file the name **frameset.html** Save it inside the **chap_10 folder**.

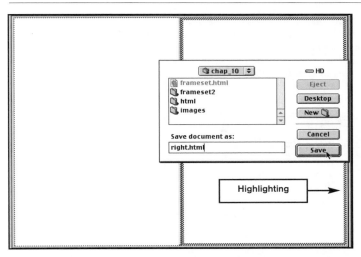

5. Dreamweaver automatically opens the Save window again. Notice how it has highlighted the right Frame? Again, this is the ONLY visual feedback the program gives you to know which file you are about to save. Since it's on the right side, I suggest naming this file **right.html**. Click **Save** again.

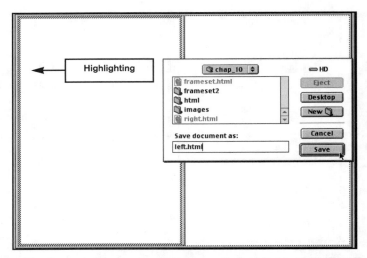

6. The Save window appears once more with the left side highlighted. This will prompt you again to notice which side you are saving. Since the highlight is on the left side, name this **left.html**. When you click **Save**, the Save window will disappear and you'll be done.

Note: *If you have any other unsaved Documents opened besides this Frameset, you will be prompted to save it or them too. You can click **Cancel** if this happens and you don't want to save the other open Documents.*

*Even though you just saved this file, notice that it says Untitled Document at the top of the Document window? What's up with that? As you learned in Chapter 4, "Basics," you've saved and named the HTML Document, but have not assigned the Title yet. In order to assign the Title, follow the exact directions below, because you are juggling three HTML Documents and you want to put the Title in the outermost page (**frameset.html**).*

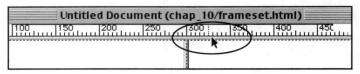

7. Click your mouse exactly where you see my cursor on this screen. This click ensures that Dreamweaver knows that you want to access **frameset.html** and not the left.html or right.html pages. Choose **Modify > Page Properties…** and give it the title **My First Frameset**. When you click **OK**, that Untitled Document title should be instantly replaced by your title.

8. Choose **File > Save All** again. Notice that you didn't see all three files like you did when you chose Save All the first time? That's the way it works—once you define the initial Frameset and Frames, you can perform one simple Save All operation and be done. Leave this file open for Exercise #2.

*I personally never use **File > Save** when I'm working with Frames because you can so easily save the wrong page and trip yourself up.*

 Note_____

Different Ways to Save Frames

This exercise taught you to save Frames by choosing **File > Save All**. There are a few different ways to save them besides this, but the way I taught you is the best because of the visual feedback it offers on which Frame is being saved. All three ways are listed in the handy chart below.

Ways to Save Frames?	
How to Save	**What You Are Saving**
File > Save	To save a Document inside a Frame, click the cursor in the Frame and use this method.
File > Save Frameset As **File > Save Frameset**	To save a Frameset file only, you may choose to use either of these methods.
File > Save All	To save all open files at once, use this method.

Note_____

No Frames!

Frames were introduced with Netscape 2.0 and Explorer 3.0. If anyone accesses your site with an older browser, they won't see your Frame content. Luckily for them and you, there's a NOFRAMES tag. Whatever is inside this HTML tag is visible to end-users who can't see Frames.

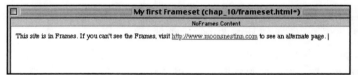

*To insert a page into your Frameset that is visible with older browsers, choose **Modify > Frameset > Edit NoFrames Content**. This window will appear, and whatever you type into it will be viewed by end-users who ordinarily wouldn't be able to see Frames. Some Web developers choose to create a whole new page for these viewers, while others redirect them to another URL, as I show above here.*

```
<HTML>
<HEAD>
<TITLE>My First Frameset</TITLE>
<META HTTP-EQUIV="Content-Type" CONTENT="text/html; charset=iso-8859-1">
</HEAD>

<FRAMESET COLS="150,461" ROWS="*" BORDER="0" FRAMESPACING="0">
  <FRAME SRC="left.html" NAME="left">
  <FRAME SRC="right.html" NAME="right">
</FRAMESET>
<NOFRAMES><BODY BGCOLOR="#FFFFFF">
This site is in Frames. If you can't see the Frames then go to <A
HREF="#">http://www.moonsnestinn</A>.com
for an alternate page. |
</BODY></NOFRAMES>
</HTML>
```

*Here's the HTML for the **NOFRAMES** content. Notice how the **NOFRAMES** tag comes after the **FRAMESET** tag? Dreamweaver writes the code automatically, and inserts whatever you specify into the HTML.*

Exercise #2_____Coloring Frames

Creating Frames is challenging because you're manipulating multiple HTML Documents in one Dreamweaver window. This exercise teaches you how to color two Frames independently. You'll also learn how to turn off the borders between them, which can help eliminate that boxy appearance that many people don't like about Frames.

STEP-BY-STEP_____

1. You should still have **frameset.html** open from the last exercise. Click on the left Frame and make sure you see the text-insertion cursor blinking.

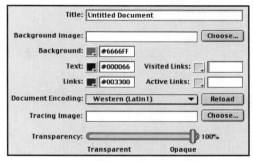

2. Choose **Modify > Page Properties... Cmd+J** (Mac) or **Ctrl+J** (Windows). Make the **Background:** a light blue color, the **Text:** a dark blue, and the **Links:** a dark green. Click **OK**. The left Frame should turn light blue.

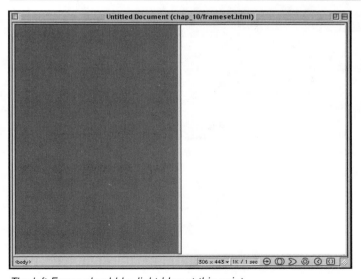

The left Frame should be light blue at this point.

3. In order to change the color for the right side, click in the right Frame and make sure you see the text-insertion cursor blinking. Choose **Modify > Page Properties...** yet again.

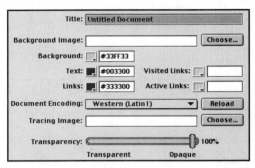

4. Make the **Background:** a light green, the **Text:** a dark green, and the **Links:** a dark yellow. Click **OK**.

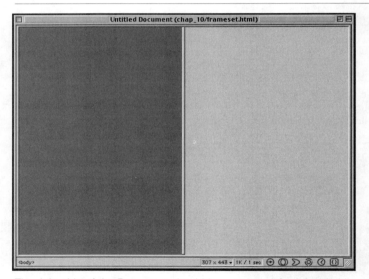

The right side of the Document should be green and the left side blue.

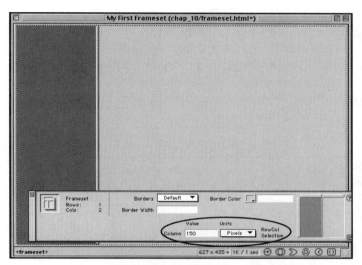

5. Click on the middle dividing Frame border and move it over to the left until the Properties Inspector reads **Column: 150 Pixels**. **Tip:** You can simply enter the value 150 into the column setting instead of dragging, if you prefer. If the Properties Inspector's not visible, go to **Modify > Selection Properties**.

6. I don't know about you, but part of what I don't like about Frames is the boxy appearance from which they usually suffer. To turn off the border on the Frame divider, select **Borders: No**, and **Border Width: 0** in the Properties Inspector. Now the dividing border should be gone. Choose **File > Save All** and leave this Document open for the next exercise.

Exercise #3_____**Links and Targets**

You've gotten through the hardest part of making a Frameset, but there's still more distance to go to the finish. This exercise will show you how to insert a link into the left side page of the Frameset. You've learned about making links, so much of this should be familiar. This exercise introduces the new concept, however—using a "target," which allows you to specify which Frame the link will trigger in your Frameset. If you're wondering what I mean by that last sentence, read on.

STEP-BY-STEP_____

1. Click inside the left Frame and make sure you see the blinking type-insertion cursor. Type the words **Our Rooms**.

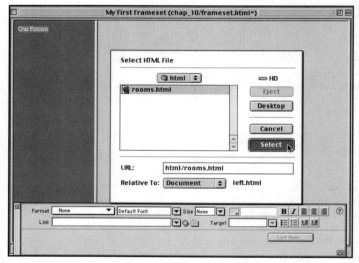

2. Select the words **Our Rooms** and click on the yellow folder for **Links** in the **Properties Inspector**. Browse to the **html** folder inside the **chap_10** folder and select **rooms.html**. Click **Select**. **Our Rooms** should now appear as an underlined link.

3. You can't preview links in Dreamweaver, so press **F12** and click on **Our Rooms**. If you get the warning shown here, it's because you didn't save before you previewed. No harm done, just check the box "Don't warn me again." Click **OK**. This way, Dreamweaver will know to automatically save your changes before you preview them, and you won't be plagued by this warning every time you press **F12**.

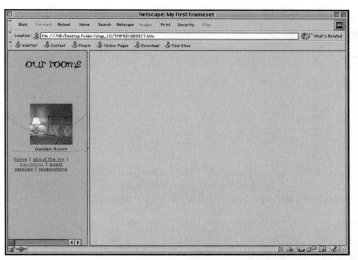

4. Once in the browser, go ahead and click the link **Our Rooms**. You might be surprised that it appears in the left Frame, the exact Frame where the link was in your Dreamweaver file! That's because you haven't yet set up a target for the link. Just like in any other Web page, once you click on a link, it's replaced by the new page that you just selected. In this situation, the narrow left Frame isn't where you want that link to appear. The left Frame should remain stationary and the links should open on the right.

If you'd prefer (as I would) that the link load in the larger right side of the Frameset, you must first name the two Frames. Giving a name to an element in HTML is something that you haven't done yet, but you'll see that it is necessary in certain instances throughout the exercises in this book. In this situation, you can't target the right Frame to receive the results of the link without first giving it a name, because it needs to know where to go.

Note: *You might be confused by the directive to give the Frame a name, because you've already saved all the Documents as **frameset.html**, **left.html**, and **right.html**. You also gave a Title, **my first frameset**, to the **frameset.html** Document. A "name" is something totally different, however, which is required in order to set custom targets in links.*

5. Return to Dreamweaver to fix the target problem. Choose **Window > Frames** to bring up the Frames window. Notice that it reads (**no name**) on both the right and left side? Click on the left side and it will become outlined with a dark line, as shown above.

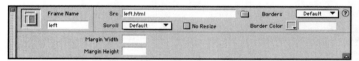

6. The Properties Inspector should now give you the setting for the Frame Name field. Enter **left**. You could name it anything you want. However, I prefer to name it something meaningful because this name will appear as text in a menu later on and I'll want to easily remember what it meant.

7. Click on the right side of the Frames window and look at the Properties Inspector again. This time it has no Frame Name because you haven't given the right side of the Frameset a name yet. Enter **right** into the **Frame Name** field. The Frames window should now read **right** and **left** in faint letters. Leave the Frames window open as you'll be needing it shortly.

8. Select the words **Our Rooms** in the left Frame. Click on the arrow next to the **Target** field to access the pop-up menu. Select **right** from the menu. The word **right** should pop into the Target field.

9. Press **F12** to preview the page again. Click on the link. The results should appear on the right side. You've just set up your first target in your first Frameset. You're on your way to mastering Frames, which is no small accomplishment!

10. Return to Dreamweaver and keep the files open for the next exercise.

Target Names

A further explanation of target names is in order, because in the last exercise you used only the custom target feature.

```
_blank
_parent
_self
_top
right
left
```

When you accessed the pop-up menu for Target, what did the terms **_blank**, **_parent**, **_self** and **_top** mean? You made the targets **right** and **left**, so you hopefully understand that those names were in the menu because you added them. The other names, however, are part of the HTML specification and always mean certain important things. Here's a handy chart to refer to.

HTML Specifications	
Target Name	**Significance**
_blank	Loads the link into a new browser window. This is the target to use if you want to keep someone inside your site, and show them another site at the same time. It opens a new browser window, so that two windows are on the screen at the same time—one containing your site, and the other containing the URL of the site you linked to.
_parent	Used when Framesets are nested, specifically, to send your end user to the parent of the nested Framesets. It's possible to put a Frameset inside another Frameset, but that's more advanced Frameset building than this book will cover. Frankly, I rarely use this target, because I rarely work with nested Framesets.
_self	Used when you want the results of the link to load in the same page that the link was in. That's default behavior of HTML anyway, so I never ever use this.
_top	Transports the end user from a Frameset to a single HTML page. This breaks the Frames and loads all of the results into a single page, in the same window.

Note_____

To Scroll or Not to Scroll?

I keep harping on the fact that Frames can look boxy, and you've already
learned how to remedy this by turning off the Frameset border. What about
scrollbars, which can also make a Frameset look boxed in? Scrollbars are
necessary if your content is larger than the size of the Frame. You can turn
scrollbars off completely or allow them to appear automatically, which is the
Dreamweaver default. I suggest you leave the program at its defaults. If the
content is big enough to warrant scrollbars, they'll appear. If not, they won't!

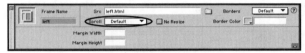

Scrollbars are set in the Properties Inspector.

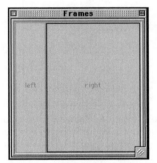

*To access the Properties Inspector's Frame Scroll options, click on the right
or left region of the Frames window. Scrollbars are set independently for
each Frame. You don't have to do this at all unless you want to force scrollbars on or off via the scroll option.*

Exercise #4_____Adding a Background Image

You've learned how to color the background of each Frame, but what about adding a Background Image? This is a pretty similar to coloring the background of each Frame, which you already did in Exercise #2. There can be unexpected alignment problems with this process, however, if the Frameset clips the Background Image on one of the Frames. In this exercise, you will learn how to set the left Frame to a specific size so that it doesn't cut off the Background Image unexpectedly.

STEP-BY-STEP_____

1. Click inside the **left.html** Frame and make sure you see the text-insertion cursor blinking to the right of the linked words **Our Rooms**. Choose **Modify > Page Properties....**

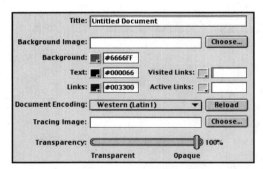

2. Click on the **Choose...** (Mac) or **Browse...** (Windows) button to the right of the Background Image to browse to the **images** folder, and select **bg_moon.jpg**. Click **Select** and then **OK**. The Background Image should appear in the left side of the Frameset.

3. Click inside the **right.html** Frame and make sure you see the text-insertion cursor blinking, then choose **Modify > Page Properties....**

4. Click on the **Choose...** (Mac) or **Browse...** (Windows) button to the right of the Background Image to locate once again **bg_moon.jpg** in the **images** folder where you just were. Click **Select** and then **OK**. The Background Image should appear in the right side of the Frameset.

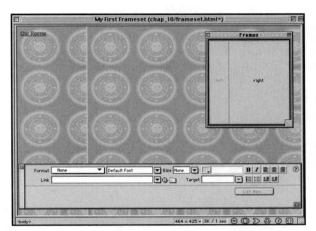

There's just one problem. It doesn't look that great, does it? The Background Image has been clipped by the size of the two Frames. To correct the problem, it's essential to know the dimensions of both the graphic and the Frameset. The following steps walk you through this process.

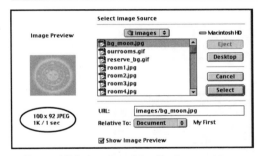

5. To establish the size of the Background Image, click on the **left.html** Frame again and make sure you see the blinking text-insertion cursor. Choose **Modify > Page Properties...** again. Click on the **Choose...** (Mac) or **Browse...** (Windows) button to the right of the Background Image to locate **bg_moon.jpg**. Notice that the dimensions 100 x 92 appear in this window? You now know that the width of the image is 100 pixels. Click **Cancel twice** to return to the Document window.

Why Cancel? The sole purpose for doing this step was to read the dimensions of the graphic, not to actually re-insert the Background Image! I often insert an image just to learn more about its size or downloading speed, and then cancel out of the process once I've gathered the information.

Next, you'll want to make the left column of the Frameset match the column size of that Background Image. Because the Background Image is 100 pixels wide, you could make the left.html column 200 pixels wide, and it would tile twice perfectly. Question is, how do you get to the information about what size the left column is? Frankly, it's a bit tricky and takes some clicking around.

6. In the Frames window (if it's not visible, go to **Window > Frames**) click to the outer border of the window. Your Frames window might already look like this before you read this step. If so, click on the left side and then click on the outer border again.

*Sometimes you have to toggle the outer border of the **Frames** window on and off to get it to show the correct information settings on the Properties Inspector. What's the goal of doing this? Changing your Properties Inspector to show you the Frameset's column size.*

*The goal of clicking on the outer border of the Frames window is to change your Properties Inspector so that it looks like this, which gives you access to the Column Values. See the **Column 150** setting? That shows the setting that you created way back in Exercise #2. You'll want to change this to accommodate the size of the Background Image in this exercise. The next steps will walk you through this process.*

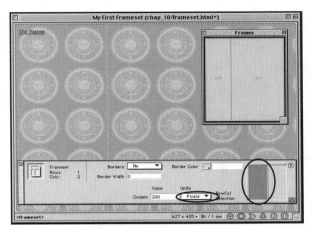

 Movie_____

frames_settings.mov

Still confused by how to access the different settings for Frames? Watch this process in action, by viewing the **frames_settings.mov** located inside of the **movies** folder on the *Dreamweaver 2 H•O•T CD-ROM.*

7. Enter the value **Column 200** into the **Properties Inspector** and press the **Return** or **Enter** key on your keyboard. The left column should have just shifted a bit to the right. Things still don't fit properly because there are more steps to follow.

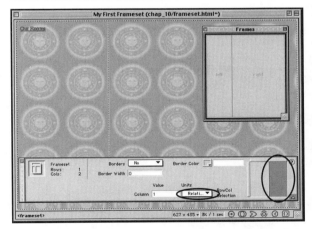

8. In the Properties Inspector, click on the right Column icon, at the right of the palette. Select **Units Relative**. Bingo! The background tile now fits perfectly!

9. Return to Dreamweaver and **Save All**. Close the file.

If the directions in Exercise #4 seemed odd and/or mysterious to you, it's because they are a little odd and mysterious! Perhaps this review will help: Clicking on the right side of the Properties Inspector's Column icon allowed you to change the settings for the right column. Choosing Relative units makes HTML allocate to the right column whatever space is left over from the fixed-pixel left column. In Exercise #4, you wanted the left side to be fixed, but the right side to scale proportionately depending on how big the end-user's monitor is.

Tip_____

Specifying a Frame Size

The last exercise showed how to specify the left Frame to be 200 pixels wide. Here are the directions to access the Frame size settings. You must have the Frames window open (**Window > Frames**).

Next, click on the outer region of the Frames window. **Tip:** You might have to click on an inner region and an outer region to jog the Properties Inspector to show the correct setting.

Click on the icon to the far right of the Properties Inspector to select the appropriate Frame. In this instance, it's the right one.

Enter the Column Value of your choice. You'll also be prompted to enter Unit Values of either Pixel, Percentage, or Relative. See the chart to the right for a description.

Note_____

Unit Value

Below is a chart that defines the choices you have when specifying a Frame size in the Properties Inspector.

Frame Size Settings	
Unit Value	**Function**
Pixels	Sets the size of the selected column or row at an absolute value. This option is the best choice for a Frame that should always be the same size, such as a navigation bar. If you set one of your Frame regions to pixels, then all the other Frames will have to yield to that size. In other words, pixels take priority over all other settings.
Percent	Specifies that the current Frame take up a specified percentage of its Frameset. This causes Frames to dynamically resize according to how wide or tall the end–user's browser was opened to. If you mix pixels and percents, pixels will be honored first.
Relative	Allocates space after Frames with units set to pixels and percent. These Frames are designed to take up all the remaining space in the browser window.

Note _____

Frame Properties

What do the Frames settings mean in the Properties Inspector? Here's a handy chart to help you understand them.

Frames Settings in Dreamweaver	
Setting	**Description**
Frame	Sets the name of the current Frame so you can use targets (remember _blank, _self, _top, and _parent?) when setting up links. This name must be a single word or use underscores (my_name) or hyphens (my-name). Spaces are not allowed.
Src	Sets the source Document for each Frame. Enter a file name or click the folder icon to browse to and select the file. You can also open a file in a Frame by clicking the cursor in the Frame inside the Document window and choosing **File > Open in Frame...**.
Scroll	Determines whether scrollbars appear when there is not enough room to display the content of the current Frame. Most browsers default to Auto. This is a good thing, because you only want scrollbars if they are necessary. Scrollbars aren't pretty, but they are necessary when there's more content than the Frameset column size can display.
No Resize	Prevents a Frame from being resizable in browsers. **Tip:** If you turn the borders off in your Frameset, end users won't be able to resize them even if the No Resize option is left off.
Borders	Controls the border of the current Frame. The options are Yes, No, and Default. This choice overrides border settings defined for the Frameset. It's important to turn the borders to No even if you've set them to 0, because of differences between Netscape and Explorer. Netscape honors 0, while Explorer honors No.
Border Color	Sets a Border Color for all borders adjacent to the current Frame. This setting overrides the Border Color of the Framesets. It's only supported on 4.0 browsers, so if you choose to use it at all, I don't recommend that you make it an integral part of your design.
Margin Width	Sets in pixels the width of the left and right margins (the space between the Frame border and the content). The default is that the Frame border and content are aligned, so unless you want an offset, you don't need to adjust this setting.
Margin Height	Sets in pixels the height of the top and bottom margins (the space between the Frame border and the content). The default is that the Frame border and content are lined up, so unless you want an offset, you don't need to adjust this setting.

Exercise #5_____Seamless Background Across Two Frames

In the previous exercise, you learned to put the same background into two Frames, and to set a Frameset's column width. Next, I'd like to repeat that same exercise with different artwork to show you some of the cool effects that you can apply to Framesets.

STEP-BY-STEP_____

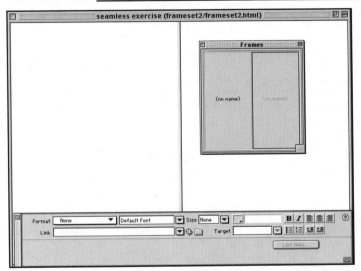

1. Open **frameset2.html** from the **frameset2** folder. This is similar to the Document you made before, but a lot of the early steps are already completed. Click on the left Frame in the Frames window (if it's not visible, choose **Window > Frames**). Next, choose **Modify > Page Properties**....

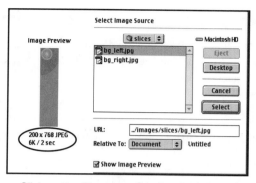

2. Click on the **Choose...** (Mac) or **Browse...** (Windows) button to the right of the Background Image and browse to the **images** folder and then the **slices** folder. Select **bg_left.jpg**. Click **OK**. Notice that the dimensions appear in the Image Preview of the Select Image Source screen and that the width of this image is 200 pixels wide. Click **Select**, then **OK**.

3. Click on the right side of the Frameset and choose **Modify > Page Properties...**. Select **bg_right.jpg** from the **slices** folder inside the **images** folder as your background image. Click **OK**. Notice that the dimensions appear in the Image Preview of the Select Image Source screen and that this image is also 200 pixels wide. Click **Select**, then **OK**.

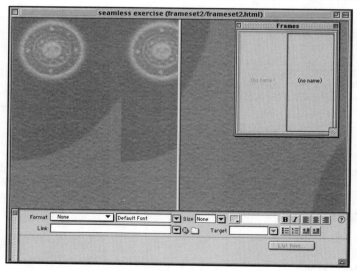

Your screen should look funky because you haven't set the Frameset's dimensions yet.

4. Make sure the Frames window is open (**Window > Frames**) and click on the outer region (if you've forgotten how, check Exercise #4, Step #6) to make your Properties Inspector display the Frameset's dimensions. Click on the left side of the Column icon (it's probably already selected) and select **Borders No**. Next enter **Border Width 0, Column Value 200**, and **Units Pixels**.

5. Next, click on the right side of the column icon, and enter **Units Relative**. Press **F12** to preview the results. When and if prompted to Save, click **OK**.

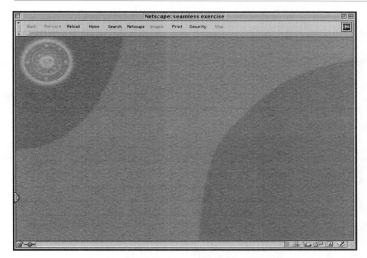

If your screen looks like this, you did everything right! If it doesn't, go back and re-read all the steps (especially the part about setting the right side to Relative!). It looks like a single page with a single background, does it not? If your audience hates the way Frames look, they should have no complaints with this little slight of hand. Onward to the next chapter, you're done here!

11.Rollovers

• **Creating Simple, Animated, and Pointer Rollovers**
• **Using JavaScript to Trigger Multiple Events**

chap_11 folder

Dreamweaver 2
H•O•T CD-ROM

One of the key challenges in Web development is to invent artwork that clearly communicates how to navigate through your site. Rollover graphics, which change when your end user puts his or her mouse over them, are great for adding visual cues that ensure your audience knows that an image has special meaning, for example, that it is a link. Rollovers are also great if you have limited space (which is true of all Web pages!) because you can put extra information within the changing graphic. For example, I could make a button that says the word "services," and when a person who visits my site places his or her mouse over the word, the word could change to list what services I offered, such as training, consulting, videos, books, lectures, etc.

Rollovers have been used for years in multimedia presentations as an effective device to indicate that an image is a button or is linked to other Documents. What you might not realize is that Rollovers are a relatively new addition to the Web, because standard HTML doesn't offer this feature. Instead, Rollovers are written in a widely used scripting language, invented by Netscape, called JavaScript.

Dreamweaver automatically writes JavaScript Rollovers for you without you ever having to write the scripts or even understand how they are constructed. This is great news, because a lot of people, myself included, don't know how to write JavaScript from scratch. Alternately, I have trained many developers who do know how to write JavaScript by hand, but enjoy Dreamweaver for its Rollover capabilities because it can literally save days of programming work. For this reason, Dreamweaver's Rollover features are helpful to both the non-programmer and the programmer.

Rollover Rules

While this book provides many exercises that teach you how to implement Rollovers, it is my hope that you'll move beyond the exercises to create your own custom Rollover graphics once you get the hang of this feature. If you plan to make your own Rollovers from scratch, you should be aware of a few important concepts.

Rollovers require a minimum of two graphics—an "off" state and an "on" state. Because this is a book on Dreamweaver, it doesn't cover how to make the graphic component of Rollovers. You would need an imaging program, such as Fireworks, Photoshop, or ImageReady, to make the images.

If you are going to make your own Rollover graphics in an image editor, one important rule to understand is that your Rollover images must be the same size in dimensions, or you risk that they will look distorted. JavaScript requires **WIDTH** and **HEIGHT** information, which Dreamweaver will add for you automatically. If you have two different-sized pieces of artwork, the JavaScript will scale both to the same width and height, causing distortion. For this reason, all the images that are provided in this chapter's exercises share the same dimensions.

Exercise #1_____Creating a Simple Rollover

This first exercise will show you how to create a simple Rollover. These types of Rollovers involve two pieces of artwork. The first graphic appears on the screen initially and the second appears when the mouse "rolls over" it. In JavaScript terminology, this is called a "swap" image. But you will not be writing any JavaScript from scratch, because Dreamweaver makes creating a simple Rollover easier than many other operations you've already learned.

STEP-BY-STEP_____

1. Define your site for Chapter 11. Copy the contents of **chap_11** to your hard drive and press **F5** to define it. If you need a refresher on this process, revisit Chapter 3, *"Site Control."*

Before the mouse moves over the star in the Web browser.

After the mouse moves over the star in the Web browser.

2. Open **basicrollfinal.html** in the **html** folder. When you move your mouse over the star, nothing happens, right? Press **F12** to preview the page. When you move your mouse over it in your Web browser, it changes to a yellow star. You can only view a Rollover inside a browser because Dreamweaver cannot preview this effect. Return to Dreamweaver and close the file. You'll get to build this same file from scratch in the following steps.

3. Choose **File > New** (Mac) or **File > New Window** (Windows) to create a new Untitled Document. It is always a good practice to save a file before you begin working with it, because Dreamweaver will give you error messages if you don't! Choose **File > Save As…** and name this file **simpleroll.html** in the **html** folder.

Movie_____

rollover_list.mov

Want to see this exercise in action? Check out the movie ***rollover_list.mov*** located inside of the **movies** folder on the *Dreamweaver 2 H•O•T CD-ROM.*

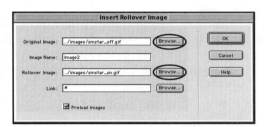

4. Choose **Insert > Rollover Image**, or click on the **Insert Rollover** button on the Objects Palette. If the Objects Palette is not visible, go to **Window > Objects**.

5. The Insert Rollover Image dialog box will appear. Use the **Browse...** buttons to locate the files **smstar_off.gif** and **smstar_on.gif** inside the **images** folder. Make sure your dialog box looks just like the one above and click **OK** when you're done.

Notice the hash mark (#) inside the Link area of the Properties Inspector? Dreamweaver inserted this symbol in order to create a link even though you didn't specify one. Why? Because a link is necessary for the JavaScript Roll-over to work. Putting a hash mark in the Link area inserts a stand-in link that doesn't link to anything. It simply acts as a place holder so that you can still click on it and see the Rollover.

6. In the Properties Inspector, click on the yellow folder icon and browse to select **rooms.html** located in the **html** folder. Press **F12** to preview the Rollover. Click on the link and voila, **rooms.html** will appear!

7. Return to Dreamweaver, and save and close the Document.

Note_____

JavaScript and Java: Separated at Birth?

You might wonder if JavaScript bears any relation to the popular programming language Java, developed by Sun Microsystems. Only in name. Netscape licensed the name from Sun in hopes that the Web community would embrace the scripting language more quickly if it had a recognizable name. Ironically, since then, JavaScript has become more widely embraced than Java, and has taken on a life and following all of its own.

One important distinction between JavaScript and Java is that the code for JavaScript is placed inside your HTML pages and Java is compiled as a separate program, meaning that you can't see the code for it inside an HTML page. This means that you can see JavaScript code inside HTML Documents if you view the source code, while the code within a Java applet is hidden. This has made JavaScript immensely popular among Web authors, as many people were able to teach themselves the language by looking at other people's Web-page source code by copying, pasting, and experimenting.

Exercise #2_____Animated Rollovers!

This next exercise uses the same technique as Exercise 1, only instead of two static images, the Rollover image is an animated GIF. You'll be putting the Rollover graphics inside a Table to ensure that they don't move around once they're in place. Working with animated Rollovers may look complicated, but it's just as easy as the last exercise you completed.

STEP-BY-STEP_____

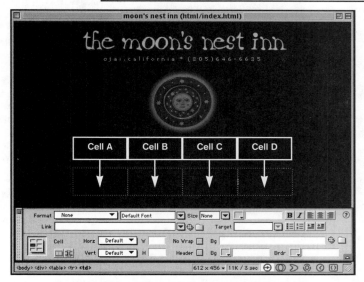

1. Open **index.html** located in the **html** folder. Notice the empty Table where the navigation elements belong? This is where you're going to insert Rollovers for each button. Click inside Cell A (row 1, column 1) and choose **Insert > Rollover Image** (you can also go to the Objects Palette and click on the **Insert Rollover** object).

2. For the **Original Image**, click the **Browse...** button to select **about.gif** located in the **images** folder. For the **Rollover Image**, click the **Browse...** button to select **about_anim.gif** located in the same folder. Click **OK**. Notice that the Table got all smooshed up after you inserted the image? You'll fix that shortly, so don't worry about it just yet.

Movie_____

smooshed_table.mov

If you would like to see a movie of how to insert these Rollovers into the Table, check out **smooshed_table.mov** located inside of the **movies** folder on the *Dreamweaver 2 H•O•T CD-ROM.*

3. Unfortunately, you can't preview the results of what you just did in Dreamweaver, so press **F12** to view it in a browser. When you move your mouse over the **about the inn** image, notice that the Rollover state is an animated GIF? Dreamweaver treats the animated GIF as it would any other GIF, yet the result when previewed in a browser is different than a Rollover created from two static GIFs. This technique produces a simple, novel effect.

4. Return to Dreamweaver and click to the right of the **about the inn (about.gif)** graphic to make sure it is deselected. With your right arrow key, insert your cursor in the next cell which is now scrunched up with the other cells on the right-hand side of the Table.

5. Once your cursor is in Cell B (row 1, column 2) choose **Insert > Rollover Image** again (or go to the Objects Palette and click on the **Insert Rollover** object). For the **Original Image**, click the **Browse...** button to select **rooms.gif** located in the **images** folder. For the **Rollover Image**, click the **Browse...** button to select **rooms_anim.gif** located in the same folder. Click **OK**.

6. Click to the right of the **our rooms (rooms.gif)** image to deselect it. Once your cursor is in Cell C (row 1, column 3) choose **Insert > Rollover Image** again. For the **Original Image**, click the **Browse...** button to select **services.gif** located in the **images** folder. For the **Rollover Image**, click the **Browse...** button to select the **services_anim.gif** located in the same folder. Click **OK**.

7. Click to the right of the **guest services (services.gif)** image to deselect it. Once your cursor is in Cell D (row 1, column 4) choose **Insert > Rollover Image** once again. For the **Original Image**, click the **Browse...** button to select **reservations.gif** located in the **images** folder. For the **Rollover Image**, click the **Browse...** button to select the **reservations_anim.gif** located in the same folder. Click **OK**.

8. Press **F12** to preview the results. I hope you agree that this was simple to execute and impressive upon completion. Return to Dreamweaver, then save and close your Document.

Note_____

Animated GIF Rollovers and Preload

The previous exercise used animated GIF files for one of the Rollover states. Dreamweaver regards these files no differently than static GIFs. If you make your own animated GIF files in an image editor and use them in Dreamweaver as Rollover states, there are a couple of gotchas I'd like to warn you about.

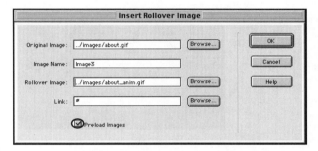

Notice that Dreamweaver automatically checks the **Preload Images** check-box in the Insert Rollover Image dialog box? What does that mean, exactly? The browser is being instructed to wait until all the graphics for the Rollover have been downloaded before the Rollover functions.

Animated GIFs can be set to play once, any number of times (2x, 3x, etc.) or loop indefinitely. If when you create your animated GIF files you set them to loop indefinitely, then leaving the **Preload Images** box checked will work just fine, as it did here. However, if you have your animated GIF play only one time, it will play when it's preloaded and by the time your end user looks at your Rollover it will no longer animate! So the rule is this: leave Preload on for looping GIFs and uncheck **Preload Images** if your GIF is set to play only one time.

Exercise #3_____**Creating Pointer Rollovers**

This next exercise shows you how to create pointer Rollovers. Pointer Rollovers re-use one piece of artwork (in this example, the star) which follows the mouse as you move over each word. This type of Rollover involves making a Table to hold all the artwork in place. You'll also get to use the Behaviors feature, instead of the Insert Rollover Image button from the Objects Palette. Are you feeling macho, or what?

STEP-BY-STEP_____

1. View the finished file first. Open **pointerfinal.html** located in the **html** folder and press **F12** to preview it inside a browser. Return to Dreamweaver and close the file. You're going to recreate this example from scratch.

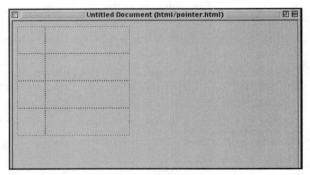

2. Open **pointer.html** in the **html** folder, which already contains an empty Table with 4 rows and 2 columns. You could have created this Table from scratch, I'm sure, but I just wanted to help you get to programming the Rollovers faster.

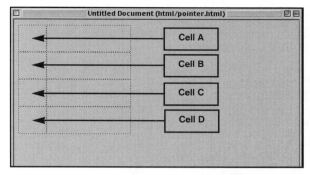

3. Click inside Cell A and select **Insert > Image** and select **blank_p.gif**. The object of this exercise is to insert the same **blank_p.gif** image in every location that the pointer will appear. Why? Because Rollovers require two images, the original state and the Rollover state. In this instance, the original state looks like nothing, but because it has to contain something, it contains an image with nothing in it.

4. Repeat this process three times, inserting the same **blank_p.gif** file inside Cells B, C, and D.

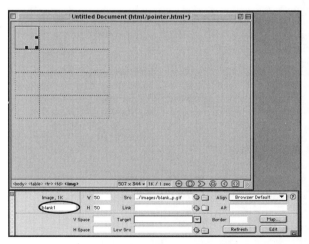

5. After you have inserted the **blank_p.gif** image into each cell, click on the top left cell, as shown above. Inside the Properties Inspector, give it the name **blank 1**. It is essential that you assign a unique name to each image by selecting each instance of **blank_p.gif** and naming it respectively, **blank 1**, **blank 2**, **blank 3**, **blank 4**. Make sure that the appropriate **blank_p.gif** image is highlighted when you name each graphic.

Note: In Exercise #3 Dreamweaver gave the Rollovers a name automatically. When you use the Swap Image Behavior, you have to give each image a unique name, or the Behavior will not work. Names in Dreamweaver (or HTML) cannot contain any spaces.

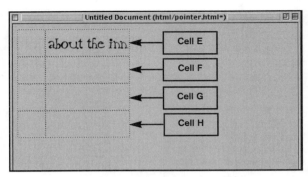

6. Click in Cell E and choose **Insert > Image**, then browse to **about_p.gif** located in the **images** folder and click **Select**.

7. While the **about_p.gif** image is selected, enter the name **about** inside the Properties Inspector. **Note:** Naming each image is essential to working with Rollovers in Dreamweaver. This is because JavaScript requires a unique name for each source graphic in order to perform Rollover functions. For this reason, you will need to add a unique name for every image that you insert into this Table.

8. Click in Cell F and choose **Insert > Image** and browse to **ourrooms_p.gif**. Inside the Properties Inspector, name this image **rooms**. Click in Cell G and choose **Insert > Image** and select **reservations_p.gif**. Inside the Properties Inspector, name this image **reservations**. Click in Cell H and choose **Insert > Image** and select **services_p.gif**. Name this image **services**.

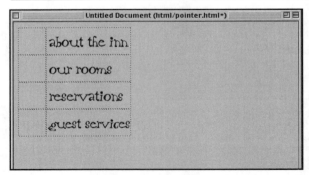

9. Click on **about_p.gif** (**about the inn**) to select it. Open the Behaviors window (if it isn't already open) by selecting **Window > Behaviors** or using the shortcut key, **F8**.

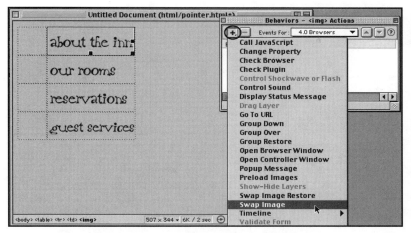

10. With the **about_p.gif (about the inn)** selected, click on the **plus** sign button in the pop-up menu above the Events column and select **Swap Image**.

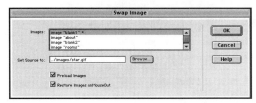

11. Make sure the **blank1** image name is highlighted at the top. Click the **Browse...** button and select **star.gif** located in the **images** folder. Click **OK**.

12. Next select **ourrooms_p.gif** and click on the **plus** sign button to select **Swap Image**. Select **blank2** inside the Images list and click on the **Browse...** button to locate **star.gif**. Repeat this process for **reservations_p.gif**, selecting **blank3**, and **service_p.gif** for **blank4**.

13. Press **F12** to preview in your browser. What you see should look just like the **pointer-roll.html** Document you opened and previewed at the beginning of this exercise. To make yourself feel really good, return to Dreamweaver and press **F10** to view the code. Hey, you didn't have to write any of that! Press **F10** to close the HTML window. Save and close the file to move on to the next exercise.

This exercise demonstrated the benefit of using a Table to hold together multiple graphics. It also reinforced the fact that you need two images for a Rollover—the original state and the Rollover state. In this instance, the original was a blank image. When you program Rollovers from the Behaviors Palette, you also must give them a name, which you did several times in this exercise!

Exercise #4_____Creating Multiple-Event Rollovers

A multiple-event Rollover uses more than two pieces of artwork in the Swap Image Behavior. In this example, three different pieces of artwork change for every Rollover. If that sounds complicated, it is! Assembling this type of Rollover can be tedious, but not nearly as tedious as writing all the HTML and JavaScript from scratch.

STEP-BY-STEP_____

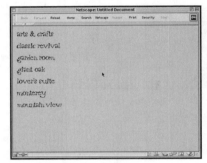

Before the Rollover.

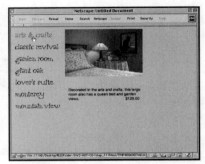

When the mouse moves over any of the names in the list, the name turns red, and a photograph and description appear at the same time.

1. Open **multiple_final.html** located in the **html** folder, and preview this finished exercise in your browser. Roll your mouse over each item in the list, and watch the rooms change. This is a very impressive type of Rollover, and you (yes you!) are going to know how to do it as soon as you follow along. Close this file.

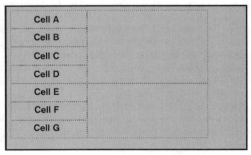

2. Open **complex.html** located in the **html** folder. Again, I got you started by making the Table for you. Because this chapter covers Rollovers, not Tables, I figured I'd once again give you a head start. You learned how to make a Table like this in Chapter 6, *"Tables."* Future steps in this exercise will refer to the various cells on this screen.

3. Click inside Cell A (row 1, column 1) and choose **Insert > Image** to browse to **arts.gif** located in the **html** folder, then click **Select**. In the Properties Inspector, name the image **arts**.

4. Click inside Cell B (row 2, column 1) and choose **Insert > Image** to browse to **classic.gif** located in the **html** folder, then click **Select**. In the Properties Inspector, name the image **classic**.

5. Click inside Cell C (row 3, column 1) and choose **Insert > Image** to browse to **garden.gif** located in the **html** folder, then click **Select**. In the Properties Inspector, name the image **garden**.

6. Click inside Cell D (row 4, column 1) and choose **Insert > Image** to browse to **giant.gif** located in the **html** folder, and click **Select**. In the Properties Inspector, name the image **giant**.

7. Click inside Cell E (row 5, column 1) and choose **Insert > Image** to browse to **lovers.gif** located in the **html** folder, then click **Select**. In the Properties Inspector, name the image **lovers**.

8. Click inside Cell F (row 6, column 1) and choose **Insert > Image** to browse to **monterey.gif** located in the **html** folder, then click **Select**. In the Properties Inspector, name the image **monterey**.

9. Click inside Cell G (row 7, column 1) and choose **Insert > Image** to browse to **mountain.gif** located in the **html** folder, then click **Select**. In the Properties Inspector, name the image **mountain**.

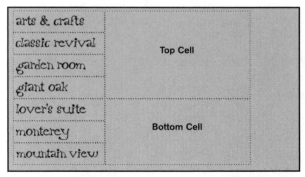

10. Click in the top cell (row 1, column 2) and choose **Insert > Image** to browse to **blank1.gif** located in the **html** folder, then click **Select**. In the Properties Inspector, name the image **blank1**.

11. Click in the bottom cell (row 2, column 2) and choose **Insert > Image** to browse to **blank2. gif** located in the **html** folder, and click **Select**. In the Properties Inspector, name the image **blank2**.

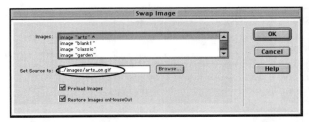

12. Select the image in Cell A (row 1, column 1). With the image selected, click the **plus** sign button in the **Behaviors** window to select **Swap Image**. **Note:** If the Behaviors window is not open, press **F8** to open it. The **Swap Image** window will open. Be sure not to click **OK** until you are instructed to! Notice that **arts** is selected in the Images list?

13. Click the **Browse...** button to **Set Source to: arts_on.gif**. This sets the Roll-over for the graphic **arts & crafts (arts.gif)** to turn red when you move your mouse over it. Don't click **OK** yet!

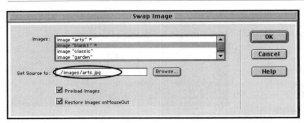

14. Select **blank1** from the same **Images** list. Click the **Browse...** button again to **Set Source to: arts.jpg**. You just instructed the Behavior to swap the **blank1 (blank1.gif)** artwork to the picture of the **arts & crafts hotel room (arts.jpg)**.

The Rollover now triggers two Behaviors: the lettering for arts & crafts has been instructed to turn red, and an image of the room will appear when the mouse moves over the original image. **Don't** *click* **OK** *yet!*

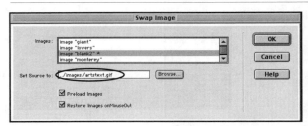

15. Scroll down the **Images** list to select **blank2**. Click the **Browse...** button again to **Set Source to: artstext.gif**. You may now finally click **OK** to end this process.

16. At this point, press **F12** and test your first Rollover! Move your mouse over the words **arts & crafts**. The lettering should turn red, and a picture of the room should appear to the upper right, with its description below. You've just set the Rollover for **arts & crafts**. There are six more items on the list to go.

17. Now return to Dreamweaver and repeat this process for the other images. Start with the Swap Image window in **Step 12**. When you're done, press **F12** to preview your work in a browser, then close the files and move on to the next chapter. Below is a chart that outlines the steps you will take.

 Movie_____

swap_image.mov

This isn't the most intuitive operation in the universe, so don't kick yourself if you don't get it right the first time. If it didn't work, please view the movie **swap_image.mov**, located inside of the **movies** folder on the *Dreamweaver 2 H•O•T CD-ROM*.

Swap Image At A Glance		
Cell	**Images**	**Set Source To**
B (row 2, column 1)	classic.gif blank1 blank2	classic_on.gif classic.jpg classictext.gif
C (row 3, column 1)	garden.gif blank1 blank2	garden_on.gif garden.jpg gardentext.gif
D (row 4, column 1)	giant.gif blank1 blank2	giant_on.gif giant.jpg gianttext.gif
E (row 5, column 1)	lovers.gif blank1 blank2	lovers_on.gif lovers.jpg loverstext.gif
F (row 6, column 1)	monterey.gif blank1 blank2	monterey_on.gif monterey.jpg montereytext.gif
G (row 7, column 1)	mountain.gif blank1 blank2	mountain_on.gif mountain.jpg mountaintext.gif

12.Forms

- **Elements of Forms • Working with Form Objects**
- **Combining Forms and Layout**
- **Opening a New Browser Window**

chap_12 folder

Dreamweaver 2
H•O•T CD-ROM

Forms are one of the most important elements of a Web site, because they enable you to ask questions of your end user and receive answers. While Forms can be identical to those we're used to in the non-virtual world (think IRS, car insurance, or loan paperwork), they can also be used for more exciting things, such as voting, guestbooks, or e-commerce. In general, Forms-based pages are much more interactive than other types of HTML pages, because they can collect and report information to you.

There are two aspects to creating Forms: creating the Form Objects (Text Fields, Checkboxes, Submit Buttons, etc.) and making the Forms function properly. This chapter focuses on the creation of Form Objects, not on the programming required to make Forms transmit data to and from your server. Unfortunately, making the Forms operational involves programming that goes beyond the scope of Dreamweaver and this book. Forms might not sound like much fun, but they are at the heart of what makes the Web different from paper and publishing mediums of the past.

Form Objects

The objects on a Form in Dreamweaver are referred to as Form Objects. These include Text Fields, Checkboxes, Images, Buttons, etc. In order to access the Form Objects, you need to change your Objects Palette from its default setting (Common) to Forms. You do this by clicking on the arrow at the top of the Objects Palette and clicking on it to access its menu.

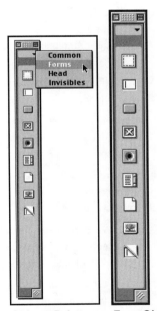

Objects Palette   **Form Objects**

*You'll find all the Form Objects on the Objects Palette. Instead of working with the Common Objects, as you have in most of the other chapters so far, this chapter will require that you set your Objects Palette to Forms, as shown above. If that menu isn't visible, go to **Window > Objects**.*

Note _____

Forms Objects

The table below outlines the different Objects available from the Form Objects Palette. As you become more familiar with Forms, you will not need this chart. Meanwhile, it should help you get a better inkling of what each of the Objects does.

	Forms Objects in Dreamweaver	
Icon	**Name**	**Function**
	Insert Form	This is the very first step in creating a Form. This inserts the **<FORM>** tag into your Document. If you do not place all your Objects inside the **<FORM>** tag, your Form will not work!
	Insert Text Field	Inserts a Text Field Object on your Form. You will use several of these in your Form. They can be set to contain single or multiple lines of data.
	Insert Button	Inserts a Submit Button Object (Dreamweaver default) on your Form. You can also make this a Reset button or set it to None.
	Insert Checkbox	Inserts a Checkbox Object on your Form. These Checkboxes are used to toggle between selecting a single option on a Form.
	Insert Radio Button	Inserts a Radio Button Object on your form. Radio buttons are used to select one item out of a list of available options.
	Insert List/Menu	Inserts a List or Menu Object on your Form. These two Objects (List or Menu) allow you to make single or multiple selections in a small area of space.
	Insert File Field	Inserts a text box and button that lets the end user browse to a file on their hard drive, for uploading.
	Insert Image Field	Inserts an image into a Form, which the user can click on. This can be used to make graphic-based buttons.
	Insert Hidden Field	Stores information that does not need to be displayed but is necessary for processing the Form on the server.

Note_____

Making Forms Function with CGI

Dreamweaver gives you complete control over the layout of your Form and the creation of Form Objects, but that is just half the battle. Getting the information from the Form to your server or database requires more than HTML can do. In order to process Forms, it's necessary to use some type of additional scripting beyond HTML. While it is possible to process Form data through JavaScript or even Java, most Web developers agree that the most foolproof way to program Forms is through CGI, PHP, or ASP.

CGI stands for **C**ommon **G**ateway **I**nterface. In essence, CGI is a protocol to get information to and from a Web server. CGI scripts can be written in a variety of programming languages, ranging from Perl, to C, to Apple-Script. If that doesn't sound complicated enough for you, add that different types of CGI scripts work with different Web servers, ranging from UNIX to MacOS to WindowsNT. Though it is complex, CGI is considered by most Web developers to be the most reliable method to work with Forms. If you have a Web site, chances are very high that your Internet service provider or Web administrator has existing CGI scripts that you can use. Because there are so many variables to CGI, and it is outside the scope of Dream-weaver, it will be up to you to coordinate obtaining and implementing the processing of your Forms.

Here are some online resources for scripts and CGI:

Matt's Script Archives
http://www.worldwidemart.com/scripts/

Selena Sol's Public Domain CGI Scripts
http://www.extropia.com/

Free Code
http://www.freecode.com/

Exercise #1_____Working with Form Objects

Even if you are not going to be adding CGI scripts yourself, you still need to set up the layout of the Form Objects on the page. In this exercise, you will get hands-on experience with each of the various Form elements. You won't be adding any scripts because doing that would require another book, but you will get everything set up so that when you do want to add a CGI script, your pages will be ready!

STEP-BY-STEP_____

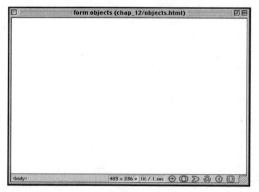

1. Define your site for Chapter 12. Copy the contents of **chap_12** to your hard drive and press **F5** to define it. If you need a refresher on this process, revisit Chapter 3, *"Site Control."*

2. Open the **objects.html** file. It's just a blank page, but at least it has a page title for you ;-).

3. Make sure the Form Objects Palette is visible. If it's not, click on the small black arrow at the top of the Objects Palette and select **Forms**.

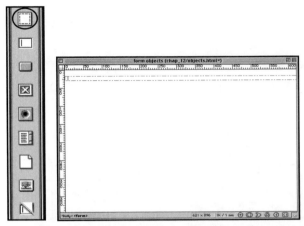

4. Click on the **Insert Form** button in the Form Objects Palette. This will insert the **<FORM>** tag into your Document. You should see red dashed lines on your page. If you don't, select **View > Invisible Elements**.

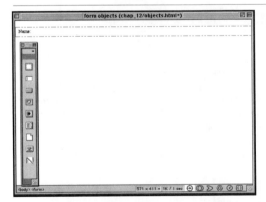

5. Position your cursor inside the red dashed lines, and type **Name:**. Press the **spacebar** once to create a single space.

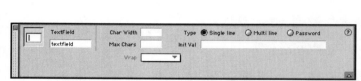

6. Click on the **Insert Text Field** button in the Form Objects Palette. This will insert a blank text field onto your page. With the text field highlighted, notice that the Properties Inspector options change.

7. In the **TextField** setting in the Properties Inspector, replace the existing text with the word **name**. This will give a unique name to this text field. Type **Char Width 35**. This sets the length of the text field. It does not limit the amount of text entered, just how much is visible. To limit the amount of text entered, you would enter a value for **Max Chars**.

8. Click to the right of the text field in your Document and press **Return**, or **Enter**. Type **Address:** and press the **spacebar** to create one space.

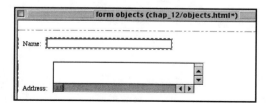

9. Click on the **Insert Text Field** button. This will insert another text field onto your page. In the Properties Inspector, enter the word **address** in the **TextField**. Type **Char Width 40**, choose **Type Multi line** and set **Num Lines 2**. You can see how the **Multi line** attribute works. This is great for larger areas of text when you don't know how much will be inserted.

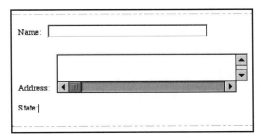

10. Click to the right of the multi-line text field and press **Return** or **Enter**. Type **State:** and insert one space by pressing the **spacebar**.

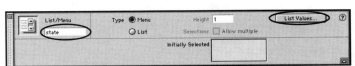

11. Click the **Insert List/Menu** button. By default, this will insert a Menu object onto your Form. In the Properties Inspector, name the object **state** beneath **List/Menu**. Next, click the **List Values...** button.

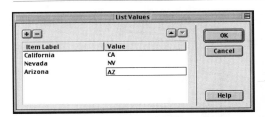

12. For the first **Item Label**, type **California**, and then press **Tab**. For the first **Value**, type **CA**, and then press **Tab**. Repeat this same process for **Nevada** and **Arizona** using the information from the image above. This Form Object will give you a pull-down menu displaying the information in the Item Label column. The information in the Value column is what a CGI or JavaScript program would process with the Form. Click **OK**.

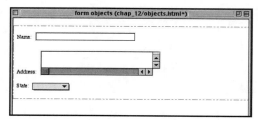

13. Click to the right of the State pull-down menu and press **Return** or **Enter**.

14. Click the **Insert Checkbox** button. This will insert a checkbox onto your page.

15. In the Properties Inspector, name the checkbox **brochure**. For the **Checked Value**, type **Send the customer a brochure**. The **Checked Value** information will appear next to the checkbox name when a CGI script processes the Form. This information is hidden from your end user, but it is useful to a programmer who is setting up the CGI because it tells him or her what the checkbox relates to.

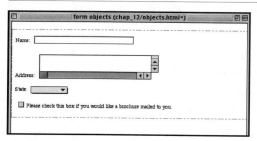

16. Click to the right of the checkbox and type **Please check this box if you would like a brochure mailed to you**. This will help the end user understand what information they are sending by checking this box. Press **Return** or **Enter**.

17. Click the **Insert Button** object. This will insert a Submit button onto your page, which is the default state that Dreamweaver automatically inserts. Because you need to have a button to submit the Form, leave the other options at their default values.

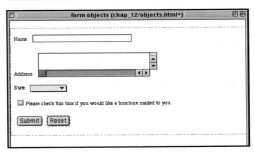

18. Click to the right of the Submit button. Click the **Insert Button** object again. This will insert another Submit button onto your page. In the Properties Inspector, change the **Action** to **Reset form**. This will create a button that clears the Form, just in case your end user makes a mistake and wants to start over. Change the **Button Name** to **reset**.

19. Save your file. Press **F12** to preview your Form in a browser. Remember, the Submit button will not work because you did not attach any CGI scripts.

20. Return to Dreamweaver, save, and close the Document.

The purpose of this exercise was to get your comfortable inserting different Form Objects and modifying some of their properties. To make a Form perform its functions, you would need to attach a program to it.

 Note_____

Creating a Pull-Down Jump Menu

If you'd like to create a pull-down menu that automatically jumps to a URL, you can download a third-party JavaScript Behavior that works with Dreamweaver. Here are two sites to help you.

Dreamweaver Depot
http://people.netscape.com/andreww/dreamweaver

Dreamweaver's Fan Page
http://www.cybernet.ch/users/massimo/

Exercise #2_____Creating a Form

The purpose of this exercise is to make you more familiar with creating a layout for your Forms. Forms can combine other HTML elements, such as Background Images and Tables. This exercise should get you comfortable with combining your new Forms-creation skills with your existing Web-layout skills.

STEP-BY-STEP_____

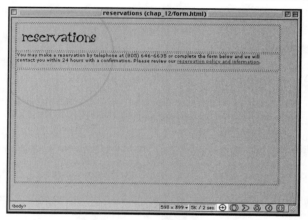

1. Open the **form.html** file. Notice that it already contains a Background Image, a graphic (**reservations**) and a Table. Click your cursor in the bottom cell of the Table.

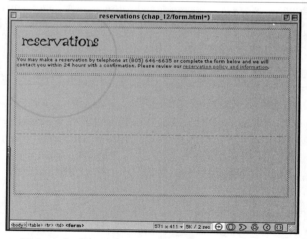

2. Click on the **Insert Form** button in the Objects Palette. Red dashes should appear in the Table cell, denoting that you have inserted a **<FORM>** tag. If you don't see red dashes, select **View > Invisible Elements**.

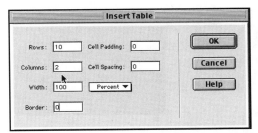

3. Select **Insert > Table**. (If you're used to clicking on the Table Object in the Objects Palette, you would need to switch it back to Common. Otherwise, for convenience's sake, just use the Insert menu right now.) Change the settings to **Rows: 10**, **Cell Padding: 0**, **Columns: 2**, **Cell Spacing: 0**, **Width: 100 Percent**, and **Border: 0**. Click **OK**.

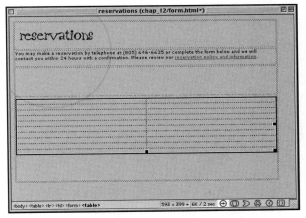

A Table will appear below the red dashes, as shown here.

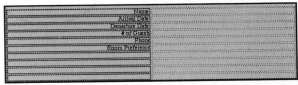

4. Click inside the first cell in column 1 and type **Name:**. Click inside the second cell in column 1, type **Arrival Date:**. Click inside the third cell in column 1, type **Departure Date:**. Click inside the fourth cell in column 1, type **# of Guests:**.Click inside the fifth cell in column 1, type **Phone:**. Finally, click inside the sixth cell in column 1, and type **Room Preference:**.

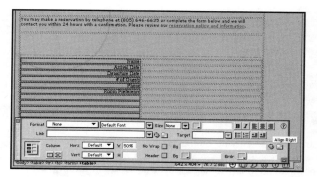

5. Click and drag to select all the cells in column 1. Once they are selected, click on the **Align Right** button in the Properties Inspector.

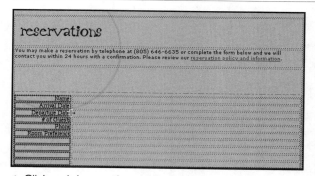

6. Click and drag on the middle divider between the two columns to move it over to the left.

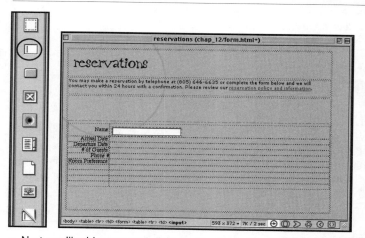

7. Next, you'll add some entry fields to the Form. Click inside column 1, row 2 and choose the **Insert Text Field** object in the Objects Palette. In the Properties Inspector, name the text field **name**.

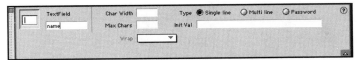

8. Repeat this same process for the next 5 cells down. Make sure you give each text field a unique name similar to the associated column.

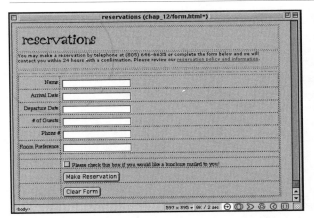

9. Position your cursor inside row 8 in column 2 and click. Next, click on the **Insert Checkbox** button in the Objects Palette and change the **CheckBox Name** to **mail** and the **Checked Value** to **mail brochure to customer**. Click to the right of the checkbox that just appeared, and type **Please check this box if you would like a brochure mailed to you!** into the Document.

10. Click in row 9 in column 2 and click the **Insert Button** button in the Objects Palette. In the Properties Inspector, change the **Label** to **Make Reservation**.

11. Click in row 10 in column 2 and click the **Insert Button** button again. In the Properties Inspector, change the **Label** to **Clear Form**, and change the **Action** to **Reset Form**.

12. *Congratulations, you've just designed a pretty-nice-looking custom Form. Go ahead and leave this file open for the next exercise. If you are brain-fried and want to quit, make sure you save your work!*

Exercise #3_____Opening a New Browser Window

Let's face it, a Web page is pretty small. There are going to be times when you just can't cram everything onto a single page. So, what are you supposed to do? One option is to open the information in another Web-page window. In this next exercise, you will open a new browser window to display some information that wouldn't fit on your page very well.

STEP-BY-STEP_____

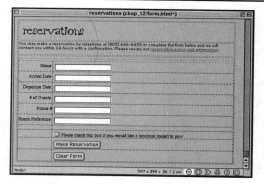

1. You should have the file open from the previous exercise.

2. Click and drag to highlight the text **reservation policy and information**.

3. In the **Properties Inspector**, next to the Link text box, notice that there is a hash mark (**#**). This is referred to as a "nowhere" link. It's a link that goes nowhere. The only purpose for this link is that certain Behaviors must be attached to links, such as the one you're about to add!

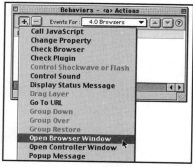

4. Press **F8**. From the **Behaviors Palette**, click on the pop-up menu and select **Open Browser Window**. This will open the Open Browser Window dialog box.

5. Click on the **Browse...** button. Browse to the **policy.html** file. Click **Select**. This is the HTML file that will be displayed in your new window. It can be an internal or external link.

6. Type in **Window Width: 310** and **Window Height: 350**. This will specify the pixel size of your window when it opens. These dimensions were chosen because they will fit the content you are going to display inside. On other projects you can use any dimensions. At the bottom of the window, type **Window Name: policy**.

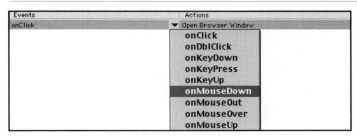

7. Click **OK**. In the Behaviors Palette, change **onMouseOver** to **onMouseDown** by clicking the pop up menu between the **Events** and **Actions**.

8. Press **F12** to preview your work.

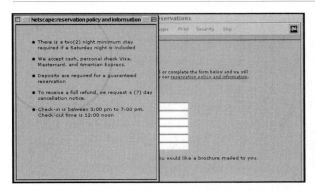

9. In the browser, click on the reservation policy and information link at the top of the page. Voila! A new browser window will open, displaying **policy.html** in a window set to 310 x 350 pixels.

10. Save and close the file. If you're not too tired, move onward to the next chapter.

13.DHTML

- **Dragging Layers**
- **Using Timeline for Animation**
- **Playing, Stopping, and Resetting the Timeline**

chap_13 folder

Dreamweaver 2
H•O•T CD-ROM

The D at the beginning of DHTML stands for "dynamic," as in **D**ynamic **H**yper**T**ext **M**arkup **L**anguage. DHTML was introduced a couple of years ago to offer more dynamic content, such as animation and interactivity, than basic HTML gives. DHTML is not really one thing, it's a combination of technologies, such as HTML, JavaScript, Style Sheets, Absolute Positioning, Plug-Ins, and DOM. For a definition of these technologies, revisit Chapter 1, *"Background."*

Unfortunately, most of the content produced by using DHTML works only on current browsers, and fails on anything below a 4.0 browser. If you plan to use techniques presented in this chapter, it's best to put them on interior pages so that visitors with older browsers can see your first page and important content. DHTML is usually reserved for entertainment-based sites, where games and/or dynamic presentations are expected and embraced. You could alternately offer DHTML content only to those end users who can see by using the browser-detection techniques discussed in Chapter 8, *"Style Sheets."* This chapter allows you to learn DHTML techniques. Whether you use them or not will likely depend on what type of site you are designing.

Warning_____

Prevent Overlaps

This chapter works with Layers, which you also worked with in Chapter 5, *"Layout."* Before you begin the exercises, open your Layers window (**F11**) and make sure that **Prevent Overlaps** is not checked. If this is left checked, the exercises in this chapter will fail.

For the purposes of converting Layers to Tables as you did in Chapter 5, it's necessary to prevent Layers from overlapping. That's because Table cells can't overlap, and the Layer information was being used to produce Tables.

In this chapter, however, you want the layers to overlap, since you will be doing animation where objects fly on top of each other. It's easy to change this setting by simply unchecking the Prevent Overlaps setting in the Layers window.

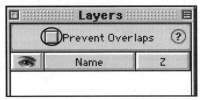

In order to successfully complete this chapter's exercises, make sure that you do not have the Prevent Overlaps setting checked.

Exercise #1_____Dragging Layers

When I was in Dallas speaking at a Macromedia seminar, my husband Bruce sat and drew this little game for our daughter. I thought the example was delightful, though she did complain that the
monkey had no shoes! Regardless of her criticism, it's a fun example of what you can do with
DHTML, and so it leads this chapter.

STEP-BY-STEP_____

1. Define your site for Chapter 13. Copy the contents of **chap_13** to your hard drive and
define it (**F5**). If you need a refresher on this process, revisit Chapter 3, *"Site Control."*

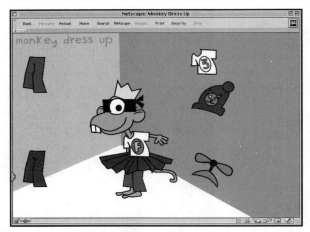

2. Open **dress_final.html** and press **F12** to preview it in a browser. Take any item and drag
it on the monkey. This game was created using Dreamweaver's Drag Layer Behavior, which
you're about to learn here. Return to Dreamweaver and close the file.

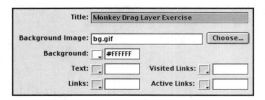

3. Choose **File > New** (Mac) or **File > New Window** (Windows) and save the Document
as **monkey2.html** into the **chap_13** folder. Choose **Modify > Page Properties...** and enter
the **Title: Monkey Drag Layer Exercise**. Select **Background Image: Choose...** (Mac) or
Browse... (Windows) **bg.gif**. Click **OK**.

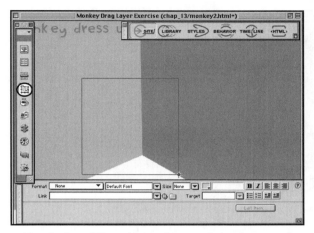

4. Use the **Insert Draw Layer** object to drag a Layer on the page.

5. Make sure the cursor is inside the Layer, and choose **Insert > Image**. Browse to **lilmonkey.gif**, and click **Select**.

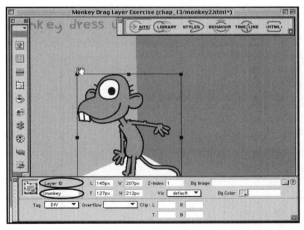

6. Click on the top handle of the Layer to select it. In the **Layer ID** area of the Properties Inspector type the name **monkey**. It's best to name your Layer something that relates to the image.

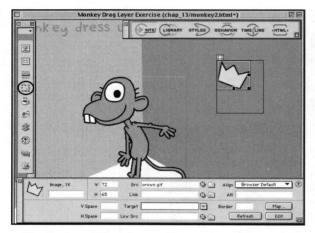

7. Use the **Insert Draw Layer** object again to drag another smaller Layer on the page. With the cursor inside the Layer, choose **Insert > Image** to locate **crown.gif**, and click **Select**.

8. Select the Layer by its handle and name it **crown** inside the **Layer ID** area of the Properties Inspector.

9. Move the crown Layer by its handle on top of the monkey's head. **Tip:** Once the Layer is selected by its handle you can use the arrow keys on your keyboard to nudge it into place.

10. Click on the image of the crown (not the crown Layer) to select it. It's essential that the image is selected, not the Layer. This has to do with the fact that the JavaScript Behavior of the Drag Layer command must be attached to the `<IMG>` tag, not the `<LAYER>` tag.

11. Open the **Behaviors** window (**Window > Behavior** or **F8**) and make sure that **3.0 + 4.0 Browsers** is selected in the pop-up menu. (By the way, even though the program claims this will work on 3.0 browsers, it will not work on all of them.) Click on the **plus** sign button and select **Drag Layer**.

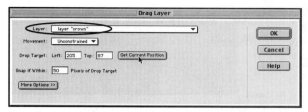

12. The Drag Layer dialog box will open. Switch to **Layer: layer "crown."** Leave the **Movement: Unconstrained**, and click on the **Get Current Position** button. This procedure will insert numbers into the Drop Target area. The program has just captured the exact position of the crown on the page. (**Note:** these numbers will vary because you might have positioned your monkey and crown differently than I did.) Leave **Snap if Within: 50 Pixels of Drop Target** and click **OK.**

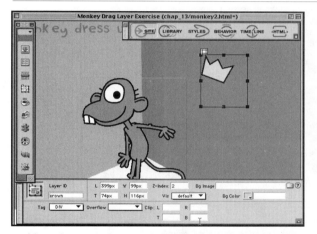

13. Move the crown Layer away from the monkey. **Note:** Wherever you place it is where it will appear in the browser. It's important to drag it away from the monkey so your end user can drag it back on!

14. Press **F12** to preview the results. Move the crown back on to the monkey.

15. See if you can complete the exercise with the rest of the dress-up artwork found in the **chap_13** folder. You'll probably be grateful that Bruce didn't make shoes, as it would be more objects to set up! When you're finished fooling around with this exercise, close the file to move on to the next exercise.

Exercise #2_____Using the Timeline for Animation

You've probably noticed the item **Timelines** in the Dreamweaver Launcher interface and wondered what it stood for. You'll finally get to find out with this exercise. This time, you'll use the same artwork, but instead of creating a drag-and-drop game, you'll create an animation of the clothes flying on to the 'lil monkey's body. If this isn't the sort of content you think you'll be adding to your site, you'll still be learning the principles of Dreamweaver animation and have a smile on your face while doing so.

STEP-BY-STEP_____

1. Open **dress_timeline1.html** in Dreamweaver, and press **F12** to preview it. This gives you the opportunity to see what you will build by completing this exercise.

2. Close **dress_timeline1.html**, and open **dress_timeline2.html**. This Document has been partially built for you.

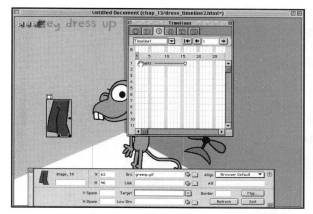

 Movie_____

keyframe.mov

To see how to make keyframes in action, check out the file **keyframe.mov** found in the **movies** folder on the *Dreamweaver 2 H•O•T CD-ROM*.

3. Make sure that the **Timelines** window is open (**Window > Timelines** or **F9**). Drag the Layer with the pants in it by its handle into **Channel 1**. It will appear inside the Timeline, as shown above.

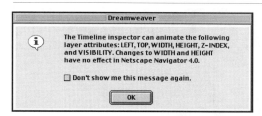

4. When this dialog box appears, just click **OK**. This is merely an information window letting you know in what different ways you can animate Layers.

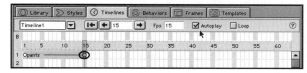

You'll see two dots in the Timeline for the pants. These are called keyframes. The first keyframe establishes where the pants are at the beginning of the animation. The second one establishes where they will be at the end.

5. Click on the second dot (keyframe) of the Pants element in the Timeline. Right now, both keyframes are set to the same position, so you haven't programmed any motion yet. The term "keyframe" means an extreme point of movement. In this case, both extremes (or keys) are set to the same position, so nothing happens.

6. With the second dot highlighted, move the pants by the Layer handle to where they belong on the monkey. Make sure you are moving the entire Layer, not just the image. **Tip:** You can use the arrow keys to nudge them into place. **Note:** See the light gray line that appears on the screen from where the pants were originally to where you just moved them? This indicates that you set up the motion properly.

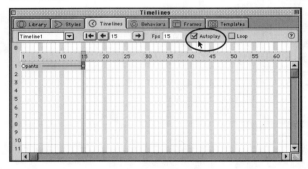

7. Make sure that the **Autoplay** checkbox is checked in the Timelines window. This tells Dreamweaver to play the animation once it is viewed from a browser.

8. Press **F12** to see the results of your labor. Unfortunately, you cannot preview animation from within Dreamweaver, only from a browser. You'll see that the pants fly on to the body, but that the hat and T-shirt remain stationary. You've gotta program those two for this to work like the first one you saw. Return to Dreamweaver.

9. Drag the hat by its Layer handle into **Channel 2**. Now, click on its second keyframe (the second dot) and move the hat by its Layer handle to the top of the monkey's head.

10. Drag the T-shirt by its Layer handle into **Channel 3**. Click on its second keyframe (the second dot) and move the T-shirt by its Layer handle to the monkey's torso.

11. Press **F12**, and voila! You've got animation.

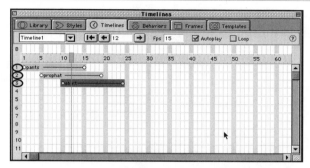

12. Return to Dreamweaver and move the Layers in the Channels like shown here. Press **F12** to see the difference. You can adjust the timing of these Layers by moving them around on the Timeline. If you click on the second keyframe of any of them, you can drag it to the right to extend the number of frames, too. When you're done playing, save and close the Document.

Note_____

Docking and Undocking Windows

The Dreamweaver Interface ships with bunch of windows and palettes arranged in a way that made a lot of sense to the people who designed the program. Fortunately, if you want your windows and palettes arranged differently, you can customize your interface in Dreamweaver 2 by docking and undocking windows in different combinations. This is a great feature because it allows you to combine just the windows you use most often.

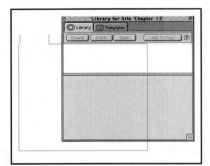 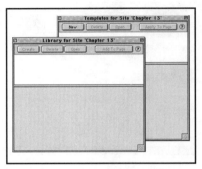

Docking Windows

Click on one of the tabs and drag outside the current window. This will give you a silhouette of the new window. Release the mouse button and wah-lah, the two have been separated!

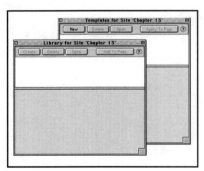 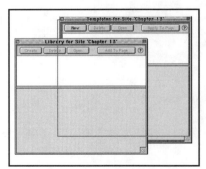

Undocking Windows

Click anywhere in the title bar of the window and drag it toward the title bar of the window with which you want to combine it. Release the mouse button and the two windows are combined!

Tip_____

The Timeline Explained

The Timeline Inspector is used to control animation in Dreamweaver. In addition, it can control many other events and JavaScript Behaviors over time, such as specifying when music starts and stops, starting and stopping a slideshow presentation, etc. To understand all the Timeline features, see the chart below.

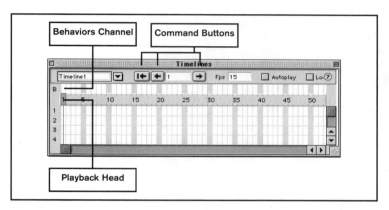

Dreamweaver Timeline Features

Feature	Explanation
Command Buttons	Three controls, Rewind, Back, and Play, let you control your Timeline.
Play Head	Allows you to drag the Play Head to preview your animation and move between frames.
Behaviors Channel	Shows any Behaviors that are attached to specific Frames.

Exercise #3_____Play, Stop, and Reset the Timeline

Let's say you wanted some buttons that could play, stop, and reset the Timeline. This next exercise shows you how to set it up.

1. Open **anim_button.html**, and press **F12** to preview it in the browser. Remember, you can't see this DHTML stuff from within Dreamweaver. Click on the link that says **GO** and watch the animation play. Click **STOP** and **RESET** to see them in action, too.

2. Return to Dreamweaver and close the file. Open **anim_button1.html**. This has been partially built for you, only you'll be adding the Behaviors.

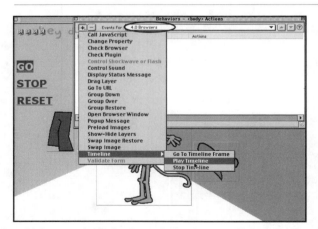

3. Make sure the **Behaviors** window is open. Switch the **Events For** to **4.0 Browsers**. Highlight the word **GO**. **Note:** In the Properties Inspector the word **GO** contains a link with the hash mark in it (**#**). This sets up a link that doesn't go anywhere. This is because many Behaviors have to be applied to links, and you don't want the link to work, just to exist.

4. With **GO** selected, click on the **plus** sign in the Behaviors window, and choose **Timeline > Play Timeline**. The Play Timeline window will appear. It should be set to **Play Timeline: Timeline1**, so click **OK.**

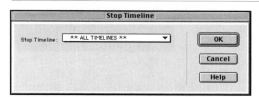

5. Highlight the word **STOP**, and click on the **plus** sign button in the Behaviors window to choose **Timeline > Stop Timeline**. The Stop Timeline window will appear. Choose **Stop Timeline: **ALL TIMELINES **** or **Timeline 1** (the only Timeline you have defined in this file). It's possible, you see, to have multiple Timelines in a Dreamweaver Document. In this exercise you are only working with a single Timeline, however. Click **OK.**

6. Highlight the word **RESET**, and click on the **plus** sign button in the Behaviors window to choose **Timeline > Go To Timeline Frame**. Enter the **Go to Frame: 1**, and click **OK.** This tells the Reset button to move the Timeline back to **Frame 1.**

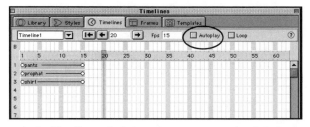

7. In the Timelines window, make sure you **uncheck Autoplay**. In this exercise, you want the links to control whether the animation plays or not, so Autoplay is no longer necessary.

*Save your work, and press **F12** to see the fruits of your Timelines labor. When you're finished, you can tell all your friends, family, and co-workers that you just made your first DHTML animation page. Don't forget to tell them where you learned it.;-)*

14.Plug-Ins

• **Linking to Sounds • Embedding Sounds**
• Inserting Flash Content • Inserting Shockwave Content
• Inserting QuickTime Content

chap_14 folder

Dreamweaver 2
H•O•T CD-ROM

Hey, you're almost through the book! There's still one more important feature of Dreamweaver to learn about before your education is complete—Plug-Ins. You might want to add sound to your page, Flash content, Director content, or QuickTime content. Dreamweaver lets you do all this via a variety of objects that are discussed in this chapter, and you can set preferences on how and when this content will play by setting parameters in the Properties Inspector.

Exciting as this sounds, it is also the area of Web development where the compatibility issues between browsers really get intense. Not everyone has the same Plug-Ins loaded, and some of the Plug-Ins work differently on Macs and Windows. Dreamweaver does a great job of letting you put this content on your site. It's the rest of the Web's limitations that you'll more likely have to struggle with!

What is a Plug-In?

In the early days of the Web, any file that wasn't an HTML file had to be downloaded and required a separate "player" for the content to be seen. This was a hassle for most Web surfers, because it meant that you had to break the flow of a good "surf" to view material in an external application. In response to this problem, Netscape introduced the idea of Plug-Ins, which extended the capability of HTML pages to display content that wasn't HTML based. Today, certain Plug-Ins ship with most browsers. These include QuickTime, Flash, and Real Audio. This chapter focuses on techniques to insert Plug-In-based content into HTML pages so it can be viewed as an "inline" element, without requiring the use of an outside player application.

 Warning_____

Plug-Ins Require Viewer Participation

As you are working through these exercises, you might find yourself being directed to download Plug-Ins from the Internet or reassign them in your browser preferences. If this seems like a hassle, remember that you are asking your audience to do the same thing when you present Plug-In-based content to them!

URLs for Downloading Plug-Ins

Plug-In	URL
QuickTime	http://www.apple.com/quicktime
Flash	http://www.macromedia.com
Director	http://www.macromedia.com

 Note_____

Plug-In Object Buttons

The methods for inserting Plug-In content are not that different than inserting other elements, such as images and Tables.

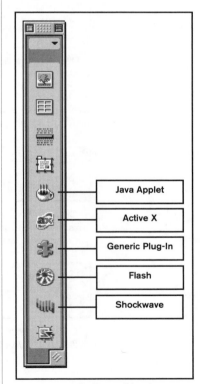

You can easily insert Plug-In content on a Web page by using the Objects Palette buttons.

Exercise #1_____Linking to Sounds

There are multiple ways to add sound to your page. In this first exercise, you will learn to add sound to your page by simply creating a link to a sound file. As you will see, there are some nuances to consider when you are working with sound files. First, there is no standard format for sounds on the Web. Sounds are handled differently between browsers and operating systems. As if designing Web pages was not difficult enough! Have no fear, by the time you do the hands-on exercises in this chapter, you will have a much better understanding of sound on the Web.

STEP-BY-STEP_____

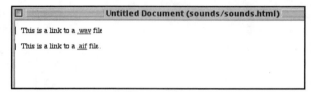

1. Define your site for Chapter 14. Copy the contents of **chap_14** to your hard drive and press **F5** to define it. For a refresher on this process, revisit Chapter 3, *"Site Control."*

2. Open **sounds.html**. You will see two links at the top of the page. These two links point directly to two different sound files. The first link points to a **.wav** file and the bottom link points to an **.aif** file.

3. Click on the **.wav** link at the top of the page. In the Properties Inspector notice that this links to the **tell-me-about.wav** file. That's all there is to it. When the user clicks on this link, the sound will be played.

4. Click on the **.aif** link. Notice that this link points to the **sound.aif** file. Nothing too complicated about this so far. Simply create a link and instead of pointing to an HTML Document, you point to the sound file.

When the page is previewed in Netscape Navigator 4.6 on the Mac, clicking on the .wav link will launch the Netscape audio player. This is the default setting for Navigator 4.6.

When the page is previewed in Netscape Navigator 4.6 on the Mac, clicking on the .aif link will launch the QuickTime Plug-In. That's because I set QuickTime as the audio player for all .aif files. This was not the default setting.

5. Press **F12** to preview this page in a browser. Click on each one of the links. Clicking on the **.wav** link will play a sound of a man saying, "Tell me about your childhood." Clicking on the **.aif** file will play a beeping sound. Depending on how your browser preferences are set up and what operating system you are using, clicking on the links might launch different audio players—or none at all!

6. Return to Dreamweaver and close the file.

Different Sound Players

Both Internet Explorer and Netscape Navigator let you choose what application or Plug-In will play audio files on Web pages. In fact, you can have different ones set for each type of audio format. For example, you might choose to have the QuickTime Plug-In play .aif and .wav files and have the Flash Plug-In play .swf files. The point is, you have complete control over this by modifying your browser preferences. You should check these settings if you experience any problems while trying to play sound files. For instructions on how to change these settings, refer to your browsers' help feature.

Tip

Different Sound Formats

One of the problems of adding sound to your Web page is deciding which format you should use. Most Web publishers use either .aif or .wav files. These two formats are the native sound formats for the Mac and Windows operating systems, meaning that you will not have to rely on Plug-Ins, but it is a good idea to be familiar with the other formats that you might run into on the Web. The chart below gives you an idea of what's out there.

Sound Formats	
Extension	**Description**
.au	This format was one of the first introduced on the Internet and was designed for NeXT and Sun Unix systems.
.aiff/.aif	The .aif (Audio Interchange Format) was developed by Apple and is also used on SGI machines. This is the main audio format for Macintosh computers.
.midi/.mid	The midi (Musical Instrument Digital Interface) format was designed to translate how music is produced. These files are usually small and low in quality.
MP3	The .MP3 (MPEG-1 Audio Layer-3) format is the newest audio file format on the Web. It offers superior compression and great quality.
.ra/.ram	The .ra (Real Audio) format was designed to offer streaming audio on the Internet.
.rmf	The .rmf (Rich Music Format) was designed by Headspace and is used in the Beatnik Plug-In. This format offers good compression and quality.
.swa	The .swa (Shockwave Audio) format was developed by Macromedia and is used in Flash.
.wav	The .wav (Wave) audio format was developed by IBM and Microsoft. This is the main audio format for the Windows operating system. Wav files will play on Macs and other systems, as well.

Exercise #2_____**Embedding Sounds**

In addition to linking to a sound file, there is another, much better, approach to adding sound to your Web pages. You can choose to embed the sound so that it shows up inside your page instead of linking to it. This will give you much more control over the sound, in that it enables sounds to appear inside HTML files with other content, too, unlike those in the last exercise, which linked to the sound file itself. By modifying specific parameters, you can control when the sound plays and how it appears on the page, if it loops or not, and several other settings. This gives you more control, which is what most people want in life, right?

STEP-BY-STEP_____

1. Open **embed.html**.

2. Select **Insert > Plug-in**. Browse to the **chap_14** folder and highlight **sound.aif**. Click **Select**. This will insert a small Plug-In icon on your page.

In this instance, it does not matter where the sound file is physically placed on the page. If you had a page where you wanted the sound controllers (play, stop, and rewind buttons) to appear, you would simply position this element like any other image or text component of any page.

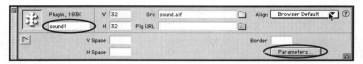

3. In the Properties Inspector, name this sound **sound1**.

4. Click on the **Parameters...** button. This will open the Parameters dialog box. This is where you will insert any of the parameters and values that are listed in the chart at the end of this exercise.

5. Under **Parameter** in the Parameters dialog box, type **autoplay** and then press **Tab**. Type **false** and then click **OK**. This will prevent the sound file from automatically playing until the user clicks on the play button. This is a very useful parameter!

6. Press **F12** to preview your page in a browser. Click on the **play** button to hear the sound play. Here you can see that QuickTime is being used to play .aif files in Netscape Navigator 4.6 for the Macintosh. **Note:** If you get a broken image icon, you might have to download the Plug-In from http://www.apple.com/quicktime.

7. Return to Dreamweaver to save and close the file.

Note_____

What's a Parameter?

Most Plug-In content is controlled by a variety of parameters, which are different for each kind of Plug-In. A parameter is an option passed to the Plug-In which tells it how to behave. In this exercise, you learned how to set autoplay to be on or off. That setting was a parameter within the QuickTime specification.

This chapter covers sound, Flash, Shockwave, and QuickTime, but there are many other types of Plug-Ins on the Web as well. In order to learn what all the parameters are for a Plug-In, it's best to visit the site from which it can be downloaded. Here's a list of sites with more information on Plug-In parameters from a variety of vendors.

LiveAudio Plug-In
http://www.emerald.net/liveaudio/

Apple's QuickTime Plug-In
http://www.apple.com/quicktime/authoring/embed2.html

Macromedia's Flash Plug-In
http://www.macromedia.com/support/flash/ts/documents/tag_attributes.htm

Macromedia's Shockwave Plug-In
http://www.macromedia.com/support/director/how/shock/objembed.html

Netscape's Plug-In Registry
http://www.home.netscape.com/plugins

Exercise #3_____Inserting Flash Content

Because both Dreamweaver and Flash are Macromedia products, it is not entirely surprising that Dreamweaver's support for Flash is superb. Instead of the generic Plug-In object that you used in the last exercise, Dreamweaver has an Insert Flash object all of its own.

STEP-BY-STEP_____

1. Create a new Document and save it as **flash.html**.

2. Click on the **Insert Flash** object, and browse to **splash.swf**. This Flash piece was donated courtesy of Greg Penny of Flower Records (http://www.flowerrecords.com) and was designed by Richard Joffray (http://www.joffray.com).

3. Notice that the Properties Inspector has a **play** button? You should be able to play the content right in Dreamweaver, unlike DHTML or generic Plug-In content. Press **F12** to view the content in the browser to check it again. It's that simple.

4. Return to Dreamweaver. Because Flash is vector-based, it can scale. Change both the **W** and **H** properties to 100%, and press **F12** again. Now change the size of your browser. The content in your browser scales, too! This only happens if you set the width and height information to a percentage.

5. Close and save the file, and move on to the next exercise, which explains how to embed Shockwave content.

Note_____

What is Flash?

Flash is a Macromedia software product that combines vector graphics, bitmap graphics and sound to create dynamic content for the Web. Just as you can insert a graphic that you created in another program to your Web page, you can author full-screen animation, sound, and interactivity within Flash, and add these features to your site without being dependent on HTML. Flash consists of both an authoring tool and a Plug-In. If you wanted to author Flash content, you would need the Flash application. If you wanted to view Flash content, you would need the Flash Plug-In installed in your browser. For more information check out the Macromedia software Web site.

Macromedia's Flash
http://www.macromedia.com/software/flash/

Exercise #4_____**Inserting Director Content**

Next, you'll get a chance to work with some Shockwave content. Once again, because this is a Macromedia product, you will have the advantage of using an Insert Shockwave object instead of the generic Insert Plug-In object.

STEP-BY-STEP_____

1. Create a new Document and name it **director.html**.

2. Click on the **Insert Shockwave** object, and browse to **leroy.dcr**.

3. Notice that the Properties Inspector has **W 32** and **H 32** as the dimensions? These are the default dimensions that you'll see in the Properties Inspector for Director or QuickTime content, because Dreamweaver can't automatically detect the size of these two formats. You'll need to plug in the correct dimensions to get this to work.

4. Enter the values **W 640** and **H 480**, and press **F12** to preview the content. How did I know that the width and height of the piece were 640 x 480? Because I asked my husband Bruce, who created it! Sadly, you must know the dimensions of the Shockwave piece before you enter the values because Dreamweaver doesn't detect them for you.

5. Try pulling Leroy's eyeglasses off. Lots of parts come off, so keep pulling on things. This is very similar to the drag-and-drop exercise you completed in Chapter 13, *"DHTML,"* only it was created in Macromedia Director by my slightly twisted (but kind and wonderful) husband, Bruce (again!).

6. Save and close the file. Time to move on to the next exercise, which shows how to insert a QuickTime movie.

 Note

What is Shockwave?

Shockwave is a Plug-In that allows a Web audience to view Macromedia Director content online. Macromedia Director, like Flash, is an authoring tool that supports better animation, sound and interactivity than the HTML-based Web. The differences between Flash and Director relate to how the authoring tool is structured, how the interactivity is programmed, and how images are formatted.

Exercise #5_____Inserting a QuickTime Movie

QuickTime content is inserted in Dreamweaver using the Plug-In object. This exercise shows you how to embed the content and preview the results.

STEP-BY-STEP_____

1. Create a new Document and name it **quicktime.html**.

2. Click on the **Plug-In** object on the Objects Palette, and browse to the file **testing.mov**. Click **Select**.

3. Change the width and height information to **W 320, H 260** in the Properties Inspector. Note how Dreamweaver could detect the dimensions of a Flash movie, but not the dimensions of QuickTime or Director content?

It's important that you know the dimensions of the file before you embed it into Dreamweaver so you can insert the correct values into the Properties Inspector. In this instance, the movie was 320 x 240, but I added an extra 20 pixels to make room for the controller below the movie, as shown above.

4. Press **F12** to preview the movie in your browser. **Note:** If you get a broken image icon, you might have to download the Plug-In from http://www.apple.com/quicktime.

5. Save and close the Dreamweaver file.

Note_____

What is QuickTime?

QuickTime is a both a file format and a Plug-In that can present sound and movies. It is one of the most versatile file Plug-Ins on the Web, because it is able to play all the formats listed in the chart below.

QuickTime Versatility
QuickTime Supports:
AIF
AU
AVI
BMP
DV Stream
FLC
Image Sequence movie exporters
JPEG/JFIF
MacPaint
MIDI
Photoshop
PICT
Picture
PNG
QuickTime Image
QuickTime Movie
SGI
System 7 Sound
Targa
Text
TIFF
WAV

.Preferences Appendix

This appendix provides numerous charts that show what each Preference in Dreamweaver 2 controls. These preferences are available by going to the **Edit > Preferences** menu.

• **Supplemental
Information** •

Dreamweaver 2

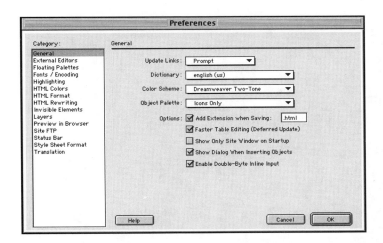

General

Option	Description
Update Links	You can have Dreamweaver automatically update, prompt to update, or never update links.
Dictionary	Lets you specify between three different dictionaries. Used for spell checking.
Color Scheme	Lets you change the color of the Dreamweaver window and palettes.
Object Palette	Changes the appearance of the Objects Palette to display Text Only, Icons and Text, or Icons Only.
Extension	Lets you specify what file extension is used when you save files.
Faster Table Editing	If checked, Dreamweaver will not update column and row changes until you click outside the table.
Show Only Site Window on Startup	If checked, Dreamweaver will display the Site window and NOT open a blank Document when Dreamweaver starts.
Show Dialog When Inserting Objects	If checked, Dreamweaver will open a dialog box allowing you to modify an object when you insert it. If not, the object is inserted with no dialog box shown.
Enable Double Byte-Line Input	If checked, you can insert double-byte text, such as Japanese text, directly into your Document. Otherwise, the text must be entered into a separate text input window.

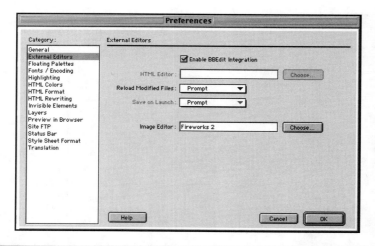

External Editors

Option	Description
Enable BBEdit Integration (Mac Only)	If checked, Dreamweaver will launch BBEdit as its external HTML editor.
HTML Editor	Lets you choose any text editor on your computer to edit HTML code.
Reload Modified Files	Lets you choose if modified images are automatically, never, or if you should be prompted before they are reloaded.
Save On Launch	Lets you choose if files are automatically, never, or promoted for save when the external HTML editor is launched.
Image Editor	Lets you choose any image editor on your computer to edit image files.

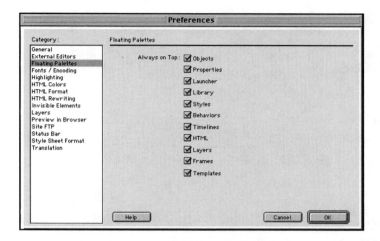

Floating Palettes	
Option	**Description**
Checkboxes	If any boxes are checked, the palettes associated with them will appear on top of the document. If not checked, then those palettes will disappear behind the document.

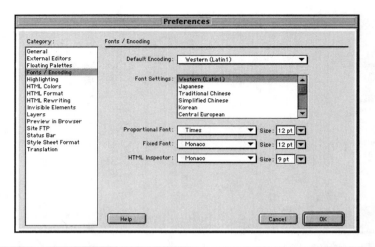

Fonts / Encoding

Option	Description
Default Encoding	Lets you select what type of font encoding is used when the page loads.
Font Setting	Sets which fonts are used for each of the Font Encoding sets.
Proportional Font	This is the font used for normal text in your documents. **Note:** that this setting only changes the font which Dreamweaver uses to display your page, not the font which your audience will see.
Fixed Font	This is the font used with the **PRE**, **CODE**, and **TT** tags when displayed by Dreamweaver.
HTML Inspector	This is the font that is used in Dreamweaver's Inspectors.

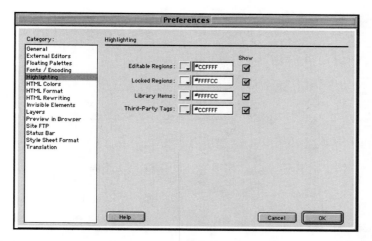

Highlighting	
Option	**Description**
Editable Regions	Lets you specify the color of editable regions in templates.
Locked Regions	Lets you specify the color of locked regions in templates.
Library Items	Lets you specify the color of library items.
Third-Party Tags	Lets you specify the color of third-party tags.

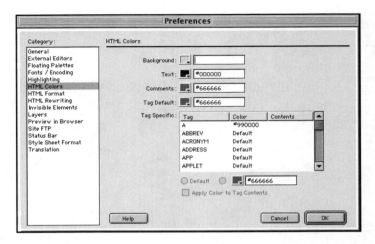

HTML Colors	
Option	**Description**
Background	Sets the background color of the HTML inspector.
Text	Sets the text color between tags.
Comments	Sets the comments tag color.
Tag Default	Sets the color for all tags except the comment tag.
Tag Specific	Lets you override the color of specific tags.

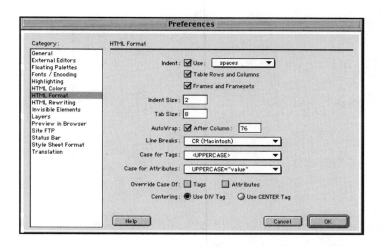

HTML Format

Option	Description
Indent Checkbox	Turns indents on and off. Also, you can specify if Dreamweaver should use either spaces or tabs.
Table Rows and Columns	Will automatically indent the **\<TD\>** and **\<TR\>** tags.
Frameset	Will automatically indent the **\<FRAME\>** and **\<FRAMESET\>** tags.
Indent Size	Sets the size of the indent. Based on tabs or spaces.
Tab Size	Lets you set the size of the tabs. Cool!
AutoWrap	Will add a hard return when text size exceeds specified length.
Line Breaks	Lets you set the type of Line Break used. Generally, it's best to set this to be the same as the type of system which will be hosting your web pages.
Case for Tags	Lets you control if tags are written as all uppercase or all lowercase letters.
Case for Attributes	Lets you control if attributes are written in all uppercase or not.
Override Checkboxes	Lets you override the case set in previous settings.
Centering	You can choose whether to use the **DIV** or **CENTER** tag to handle center alignment.

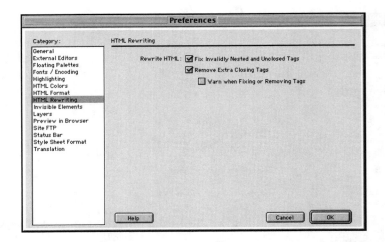

HTML Rewriting

Option	Description
Fix Invalidly Nested and Unclosed Tags	If checked, errors with tags will be corrected. Very cool!
Remove Extra Closing	If checked, extra closing tags will be removed.
Warn Fixing / Removing	Will display a list of invalid tags, warning you when they're being prepared.

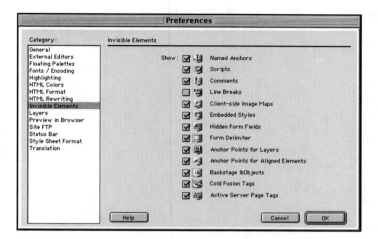

Invisible Elements	
Option	**Description**
Show	For each checked element, a display marker will be displayed in your document.

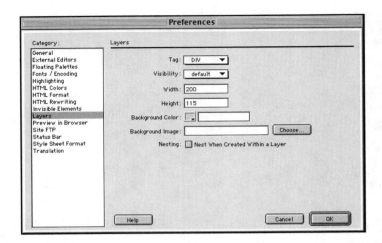

Layers

Option	Description
Tag	Sets which tag is used to create layers in your document.
Visibility	Sets the default visibility of layers.
Width / Height	Sets the default width and height of layers
Background Color	Sets the default background color of layers.
Background Image	Sets the default background image of layers.
Nesting	Sets if layers are nested inside one another or not.

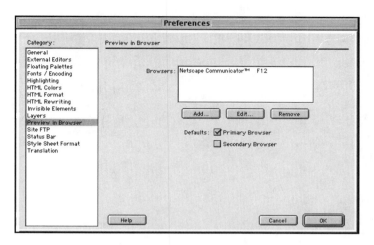

Preview in Browser	
Option	**Description**
Add	Lets you add another browser to the list.
Edit	Lets you edit an existing browser in the list.
Remove	Lets your remove a browser from the list.
Primary Browser	Sets the Primary Browser, opened with **F12**.
Secondary Browser	Sets the Secondary Browser, opened with **Cmd+F12** (Mac) or or **Ctrl+F12** (Windows).
Preview Using Local Server	If you're running a Web server on your computer, check this to view the site through it (Windows only).

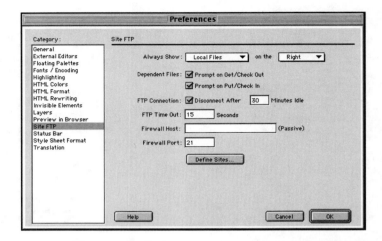

Site FTP	
Option	**Description**
FTP Time Out	Sets how long Dreamweaver will try to connect to the remote FTP server before giving up.
Firewall Host	Address of a proxy server to be used for FTP. Only used if you are behind a firewall, otherwise it should be left blank.
Firewall Port	Sets the port if something other than 21 is being used.
Define Sites	Will open the Define Sites window.

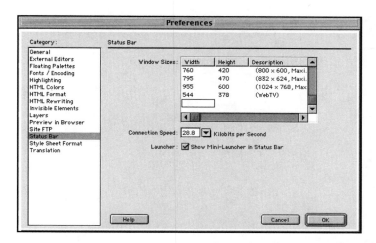

Status Bar

Option	Description
Window Size	Lets you add, modify, or delete from the list of window sizes.
Connection Speed	Sets the connection speed at which Dreamweaver will estimate the download time of your pages.
Launcher	If checked, Dreamweaver will display the mini-launcher in the status bar.

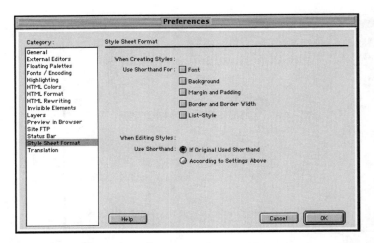

Style Sheet Format	
Option	**Description**
Use Shorthand For	Each style attribute checked will be written by Dreamweaver in shorthand form, which is not well supported by all browsers.

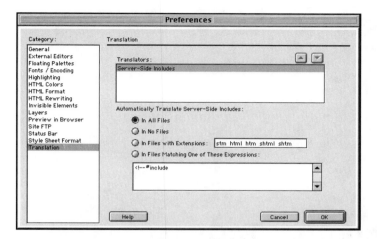

Translation

Option	Description
Translators	Allow you to specify which files are processed, or to turn off processing of server-side includes.

.Troubleshooting FAQ

• Frequently Asked Questions •

Dreamweaver 2

If you've run into any problems while following the exercises in this book, this F.A.Q. is intended to help. This document will be maintained and expanded upon at this book's companion Web site:

http://www.lynda.com/books/dw2hot

If you don't find what you're looking for here or there, please send an email to: dw2faq@lynda.com.

If you have a question related to Dreamweaver, but unrelated to a specific step in an exercise in this book, visit the Dreamweaver Site at: http://www.macromedia.com/support/ dreamweaver/ or call their tech-support hotline at (415) 252-9080.

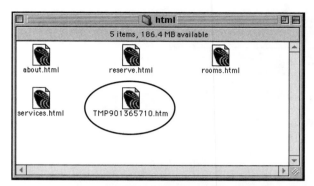

Q: Why do strangely named files appear inside my exercise folders?

A: Whenever you preview a page in a browser, Dreamweaver creates a temporary HTML file. You can delete these files when they appear, or leave them alone, since they don't hurt anything. When and if you upload your finished work to a Web server, you will want to delete them or not upload them. If you do accidentally upload them to your server, however, they won't hurt anything since they aren't truly linked to any of your site.

Window	
Objects	⌘F2
Properties	⌘F3
Launcher	
Site Files	F5
Site Map	Shift F5
Library	F6
Styles	F7
Behaviors	F8
Timelines	F9
HTML	F10
Layers	F11
Frames	⌘F10
Templates	⌘F11
Arrange Floating Palettes	
Hide Floating Palettes	F4
Dreamweaver Online	⌘F1

Q: How do I call up the Properties Inspector?

A: If you can't see the Properties Inspector or, for that matter, any of Dreamweaver's palettes, pull down the **Window** menu. A list of shortcut keys that will help you quickly access all of Dreamweaver's palettes can be found at the end of Chapter 2, *"Interface,"* on page 29.

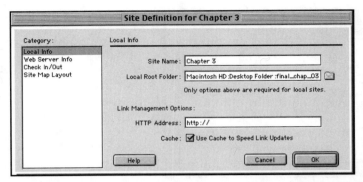

Q: I defined my site for a chapter, but files that are listed in the exercises aren't there. What happened?

A: This could be because when you were defining the site you specified a folder that was inside the chapter folder, instead of the chapter folder itself. Go ahead and redefine the site. (If you need to revisit these steps, visit Exercise #1 in Chapter 3, *"Site Control."*) **Note:** Selecting the correct folder is done differently on Mac and Windows.

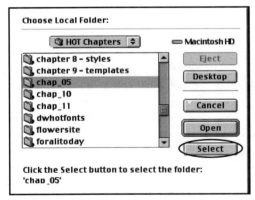

• (Mac) When you're browsing to define the chapter folder and the **Choose Local Folder** dialog box pops up, notice how there's both an **Open** and a **Select** option. Highight the chapter folder, and click **Select**. Don't click **Open**, because you would then define as your site an interior folder, instead of the main folder. This is opposite to the way Windows users define their sites.

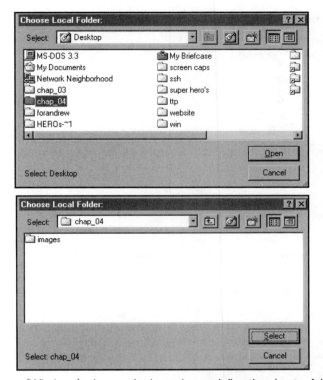

• (Windows) when you're browsing to define the chapter folder and the **Choose Local Folder** dialog box pops up, select the chapter folder. First click **Open**. After the folder is opened, click **Select**. This is the opposite way that Macintosh users define their site.

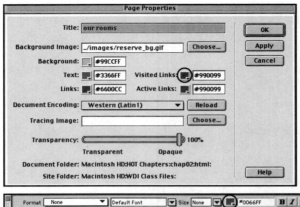

Q: Where's the Color Palette?

A: Because it's context sensitive, the Color Palette only appears when you click in one of Dreamweaver's color wells. Color wells appear inside the Properties Inspector and the Page Properties.

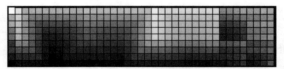

Q: I thought the browser-safe palette contained 216 colors, but the Color Palette in Dreamweaver looks like it contains a lot more colors than that. What's up?

A: Dreamweaver's Color Palette repeats certain colors in order to create an array that is helpful for color picking. The colors are organized by hue from left to right, and by value from top to bottom. This palette is helpful for seeing all the hues together (such as all the blues, reds, yellows, or greens) or evaluating which colors to choose from light to dark.

Q: I just specified a Tracing Image in my Page Properties window, but I can't see it when I preview the page in my browser. Panic is starting to set in!

A: If you cannot see a Tracing Image… that's the whole point! The Tracing Image will appear in your Dreamweaver Document window, but not in the browser. It's there for your reference only, and your end users will never see it.

Q: On the Mac, Dreamweaver can't seem to find any of my files when I preview in the browser, and/or my Dreamweaver Document window has the Objects Palette embedded in it and I can't get rid of it.

A: You've probably run into a memory leak. Dreamweaver requires at least 35 MB of RAM. I actually use 50 MB on my Mac. RAM is a lot cheaper than it used to be, so if you plan to use Dreamweaver you can save yourself a lot of heartache by biting the bullet and buying more! **Warning:** There may be times you may have to reinstall the program to fix the problem, even if you do assign it more RAM.

Q: I put one Layer on top of another! How do I delete it?

A: To delete a Layer, select it by the handle at its top and hit **Delete**. Of course, there's always the universal undo command, **Cmd+Z** (Mac) or **Ctrl+Z** (Windows), too.

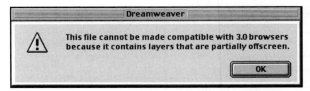

Q: When I convert Tables to Layers, I get an error message stating that one of the Layers is offscreen. How did this happen, and how do I fix it?

A: It is possible to create a Layer and move it so that it is partially or fully offscreen using the arrow keys. This is actually handy for images that you want to have bleed off the edge, or animations that begin offscreen. For converting to Tables, however, it won't work! If you can locate the offending Layer, click on its edge and use the arrow keys to move it back into the screen area. If you can't find the Layer to delete it, try opening the Layers window (**Window > Layers**) and selecting each Layer name that appears inside the window. Eventually, you'll be able to figure out which is on or off the screen by process of elimination.

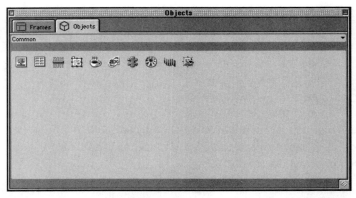

Q: My Objects and Frames palettes are showing up in the same tabbed window, and I'd rather they were separate.

A: Simply click on the top of one of them, and drag it away from the other. Conversely, you can drag several of them together for one uniform palette. Just grab it from its top. To see how to dock and undock palettes, visit Chapter 13, *"DHTML,"* page 266.

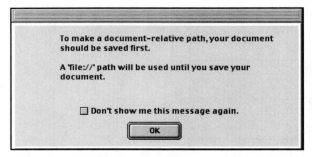

Q: Why do I get the message, "To make a document-relative path, your document should be saved first"? I can't figure out what this gibberish means!

A: I agree, the dialog box could have simply stated, "Save your file now, or Dreamweaver can't keep track of your files," because that's all it's asking you to do. Sigh. If only developers knew how to speak in non-technical terms at times, eh? All you need to do is click **OK**, and save your file (inside the defined site), and Dreamweaver won't bark any more.

Q: Why do I get the message that my file is located outside of the root folder?

A: Dreamweaver is asking you to move the file that you're inserting into the root folder that you've defined as your site. If you work with files outside your defined root folder, Dreamweaver cannot keep track of your links and site management, which is counter productive to the way the program is structured and to your workflow. Though this message is annoying, it is actually helping you maintain a healthy site without broken links and upload problems when you publish it. **Note:** There are different ways to handle this message depending on the system you are running.

- (Mac) you should click **Yes**, and then browse to the correct folder. At that point will be prompted to **Save**, which you should do.
- (Windows) you should click **Yes**, and Dreamweaver will automatically pop you into the correct folder. Click **Save** and the file will be moved.

Q: Why aren't my Templates working?

A: If you leave a Template file open and work on another site (such as another chapter in this book that you've defined as a different site), Dreamweaver can't keep track of your Templates. It's best to work on a single site at a time, and not flip between them while leaving files open from another defined site. This is true with all Dreamweaver Documents, though Templates and Libraries are particularly sensitive to site-definition confusion.

Q: When I try to locate class files, why can't I see the file extensions at the end of file names, such as .gif, .jpg and .html?

A: On Windows, you will need to change your preferences to view file name extensions. Instructions to do this are inside the Chapter, *"Introduction"* on Pages XII-XIII.

.Index

• Subjects and Locations •

Dreamweaver 2

Symbols

A

absolute links
    creating, 68
    defined, 36
    illustrated, 38
    image maps, 128
    in path structure, 42
    in site map, 45
    URL, 39
    See also links
active links, 64, 170
Adjust Tracing Image Position window, 78
.aif extension, 272, 273, 274
alignment
    Absolute Bottom, 143
    Absolute Middle, 143
    Baseline, 143
    Bottom, 143
    Browser Default, 143
    center, 60
    features, 143
    images/text with Tables, 110-116
    Layer, 82, 89
    Left, 143
    Middle, 143
    object, 23
    options, 142
    percentage-based Table, 118-120
    Right, 143
    Table, 89, 113-114
    text, 142-143
    Text Top, 143
    Top, 143

Alt-key shortcuts, 17
animated GIFs, 230, 231
animated Rollovers, 229-231
    Preload Images and, 231
    states, 230, 231
    See also Rollovers
animation
    full-screen, authoring, 279
    keyframes, 263
    playing, 264
    previewing, 264
    Timelines for, 262-267
Apple System Color Picker, 62
assembling images, 121-123
attributes (HTML), 6
.au extension, 274

B

background images, 65, 80, 250
    dimensions, 215
    Frameset, 214-217
    Tracing Images and, 80
backgrounds
    colors, 65, 80
    in multiple Frames, 198, 221-223
BBedit, 26
Behaviors, 159
    applying, 177
    Drag Layer, 258, 260
    Swap Image, 233, 236
    triggering, with Rollovers, 238
Behaviors Palette, 235, 254

P

.Notes

• **Free Space** •

Dreamweaver 2

CD-ROM LICENSE AGREEMENT

THIS SOFTWARE LICENSE AGREEMENT CONSTITUTES AN AGREEMENT BETWEEN YOU AND, LYNDA.COM, LLC. . YOU SHOULD CAREFULLY READ THE FOLLOWING TERMS AND CONDITIONS BEFORE OPENING THIS ENVELOPE. COPYING THIS SOFTWARE TO YOUR MACHINE, BREAKING THE SEAL, OR OTHERWISE REMOVING OR USING THE SOFTWARE INDICATES YOUR ACCEPTANCE OF THESE TERMS AND CONDITIONS. IF YOU DO NOT AGREE TO BE BOUND BY THE PROVISIONS OF THIS LICENSE AGREEMENT, YOU SHOULD PROMPTLY DELETE THE SOFTWARE FROM YOUR MACHINE.

TERMS AND CONDITIONS:

1. GRANT OF LICENSE. In consideration of payment of the License Fee, which was a part of the price you paid for this product, LICENSOR grants to you (the "Licensee") a non-exclusive right to use and display this copy of a Software program, along with any updates or upgrade releases of the Software for which you have paid (all parts and elements of the Software as well as the Software as a whole are hereinafter referred to as the "Software") on a single computer only (i.e., with a single CPU) at a single location, all as more particularly set forth and limited below. LICENSOR reserves all rights not expressly granted to you as Licensee in this License Agreement.

2. OWNERSHIP OF SOFTWARE. The license granted herein is not a sale of the original Software or of any copy of the Software. As Licensee, you own only the rights to use the Software as described herein and the magnetic or other physical media on which the Software is originally or subsequently recorded or fixed. LICENSOR retains title and ownership of the Software recorded on the original disk(s), as well as title and ownership of any subsequent copies of the Software irrespective of the form of media on or in which the Software is recorded or fixed. This license does not grant you any intellectual or other proprietary or other rights of any nature whatsoever in the Software.

3. USE RESTRICTIONS. As Licensee, you may use the Software only as expressly authorized in this License Agreement under the terms of paragraph 4. You may physically transfer the Software from one computer to another provided that the Software is used on only a single computer at any one time. You may not: (i) electronically transfer the Software from one computer to another over a network; (ii) make the Software available through a time-sharing service, network of computers, or other multiple user arrangement; (iii) distribute copies of the Software or related written materials to any third party, whether for sale or otherwise; (iv) modify, adapt, translate, reverse engineer, decompile, disassemble, or prepare any derivative work based on the Software or any element thereof; (v) make or distribute, whether for sale or otherwise, any hard copy or printed version of any of the Software nor any portion thereof nor any work of yours containing the Software or any component thereof; (vi) use any of the Software nor any of its components in any other work.

4. THIS IS WHAT YOU CAN AND CANNOT DO WITH THE SOFTWARE. Even though in the preceding paragraph and elsewhere LICENSOR has restricted your use of the Software, the following is the only thing you can do with the Software and the various elements of the Software:DUCKS IN A ROW ARTWORK: THE ARTWORK CONTAINED ON THIS CD-ROM MAY NOT BE USED IN ANY MANNER WHATSOEVER OTHER THAN TO VIEW THE SAME ON YOUR COMPUTER, OR TO POST TO YOUR PERSONAL, NON-COMMERCIAL WEB SITE FOR EDUCATIONAL PURPOSES ONLY. THIS MATERIAL IS SUBJECT TO ALL OF THE RESTRICTION PROVISIONS OF THIS SOFTWARE LICENSE. SPECIFICALLY BUT NOT IN LIMITATION OF THESE RESTRICTIONS, YOU MAY NOT DISTRIBUTE, RESELL OR TRANSFER THIS PART OF THE SOFTWARE DESIGNATED AS "CLUTS" NOR ANY OF YOUR DESIGN OR OTHER WORK CONTAINING ANY OF THE SOFTWARE DESIGNATED AS "DUCKS IN A ROW ARTWORK" NOR ANY OF YOUR DESIGN OR OTHER WORK CONTAINING ANY SUCH "DUCKS IN A ROW ARTWORK," ALL AS MORE PARTICULARLY RESTRICTED IN THE WITHIN SOFTWARE LICENSE.

5. COPY RESTRICTIONS. The Software and accompanying written materials are protected under United States copyright laws. Unauthorized copying and/or distribution of the Software and/or the related written materials is expressly forbidden. You may be held legally responsible for any copyright infringement that is caused, directly or indirectly, by your failure to abide by the terms of this License Agreement. Subject to the terms of this License Agreement and if the software is not otherwise copy protected, you may make one copy of the Software for backup purposes only. The copyright notice and any other proprietary notices which were included in the original Software must be reproduced and included on any such backup copy.

6. TRANSFER RESTRICTIONS. The license herein granted is personal to you, the Licensee. You may not transfer the Software nor any of its components or elements to anyone else, nor may you sell, lease, loan, sublicense, assign, or otherwise dispose of the Software nor any of its components or elements without the express written consent of LICENSOR, which consent may be granted or withheld at LICENSOR's sole discretion.

7. TERMINATION. The license herein granted hereby will remain in effect until terminated. This license will terminate automatically without further notice from LICENSOR in the event of the violation of any of the provisions hereof. As Licensee, you agree that upon such termination you will promptly destroy any and all copies of the Software which remain in your possession and, upon request, will certify to such destruction in writing to LICENSOR.

8. LIMITATION AND DISCLAIMER OF WARRANTIES. a) THE SOFTWARE AND RELATED WRITTEN MATERIALS, INCLUDING ANY INSTRUCTIONS FOR USE, ARE PROVIDED ON AN "AS IS" BASIS, WITHOUT WARRANTY OF ANY KIND, EXPRESS OR IMPLIED. THIS DISCLAIMER OF WARRANTY EXPRESSLY INCLUDES, BUT IS NOT LIMITED TO, ANY IMPLIED WARRANTIES OF MERCHANTABILITY AND/OR OF FITNESS FOR A PARTICULAR PURPOSE. NO WARRANTY OF ANY KIND IS MADE AS TO WHETHER OR NOT THIS SOFTWARE INFRINGES UPON ANY RIGHTS OF ANY OTHER THIRD PARTIES. NO ORAL OR WRITTEN INFORMATION GIVEN BY LICENSOR, ITS SUPPLIERS, DISTRIBUTORS, DEALERS, EMPLOYEES, OR AGENTS, SHALL CREATE OR OTHERWISE ENLARGE THE SCOPE OF ANY WARRANTY HEREUNDER. LICENSEE ASSUMES THE ENTIRE RISK AS TO THE QUALITY AND THE PERFORMANCE OF SUCH SOFTWARE. SHOULD THE SOFTWARE PROVE DEFECTIVE, YOU, AS LICENSEE (AND NOT LICENSOR, ITS SUPPLIERS, DISTRIBU-TORS, DEALERS OR AGENTS), ASSUME THE ENTIRE COST OF ALL NECESSARY CORRECTION, SERVICING, OR REPAIR. b) LICENSOR warrants the disk(s) on which this copy of the Software is recorded or fixed to be free from defects in materials and workmanship, under normal use and service, for a period of ninety (90) days from the date of delivery as evidenced by a copy of the applicable receipt. LICENSOR hereby limits the duration of any implied warranties with respect to the disk(s) to the duration of the express warranty. This limited warranty shall not apply if the disk(s) have been damaged by unreasonable use, accident, negligence, or by any other causes unrelated to defective materials or workmanship. c) LICENSOR does not warrant that the functions contained in the Software will be uninterrupted or error free and Licensee is encouraged to test the Software for Licensee's intended use prior to placing any reliance thereon. All risk of the use of the Software will be on you, as Licensee. d) THE LIMITED WARRANTY SET FORTH ABOVE GIVES YOU SPECIFIC LEGAL RIGHTS AND YOU MAY ALSO HAVE OTHER RIGHTS WHICH VARY FROM STATE TO STATE. SOME STATES DO NOT ALLOW THE LIMITATION OR EXCLUSION OF IMPLIED WARRANTIES OR OF INCIDENTAL OR CONSEQUENTIAL DAMAGES, SO THE LIMITATIONS AND EXCLUSIONS CONCERNING THE SOFTWARE AND RELATED WRITTEN MATERIALS SET FORTH ABOVE MAY NOT APPLY TO YOU.

9. LIMITATION OF REMEDIES. LICENSOR's entire liability and Licensee's exclusive remedy shall be the replacement of any disk(s) not meeting the limited warranty set forth in Section 8 above which is returned to LICENSOR with a copy of the applicable receipt within the warranty period. Any replacement disk(s)will be warranted for the remainder of the original warranty period or thirty (30) days, whichever is longer.

10. LIMITATION OF LIABILITY. IN NO EVENT WILL LICENSOR, OR ANYONE ELSE INVOLVED IN THE CREATION, PRODUCTION, AND/OR DELIVERY OF THIS SOFTWARE PRODUCT BE LIABLE TO LICENSEE OR ANY OTHER PERSON OR ENTITY FOR ANY DIRECT, INDIRECT, OR OTHER DAMAGES, INCLUDING, WITHOUT LIMITATION, ANY INTERRUPTION OF SERVICES, LOST PROFITS, LOST SAVINGS, LOSS OF DATA, OR ANY OTHER CONSEQUENTIAL, INCIDENTAL, SPECIAL, OR PUNITIVE DAMAGES, ARISING OUT OF THE PURCHASE, USE, INABILITY TO USE, OR OPERATION OF THE SOFTWARE, EVEN IF LICENSOR OR ANY AUTHORIZED LICENSOR DEALER HAS BEEN ADVISED OF THE POSSIBILITY OF SUCH DAMAGES. BY YOUR USE OF THE SOFTWARE, YOU ACKNOWLEDGE THAT THE LIMITATION OF LIABILITY SET FORTH IN THIS LICENSE WAS THE BASIS UPON WHICH THE SOFTWARE WAS OFFERED BY LICENSOR AND YOU ACKNOWLEDGE THAT THE PRICE OF THE SOFTWARE LICENSE WOULD BE HIGHER IN THE ABSENCE OF SUCH LIMITATION. SOME STATES DO NOT ALLOW THE LIMITATION OR EXCLUSION OF LIABILITY FOR INCIDENTAL OR CONSEQUENTIAL DAMAGES SO THE ABOVE LIMITATIONS AND EXCLUSIONS MAY NOT APPLY TO YOU.

11. UPDATES. LICENSOR, at its sole discretion, may periodically issue updates of the Software which you may receive upon request and payment of the applicable update fee in effect from time to time and in such event, all of the provisions of the within License Agreement shall apply to such updates.

12. EXPORT RESTRICTIONS. Licensee agrees not to export or re-export the Software and accompanying documentation (or any copies thereof) in violation of any applicable U.S. laws or regulations.

13. ENTIRE AGREEMENT. YOU, AS LICENSEE, ACKNOWLEDGE THAT: (i) YOU HAVE READ THIS ENTIRE AGREEMENT AND AGREE TO BE BOUND BY ITS TERMS AND CONDITIONS; (ii) THIS AGREEMENT IS THE COMPLETE AND EXCLUSIVE STATEMENT OF THE UNDERSTANDING BETWEEN THE PARTIES AND SUPERSEDES ANY AND ALL PRIOR ORAL OR WRITTEN COMMUNICATIONS RELATING TO THE SUBJECT MATTER HEREOF; AND (iii) THIS AGREEMENT MAY NOT BE MODIFIED, AMENDED, OR IN ANY WAY ALTERED EXCEPT BY A WRITING SIGNED BY BOTH YOURSELF AND AN OFFICER OR AUTHORIZED REPRESENTATIVE OF LICENSOR.

14. SEVERABILITY. In the event that any provision of this License Agreement is held to be illegal or otherwise unenforceable, such provision shall be deemed to have been deleted from this License Agreement while the remaining provisions of this License Agreement shall be unaffected and shall continue in full force and effect.

15. GOVERNING LAW. This License Agreement shall be governed by the laws of the State of California applicable to agreements wholly to be performed therein and of the United States of America, excluding that body of the law related to conflicts of law. This License Agreement shall not be governed by the United Nations Convention on Contracts for the International Sale of Goods, the application of which is expressly excluded. No waiver of any breach of the provisions of this License Agreement shall be deemed a waiver of any other breach of this License Agreement.

16. RESTRICTED RIGHTS LEGEND. Use, duplication, or disclosure by the Government is subject to restrictions as set forth in subparagraph (c)(1)(ii) of the Rights in Technical Data and Computer Software clause at 48 CFR § 252.227-7013 and DFARS § 252.227-7013 or subparagraphs (c) (1) and (c)(2) of the Commercial Computer Software-Restricted Rights at 48 CFR § 52.227.19, as applicable. Contractor/manufacturer: LICENSOR: LYNDA.COM, LLC, c/o PEACHPIT PRESS, 1249 Eighth Street, Berkeley, CA 94710.